D1548457

The Golem Remembered, 1909–1980

The Golem Remembered, 1909–1980

Variations
of a
Jewish Legend

by
Arnold L. Goldsmith
Wayne State University

Wayne State University Press
Detroit, 1981

Library of Congress Cataloging in Publication Data

Goldsmith, Arnold L.
  The golem remembered, 1909-1980.

  Bibliography: p.
  1. Golem in literature. I. Title.
PN57.G56G6   398.2'2'089924   81-7458
ISBN 0-8143-1683-2   AACR2

Frontispiece courtesy Museum of Modern Art/Film Stills Archive, 1 W. 53rd Street,
New York City.

Grateful acknowledgment is made to the Morris and Emma Schaver Publication Fund
for Jewish Studies for financial assistance in the publication of this volume.

A slightly different version of chapter 2 of this book was previously published in the
Midrasha Journal 2 (Winter 1979):3–14. The author and publisher would also like to thank
the following individuals and institutions for permission to reprint material which first
appeared in their publications: W. H. Auden, "Musée des Beaux Arts," in *Collected
Poems*, ed. Edward Mendelson. Copyright © Random House, Inc.; E. F. Bleiler, ed.,
*"The Golem" by Gustav Meyrink and "The Man Who Was Born Again" by Paul Busson: Two
German Supernatural Novels*. Copyright © 1976 by Dover Publications, Inc.; Chayim

To Glad,

who taught me to love

my heritage

Contents

Illustrations

Preface

IN the last few years, as I have lectured on the subject of the golem to synagogue and college audiences, I have frequently been asked three questions. Is there more than one golem? Do you really believe that the golem existed? How did you get started on such an unusual subject? The answer to the first question, which will be discussed in full in the Introduction, is yes. There is more than one golem. The second question continues to amaze me. Even though I am convinced that we are dealing with legend, not fact, many people in this modern age of reason, science, and advanced technology still believe in the supernatural and mystical. If legends are repeated often enough, there will always be listeners who believe in them. The third question is a pleasure to answer. My interest in the golem can be traced back to a visit five years ago to the library of Congregation Beth Shalom, Oak Park, Michigan. Librarian Eleanor Smith, to whom I shall always be indebted, showed me an old copy of *The Golem: Legends of the Ghetto of Prague,* written by Chayim Bloch and translated into English in 1925, but originally published in German, in Vienna, in 1919. The binding was broken and sections of the book were loose, but because of my interest in Jewish literature, Mrs. Smith correctly anticipated that I would find these tales delightful. That was how it all got started.

As soon as I began reading these wonderful legends, I remembered that I had heard the word *golem* many times in my childhood. My mother had used it as an affectionate insult whenever I did something clumsy or stupid. She would call me a *laymener gaylom* (literally, a "clay golem"; freely rendered, "a clumsy fool"). Little did I know then that in Jewish folklore a famous sixteenth-century rabbi was reputed to have created a man of clay from the banks of the Moldau in Bohemia (now Czechoslovakia) to protect the Jewish people in times of persecution. This Jewish robot, homunculus, or Frankenstein monster, incapable of speech in many of the early legends, cutter of wood and hauler of water, clumsy of gait and seemingly dull of wit, was being remembered in Yiddish vernacular as a *schlemiel.* What a surprise it was to discover that some of the twentieth-century stories about this remarkable creature portrayed him as sensitive, articulate, and intelligent.

11

The more I probed the legends of the golem, the more fascinating they became. The enthusiastic reception of my first few lectures in Michigan and Ohio made me realize that there was a large, intelligent audience of lay readers who were as curious about them as I was. Some of the older people, usually of Eastern European origin, wanted to share with me oral legends (even golem jokes) which they remembered. The younger people knew little or nothing about the golem and wanted to learn more about its origin and about the many different versions of this legend in modern literature. Fortunately for them and for me, in the 1970s four of the five major twentieth-century book-length works dealing with the golem became easily available in English translations or new editions. The fifth, America's major contribution to the golem legend, *The Sword of the Golem,* is a novel by Abraham Rothberg, published at the end of 1970.

Essentially, my plan was to recapture for a modern audience the flavor of these incredible legends so important in the Jewish cultural past. Throughout this study I am indebted to various scholars for their pioneering work on the history of the golem. Foremost among them is the venerable Gershom Scholem, one of the leading scholars of Jewish mysticism, whose learned commentaries on the development of the legends is indispensable. However, Scholem was not interested in my own specialty—literary analysis. As I investigated the life of Rabbi Judah Loew, the sixteenth-century scholar allegedly the creator of the Golem of Prague, the most famous of all the golemim in the twentieth century, I found myself indebted to Rabbi Ben Zion Bokser and Frederic Thieberger, but neither of these men undertook the kind of study I have made. To Thieberger I owe the theory of how these legends became transferred from one Eastern European rabbi to another as late as the eighteenth century, but the analysis of their literary treatment is my own. To another scholar, Donald F. Glut, I owe much of my information about the appearance of the golem legends in popular culture, but I have been able to turn up some information on both a new film and a sequel to the *Superman* comic book adventure unavailable to him at the time his comprehensive study of the Frankenstein legend went to press.

Finally, because the number of other people who have helped me is too long to list, I would like to single out the following: Eleanor Smith, for introducing me to the Golem of Prague; Phyllis Young and my colleague Joseph Prescott, for sharing with me their love of and expertise in Yiddish; Charles Semarjian, a student in Professor John Reed's monster literature course, who, after hearing my guest lecture, showed me and then allowed me to borrow his rare copies of *Superman* comics; Mae Sweet, for supplying me with pertinent information on her son's short film, *Black Golem*; Rabbi Emeritus Max Weine, one of the editors of the *Midrasha Journal*, for his encouragement of my work; my colleagues, Professors Harold Goldman and Joseph Gomez, for their friendly interest and help in my project; my son Steven, for introducing me to the poetry of Borges; the reference librarians at the Purdy Library at Wayne State University, for their patience in helping me find obscure information; Jean Owen and Sherwyn Carr, of the Wayne State University Press, for being two of the best editors a writer could ever hope to have; and Mary Gilbert, who typed the original manuscript. My greatest debt is to my wife, Gladys, to whom this book is dedicated, for her wisdom, good sense, and understanding. Like the rebbetsin in the legends, she was willing to put up with the golem.

Introduction

The word *legend* is derived from the Latin *legenda* meaning to be read. The term originally applied to narratives of the Middle Ages, such as lives of the saints, which had *to be read* as a religious duty. However what the word suggests need not be limited to its ecclesiastical usage. In a broader sense, legend may be taken to imply whatever will come to be read by successive ages into an event or record of the past: the ever-new and ever-changing re-reading of old sources by new generations of men. Great events and great books have a posthumous story of their own. Each following period puts its inner life into the patient and pliant texts of old. In turn the familiar documents reward and surprise new inquirers with new answers.

Spiegel, Introduction to *Legends of the Bible*

IN this book I am concerned with a single golem, the most famous one in modern times, the prototype of most of the golemim in twentieth-century literature—the incredible Golem of Prague. This strange crea-ture sometimes appears as an ominous, slant-eyed, clean-shaven, bald man in a shapeless gray coat, his face half hidden in darkness; some-times he looms ten feet tall, wearing a huge wig like an inverted wing nut framing his square face, a five-pointed amulet fastened to his massive chest; others see him as a white-bearded, mummylike figure with a green Hebrew letter drawn on his stony forehead. He has even appeared in the shape of a goggle-eyed robot made of gleaming brass nuts, bolts, wheels, and valves. The form changes, but the appeal of the golem in this century to the imagination of artists and their audi-ence is undeniable.

Perhaps the strangest modern manifestation of the sixteenth-century golem, however, was unveiled by one of the leading scholars of Jewish mysticism and the symbolism of the Kabbalah, Gershom Scholem. This venerable scholar, dedicating the newly built Israeli computer at the Weizmann Institute at Rehovot on June 17, 1965, named it Golem No. 1 (Golem Aleph). In his address Scholem traced a direct line of descent from the legendary golem to the new one. He began with the story of Rabbi Judah Loew, who in 1580 is said to have created a man from clay to protect the Jewish community against the

15

increasing threat of anti-Semitism and a pogrom. Although this famous golem is unable to speak, he is apparently able to carry out all of his master's orders. In some subsequent versions of the story this golem runs amuck, and Rabbi Loew has to tear the holy Name of God from the creature's mouth or remove a mystical letter from his forehead to reduce him to a pile of clay. In most of these legends man triumphs over the robot, but Scholem wondered whether the outcome would be the same in the case of the golem of Rehovot. Whereas the old golem brings water to the rabbi's house, the new golem of Rehovot calculates the movement of the ocean tides. Though the new golem is superior in memory and ability to communicate, unfortunately it suffers occasional memory lapses and breakdowns and makes the modern scholar pray that it will help bring peace to the world, not destruction.

The history of the golem goes back long before 1580. The origin of the word can be traced to the Hebrew *golem,* which means "shapeless matter," "ignorant person," "dummy." In Yiddish it usually has the last two meanings and is often an affectionate insult. The word appears only once in the Hebrew Bible, in Psalm 139:16. There the speaker, perhaps Adam, praises the Creator, acknowledging how God secretly formed his body "in the lowest parts of the earth," from which came his "unperfect substance" (that is, *golem*). This single reference led the compilers of the talmudic Aggadah to use *golem* to mean something unformed and imperfect—in short, matter without form. The word has even been used in talmudic commentary to refer to a woman who has not conceived.

Since Scholem and others have traced the appearance of golem references from a Sanhedrin passage (38b) describing Adam's first day through medieval commentaries to modern portrayals of the Golem of Prague, there is no need to repeat this history here, but a few important motifs in the earlier legends must be mentioned as background for their reappearance and variation in twentieth-century literature. The first is the golem's huge size. The second is the special power, a tellurian force, which enables him to have a vision of the future of mankind. The third is the danger of man's conceit in creating artificial life and thus competing with God. To these should be added one other motif which plays an important part in almost all of the twentieth-century stories about the golem—his eventually having to be returned to the clay from which he was created. In Yudl Rosenberg's collection of legends, *Nifla'ot Maharal im ha-Golem* (1909), the golem is removed because his mission has been successfully completed, but in most of the other twentieth-century versions this creature's life must be taken because he has become a threat either to his creator or the Jewish community.

The motif of the golem as a physical threat to his creator first appears in the writings of German students of Jewish lore in the seventeenth-century, but it does not occur in Hebrew literature until the eighteenth. Rabbi Elijah Baal Shem of Chelm, who died in 1583, is the subject of these new stories in both cases. The earliest account of Rabbi Elijah's activities is given in a letter written in 1674 by Christoph Arnold. In this letter, Arnold first generalizes, explaining how the Polish Jews bring life to a man of clay after reciting prayers, fasting, and saying the *Shem ha-meforash* (the most sacred name of God) over the prostrate form. The Jews command this golem to do their housework. As he grows in size daily and becomes a threat to them, they remove the aleph from his forehead, reducing him to clay. Arnold then tells a story he has heard about Rabbi Elias (that is, Elijah), a baal shem in Poland, who can no longer reach the aleph on his golem's forehead. Threatened by this creature's daily growth, he tricks him by commanding him to remove his master's boots. The ruse works, enabling Rabbi Elias to remove the aleph when the golem stoops, but the resulting pile of mud falls on his creator and crushes him. When two centuries later, in his autobiography and elsewhere in his writings, Jacob Emden records this story, which he heard from his father, he allows the rabbi to escape with only cuts and bruises.

In the twelfth- and thirteenth-century legends, the destructive power of the golem does not lie in physical violence to his creators, but in the possibility of idolatry. The actual danger, according to Gershom Scholem in *On the Kabbalah and Its Symbolism,*

> is not the golem or the force emanating from him, but the man himself. The danger is not that the golem, become autonomous, will develop overwhelming powers; it lies in the tension which the creative process arouses in the creator himself.

This motif is best seen in two versions of the golem story recorded in the thirteenth century but going back to Jeremiah and his so-called son, Ben Sira, in the fourth century B.C.E. In the first, an early thirteenth-century text, Jeremiah and Ben Sira, warned by the golem of the danger of being worshiped by their admiring followers, reverse the combination of letters used in his creation, erase the aleph (which, strangely, is not even mentioned in their act of creation), and the creature dies. In Hebrew the word for "truth," *emet*, is spelled aleph-mem-taw. When, in the second version, the golem himself uses a knife to remove from his forehead the aleph beginning the last word in *YHWH elohim emet* ("God is Truth"), "truth" is reduced to "dead" (mem-taw). Jeremiah, fearing blasphemy as he reads the new message, "God is dead," on the golem's forehead, heeds the creature's warning that people might worship him and Ben Sira for their awesome power. Reversing the alphabet, he reduces the golem to dust. " 'Then Jeremiah said: Truly, one should study these things only in order to know the power and omnipotence of the Creator of the world, but not in order really to practice them.' " In the twentieth century, it is H. Leivick, in *The Golem: A Dramatic Poem in Eight Scenes* (1921), and Abraham Rothberg, in *The Sword of the Golem* (1970), who develop this tension, this inner conflict on the part of the creator, adding a rich new dimension only hinted at in some of the talmudic legends.

No introduction to the legends of the Golem of Prague would be complete without some mention of the *Sefer Yezirah*, one of the fundamental books of Jewish mysticism. This enigmatic book, which Scholem believes was written by a Jewish neo-Pythagorean between the third and sixth centuries, is central to the development of the Kabbalah. According to Rabbi Ben Zion Bokser in *From the World of the Cabbalah*, the *Sefer Yezirah*

> traces God's creative presence to the harmonies of numbers and their equivalent symbolism in the Hebrew alphabet. Joining the primary numbers from one to ten and the twenty-two letters of the Hebrew alphabet, we get "thirty-two secret paths of wisdom," as this book describes it, through which God created all that has existence. The ten primary numbers are here called *sefirot*, and it is from this text that the concept of the *sefirot* was introduced to the later Cabbalah.

Though the ten *sefirot* and later kabbalistic symbolism of the *sefirot* are not directly related to the making of a golem, some medieval commentators took the *Sefer Yezirah* as a practical "manual of magic" rather than as a theoretical guide to wisdom. It is Scholem's contention that this strange book was meant to supply a broad outline, "with certain astronomico-astrological and anatomical details," of how the cosmos was created basically from the twenty-two letters, each one of which " 'governs' a part of man or a realm of the great world."

In the medieval period the belief in the creation of a golem was common. This belief can be partly attributed to kabbalistic doctrine.

Scholem clarifies the link between the Kabbalah and the golem legends in his dedication speech, reminding his audience that the Kabbalists saw the universe as

> built essentially on the prime elements of numbers and letters, because the letters of God's language reflected in human language are nothing but concentrations of His creative energy. Thus, by assembling these elements in all their possible combinations and permutations, the Kabbalist who contemplates the mysteries of Creation radiates some of this elementary power into the Golem. The creation of a Golem is then in some way an affirmation of the productive and creative power of Man. It repeats, on however small a scale, the work of creation.

In short, in his successful performance of this mystical ritual of initiation, culminating in the ecstatic act of creating a golem, the scholar proves his mastery of secret knowledge.

Over the centuries, Kabbalists have argued over the quality of existence found in a golem. One talmudic text, Pseudo-Saadya, written in the thirteenth century, credits this creature with the highest level of being and claims that man has the divine power to give the golem both vitality and a soul. A sixteenth-century Talmudist argues that a golem has no *ruah* (soul) because the Talmud says that he is speechless, but that such a mute creature does have *nefesh* (the lowest degree of soul; that is, life), for he has vitality and movement. To another, Moses Cordovero, the golem has only *hiyyuth*, a special kind of vitality which is higher than the soul of animals. For this reason a golem does not die in the sense that an animal does, but simply returns to the earth, his natural element. Thus Cordovero can argue that the person who kills a golem should not be punished because he has broken no law of the Torah.

Jewish writers were not the only ones to be fascinated by the golem. Christian writers over the centuries have shared this interest, as evidenced by Christoph Arnold's letter. Both Scholem and Bokser refer to parallels to the golem legends in the Christian community, stories involving Albertus Magnus, Saint Thomas Aquinas, and Paracelsus. According to Bokser, "The feats of Paracelsus furnished Goethe with the material for his Faust legend. Christian mystics shared the basic doctrinal presuppositions as well as the folk-lore which flowed from them with their Jewish colleagues of the same period." Scholem even relates some of the golem legends to Christian tales involving "the resurrection of the dead by putting the name of God in their mouths or on their arms, and by removing the parchment containing the name in reverse and thus causing their death. Such legends," he adds, "were wide-spread in Italy from the tenth century."

As mentioned earlier, the rabbi most prominently identified with the legends of the golem was Judah Bezalel Loew (ca. 1512–1609). Somehow the Polish legend about Rabbi Elias of Chelm became transferred to Prague and to Rabbi Loew during the second half of the eighteenth century, shortly before Jacob Grimm published his collection of tales. Bokser believes that this transference took place because of Rabbi Loew's reputation for simplifying and popularizing some of the esoteric doctrines of Jewish mysticism. The popularity of this great figure "led the people to endow him with the supernatural powers which supposedly inhered in the mastery of the Cabbalah. Folk imagination is never deterred by facts when it is launched on its work of legend building." That Bokser was apparently on the right track will be seen in chapter 1 of this study, which explores the life and legends of "the Great Rabbi Loew."

Chapter One

The Two Judah Loews:
Historical and Legendary

ANYONE interested in the Golem of Prague is faced with some intriguing mysteries. Certain tantalizing questions demand answers. How, for example, do scholars explain the cluster of fantastic legends developing around a sixteenth-century rabbi two hundred and more years after his death? How does one account for Judah Loew's becoming wrapped in a mantle of magic? Why Judah Loew? To shrug off the mystery and simply refer to the vagaries of folk imagination does not satisfy the inquisitive mind. Too many ironies emerge.

First, it is one of the fascinating ironies of Jewish literary history that a man who in real life did not believe in miracles became in legend responsible for one of the greatest miracles ever allegedly performed—the creation of a man from clay. Second, it is equally ironic that this same sixteenth-century rabbi who condemned magic should, since the eighteenth century, be identified in legend with feats of magic that dazzled an emperor and his court. And third, it is somewhat miraculous itself that this same man, during his lifetime and centuries later, should have had such immense appeal to both rational scholars and mystics, to believers both in the Enlightenment and in the Kabbalah. It is this historical figure, Rabbi Judah Bezalel Loew (sometimes spelled Low, Löw, Loewe, Loeb, Liva, Loevy, or Levi), frequently called "the Maharal" (an acronym for the Hebrew *Moreinu ha-Rav Rabbi Liva,* "Our teacher, the master Rabbi Loew"), who became so popular in Jewish legends that he eventually made his debut in drama, novel, short story, film, opera, and ballet. This chapter, then, serves to introduce the real Judah Loew and the legendary. Sometimes the two figures seem inseparable; sometimes they are worlds apart.

The Historical Rabbi Loew

Throughout their history, the Jews of the Diaspora looked for heroic figures who could mitigate their suffering and lead them to the messianic redemption their religion taught them to expect. Sixteenth-century Bohemian Jews had more than their share of enemies both within and outside their religion. Apostate Jews who broke under persecution and converted to Christianity (unlike the Marranos, those converts who tried to practice their original religion covertly) turned on their coreligionists, partly as a result of their guilty consciences. In addition, of course, there was the long-standing conflict with Christianity, a polemical dispute which erupted periodically with dire consequences for the vulnerable minority. In *From the World of the Cabbalah*, Rabbi Ben Zion Bokser describes the nature of this persecution.

> In 1559 all Hebrew books in Prague were seized, to be examined for possible anti-Christian reference. The contemporary historian, David Ganz, reports that not even a single prayer book was left and that the cantor had to chant the prayers orally [that is, from memory]. The Talmud was burned six times in the course of the 16th century, in 1553, 1555, 1559, 1566, 1592, and 1599. A Christian censorship of Hebrew books was introduced in 1562. In 1561 under the instigation of the Jesuits an order was issued forcing Jews to listen to Christian sermons, which disparaged their own faith and extolled the virtues of Christianity.

Even Martin Luther, who began his ministry with the apparent intention of improving the lot of the Jews, was really trying to soften their resistance to Christianity as a first step to conversion, and he then turned bitterly against them. According to Frederic Thieberger, though the Jews were forced to wear yellow badges, were not allowed to trade in many articles, and suffered from horrible pogroms and expulsion orders, "the worst could always be averted by playing on the threat of Turkish aggression and by the religious wars amongst the Christians." Another mitigating factor "was a certain humanitarian attitude amongst the sovereigns," such as Ferdinand I, Maximilian I, and Rudolf II. For example, in 1580, Rudolf II repealed the restrictions forbidding Jewish furriers to make fur coats or fur-trimmed dresses and allowed Bohemian Jews to trade freely, but, at the same time, "he renewed the edict that the Jews had to wear on their attire the yellow badge of identification, and in 1585 he even sanctioned the expulsion of the few Jews in Schönberg in Moravia."

One of the most interesting documents recording the religious disputations between the Catholic church and the Jews, which occurred even before Rabbi Loew arrived in Prague in 1573, is *Nizahon*, by Rabbi Yom Tob Muehlhausen, who frequently debated with both Christian priests and apostate Jews currying favor with their new church by slandering their old religion. Rabbi Muehlhausen's career is probably the prototype for the many legends which later circulated about Rabbi Loew and his polemical disputes with the spokesmen for Catholicism. The most famous of these depicts Judah Loew as the champion of his religion in a debate with three hundred priests, whom he took on in groups of ten for thirty days. Though, as Bokser points out, "there is no evidence that such a debate ever occurred, . . . the folk-imagination was on solid ground in the essential ingredients out of which it built its story. One of the greatest themes in the writing of Rabbi Judah was the defense of Judaism against the challenge of Christianity." This theme is central to most of Yudl Rosenberg's and Chayim Bloch's tales.

Though Rabbi Loew was a prolific writer (fifteen works were published during his lifetime and one was published posthumously, while a number of his manuscripts were lost in a fire in 1689), he told very little about himself. Personal notes are rare in his writings. According to Bokser, "Our principal sources of knowledge about him are indirect—occasional comments by contemporaries, a tombstone inscription, which extols his many-sided accomplishments, and family chronicles in which an oral tradition is reduced to writing for the benefit of posterity." The author of the family chronicles, *Megillath Yuchasin,* was Meir Perles (or Pereles), a descendant who, as secretary of the Prague Jewish community, was asked in 1727 by Rabbi Isaiah Katz of Brod in Moravia to write about his famous ancestor. The chronicles were not published until 1745, when they appeared as a supplement to *Mate Moshe,* by Moses Katz, Rabbi Katz's son. It is important to make clear immediately that in this work, published almost a century and a half after Rabbi Loew's death, there is no mention of any of the legends which today are so well known.

There is some uncertainty as to the date of Rabbi Loew's birth, but it was probably around 1512. Whatever the exact date, it is agreed that Judah Loew ben Bezalel was born into a distinguished Jewish family which was originally from Worms but settled in Poland because of anti-Semitism. His three older brothers, Hayim, Sinai, and Samson, also became accomplished scholars. One of the personal stories told by Perles (and repeated by Rosenberg and Bloch) concerns Judah Loew's engagement to Perl (or Pearl) Reich, a young woman four years older than he. When her father suffered financial reverses, he offered Judah the chance to break the engagement, but Judah refused. The wedding was put off for ten years while Perl established herself in a bakery to help support her family. Though Perl was already thirty when she finally married Judah, she bore him seven children, six girls and a boy. The daughters, all of whom married well, are telescoped into one (or changed to a granddaughter) in the legends and stories about their famous father two to four hundred years later. The son, Bezalel, mentioned in a small but significant way in Abraham Rothberg's *Sword of the Golem,* became a rabbi in Cologne and then became embittered when he was turned down as his father's successor in Prague. He left the city to head a rabbinical academy in Kolín before he died in 1600, nine years before his father.

From 1553 to 1573, Judah Loew served as rabbi of the province of Moravia. Little is known about his career during this time, but when he left Nicolsberg for Prague in 1573, he was independently wealthy and seeking new challenges. Over sixty, but apparently in good health, he set out to continue his career as educator and rabbi, determined now to publish some of his writings. Why Rabbi Loew came to Prague is unclear, however. He had not been invited to become the city's chief rabbi. In fact, contrary to the impression given in legend and fiction, he held that position for only a small fraction of his career. Why, then, did he come? Thieberger is probably correct in suggesting that the main attraction was the exciting intellectual life which the city offered. Prague was an important cultural center of Judaism long before Rabbi Loew arrived. The most important books of the sixteenth century were being printed in Prague by the descendants of a printer named Gerson, who at the beginning of the century had been designated by the emperor as the only printer of books written in Hebrew. The availability of a Hebrew press is a factor that cannot be underestimated. It was this press that published most of Rabbi Loew's works in his old age.

Another attraction in Prague was the new Klaus Synagogue, built through the generosity of Mordecai Maisl, the great philanthropist and Rabbi Loew's devoted friend, in commemoration of Emperor Rudolf's friendly visit to the Jewish ghetto in 1571. Rabbi Loew became the head of the new academy attached to the synagogue and served with distinction in this capacity for eleven years, making significant changes in the sterile pedagogy of the time and becoming known throughout Central Europe as a leading Jewish educator. His writings dealt with questions of Halakah (that is, interpretations of scriptural law), but it was his love for Aggadah (the Jewish tradition of stories and legends which were used to teach talmudic wisdom) that endeared him to his followers. Among his published writings are several sermons, a popular book on piety and morals, and studies of Rashi's biblical commentaries, divine providence in the early history of Israel, scriptural law, the messianic hope of Judaism, the Book of Esther, and the Hanukah festival.

Despite his renowned brilliance and other eminent qualifications, Judah Loew was not elected chief rabbi of Prague in 1583. Isaac Hayot, his brother-in-law, was chosen instead. Apparently Rabbi Loew had offended too many of the lay leaders of the Jewish establishment with his independent and outspoken views, for he had accused the oligarchy in Prague of making their rabbis spineless beggars. Moreover, traditionalists were offended by his attempt to introduce kabbalistic ideas into his sermons and writings. One of his objections was to the hallowed High Holy Day prayer in which man asks the angels to act as mediator between him and God. Rabbi Loew felt that man did not need any intermediaries in communicating with his Maker.

In 1584, Rabbi Loew returned to Posen, where he was chief rabbi until 1588. After the resignation of his rival and relative, Rabbi Isaac Hayot, he returned to Prague, but was again denied the prestigious position of chief rabbi and resumed his old post at the college at Klaus Synagogue. In 1589, he did return briefly to the Altneuschul to deliver a scathing sermon excommunicating those Jews guilty of slandering certain distinguished Jewish families. The details of this unpleasant situation would reappear about three hundred years later in one of the golem legends.

In 1592, a few weeks before his return to Posen as the new chief rabbi, probably the most famous event in Rabbi Loew's life occurred. He was invited for an audience with Emperor Rudolf II. Thieberger emphasizes the great significance of this short visit.

> One cannot be surprised that this audience greatly stirred the mind and the imagination of the Jews. For them the Sovereign was not only the personification of unlimited power, on which their very life depended, but according to their religious conception he embodied something holy, assigned to him directly from God, no matter whether he was a cruel or a gracious ruler. Suddenly a member of the despised and persecuted Jewish people, considered as being outside the pale of the ordinary law, is granted the privilege of talking to a great sovereign of the time, not as a financial adviser, not as a political go-between, not as a physician, but as a Jew and 'as a friend'.

There is no factual evidence as to the subject of the conference, though there are many legends, but two of Rabbi Loew's contemporaries have confirmed that the meeting did take place. The first is David Ganz, one of the rabbi's students, a historian and scientist, who reported in his chronicles that Emperor Rudolf sent for Rabbi Loew and had a long, friendly, confidential conversation with him on Sunday, 10 Adar 5352. According to Thieberger, Ganz's date is in error by one week. The other contemporary source is the eyewitness report of Yitzchak Kohen, Rabbi Loew's son-in-law. Chayim Bloch prints it in full as a long footnote to his chapter, "The Audience with the Kaiser," in *The Golem*. He explains that it appeared in the fourth issue of the Hebrew paper *Hamagid* in Lyck in 1872, edited by a Dr. L. Silberman. Thieberger supplies additional information. Apparently Yitzchak Kohen originally recorded his experience in his Venetian Bible, the newly discovered source of the report in *Hamagid*.

According to Kohen, Rabbi Loew was invited to appear in Prince Bertier's apartment adjoining Emperor Rudolf's castle. He went there accompanied by his brother, Rabbi Sinai; his son-in-law; and Isaac Weisl, the head of the Jewish community. The prince treated his guests cordially, even allowing them to keep on their skullcaps. While Rabbi Sinai and the author were seated in one room, Rabbi Loew was escorted into an adjoining room where he sat facing the prince, who conversed with him "about mystical matters" in tones loud enough for the others to hear every word. The loudness

> "was especially intended by the Prince so that our Sovereign, the Emperor, who was standing behind a curtain at the back of my father-in-law, could hear everything. All at once there was silence. One could hear the noise caused by the scraping of the chairs, when our Sovereign the Emperor lifted the curtain, advanced in all his majesty and exchanged a few words with my father-in-law about the previously mentioned matters. He then retired again. All this took place at a distance of 6 to 8 ells from us."

After another brief conversation with the prince, Rabbi Loew was led back to his companions, hands were shaken all around, and the guests accompanied to the courtyard. Kohen's entry for that day ends,

> "As to the subject of the conversation, it is only correct, in matters affecting the Sovereign, to be silent about it. But if God

grants us life we shall disclose the subject when the time is ripe. I have recorded everything only quite shortly, also the politeness shown us by the Prince."

The next day Kohen added that Prince Bertier informed Isaac Weisl that the emperor had enjoyed his talk with Rabbi Loew.

Yitzchak Kohen never did keep his promise to reveal the subject of the discussion, but it seems likely from his use of *nistarot*, translated by Bloch as "confidential matters" and Thieberger as "mystical matters," that the emperor, who was known to be an intellectual and lover of the arts and sciences, a cultured man who surrounded himself with famous figures like Georg Hufnagel, Jan Breughel, Tycho Brahe, and Johann Kepler, was interested in the rabbi's deep knowledge of the Kabbalah. Many of the legends and stories involving this historical meeting mention the emperor's fascination with alchemy and his interest in the *Zohar*. According to Thieberger, "Cabbalistic fantasy found the motive for the audience in the Rabbi's magical devices or in his elucidation of certain riddles in the life of the Emperor. The single audience grew into repeated mutual visits and the intercourse with the Emperor into intercourse with other aristocrats." Some say that Rabbi Loew sought the audience with Rudolf II to end libels against the Jews and thus avoid any more mob violence and repressive legislation. But whatever the explanation, in history, legend, or fiction, it is hard to disagree with Bokser, who sees the audience with the emperor as a sign of Judah Loew's stature at this time.

Information on the last seventeen years of Rabbi Loew's life is also sparse. He finally became chief rabbi of Prague in the closing years of the sixteenth century. During this period he also published five of his books, which had been written earlier but needed revision. Rabbi Loew remained active until 1600. He continued to lecture on the Mishnah at Klaus College, worked on his writings, and spent considerable time settling disputes. In 1604, he resigned his post because of ill health and age. On August 22, 1609, seven years before the death of William Shakespeare, Judah Loew died. Thirty of his students eventually had the honor of being buried beside their teacher.

A definitive study of Judah Loew's philosophy remains to be written. He was an extremely well-read man with the wide-ranging interests of a Renaissance scholar. One book in particular which he enjoyed studying deserves special mention here, the *Zohar*, the central work of Jewish mysticism, perhaps authored in the second century of the Common Era, and thus antedating the *Sefer Yezirah*. First published in

Spain by Moses de Leon, the *Zohar* is considered by Kabbalists of many continents to be as holy as the Bible and Talmud. Bokser explains Judah Loew's fascination with the *Zohar*.

> Whereas the Talmud said very little, at least not directly, about God and how we are to find a way to Him, here he found a continued preoccupation with the very questions which stirred him most, questions about man and his destiny, questions about God Who was both hidden and near, beyond the universe, and yet the very breath of its being. A poetic glow, suffused with warmth and the romance of deep faith was distilled by the Cabbalistic writings. They struck a responsive chord in the imaginative Judah.

Mysticism, a major component of Renaissance humanism, fascinated Christian as well as Jewish scholars in the sixteenth century. According to Bokser, "The political and religious instability of the time and the collapse of the familiar conceptions of the universe undermined man's sense of personal security." Man's "quest for God as an object of personal experience, rather than of dogmatic knowledge" spurred his interest in mysticism.

The practical mystic, explaining God's work of creation in terms familiar to man's own experience, tried to unite himself with the divine forces governing all life. In this attempt he performed secret rites, usually invoking the secret name of God and special combinations of letters and numbers which would supposedly empower him to control events in the natural world. This attempt to control nature, to turn base metals into gold or to discover the elixir of life, led, in the sixteenth century, to widespread interest in alchemy. Rabbi Loew, however, rejected this mixture of science and magic and relied solely on the Torah as the ultimate source of all man's knowledge about the world. It was the Torah, Thieberger explains, that was the core of Rabbi Loew's philosophy.

> The text of the Torah, through its unique combination of letters and words, conveys to man everything he needs to know in order to find his way both in thought and action through the perplexities of life, without being obsessed by the fear of getting lost in the Universe. At the same time every particle of the text is of cosmic significance which man can only surmise with awe.

Man's knowledge and love of the Torah, the revealed word of God, enable him to combine the material and the spiritual worlds.

Rabbi Loew's disbelief in miracles is especially important to this study because of the way the behavior of the legendary rabbi contradicts the philosophy of the historical figure on whom he is based. According to the real Rabbi Loew, man must not call an event a miracle because it is beyond his comprehension. There can be no such thing as a sudden change of the natural course of events, because the order of such events is fixed. Rabbi Loew saw two distinct worlds, the one lacking corporeality and time as we know them, following its own divinely given laws, the other visible to our senses. How, then, does man explain what has appeared to be a miracle, such as water turning to blood or the parting of the Red Sea? To Rabbi Loew, these apparent miracles are only sudden glimpses man is given of events in the spiritual world. They actually have not happened here. Unlike Maimonides, who sought a rational explanation for everything, Rabbi Loew based his faith on intuitive acceptance. In *Tiphereth Yisrael* he wrote,

> If we are able to find the reason, then the Torah would be no more than a textbook of medicine or natural history. It is here, however, not a question of the order of nature, i.e., of material causes and effects, but of a divine, supernatural order. By fulfilling the commandments, we fulfill their supernatural purpose, cling to God and purify ourselves.

Rabbi Loew's use of the Torah as a bridge to connect the physical and spiritual worlds is a good example of the mystic's love of numbers. The importance of numbers in the interpretation of Jewish religious literature is well known and can be observed especially in the Middle Ages, when both Christian and Jewish scholars studied the *Zohar* because of their fascination with Kabbalah. In *Tiphereph Yisrael*, Rabbi Loew based his philosophy on the tradition that there are 613 precepts in the Torah, 365 of them negative commands and 248 positive. The 365 "thou shalt nots" correspond with the days of the year which determine the movement of time in the corporeal world. When man observes these commandments, he keeps order in the lower, material world. The 248 positive precepts, according to an old Jewish belief, correspond to the bones in the human body. The man who observes these precepts in his daily life, Rabbi Loew argued, is striving for perfection with every bone in his body and thus approaches the perfection of the divine order in the spiritual world. As Thieberger points out, "The negative precepts were meant to reduce the dangers lurking in the concrete world, whilst the positive ones, the number of which is noticeably smaller, are directed towards the absolute truth, outside of space and time."

Although the above is only a brief summation of some of the highlights of Rabbi Loew's thoughts, it indicates this venerable scholar's connection to Renaissance humanism. With his emphasis on the centrality of individual experience in man's quest for truth, his belief in the importance of educating the poor man as well as the rich, his shifting away from the sterile pedagogy of traditional talmudic study to the broader elements of Jewish education, Judah Loew stands, as Bokser says in the concluding statement of his book, "as a Jewish representative in the movement of transition from medieval to modern times." More important to the purpose of this study is Thieberger's conclusion in evaluating the range of Judah Loew's thought. "By combining in his mental outlook, and no doubt also in his daily life, mysticism with realism, [Loew] became enveloped in an aura of magic which not only greatly impressed posterity, but also provided it with that great legendary character it needed in its longing for redemption."

The Legendary Creator of the Golem

With the image of the historical Judah Loew, Renaissance scholar-rabbi-mystic, in the background, it is possible to address the question of how the legend of the Golem of Prague became identified with this man over one hundred years after his death. Perhaps the final answer will never be known, but Thieberger has put together enough pieces of the puzzle to show the way future scholars will have to go to solve the mystery. The explanation begins with the decision in the early eighteenth century to write the Loew family chronicle.

Because the tombstone over the graves of Judah and Perl Loew (who was 104 when she died) had deteriorated and sunk into the ground over the years, it was restored in 1724 with contributions from the rabbi's descendants and admirers. At the same time, some of the descendants decided "to collect reminiscences of the family and to fix the actual line of descent. The strong Kabbalistic movement then prevailing, combined with the fascination exercised by Jonathan Ebeyschütz on the youth of Prague, brought to the fore once again the memory of the great master of the Aggadah." Many pilgrims visited the now restored grave and "the Great Rabbi Loew" gradually "became the central figure of a whole series of legends." It is important to remember that Meir Perles makes no mention of the golem or any of the other legends in the *Megillath Yuchasin*. According to Thieberger,

"The first indication of Rabbi Loew's supernatural activity appears in 1709, just one hundred years after his death." Rabbi Loew's great-great-grandson, Naftali Kohen, a rabbinical authority, in correspondence with Rabbi Zvi Chacham over a religio-juridical question, referred to his "ancestor, the Maharal of Prague, who, as is well known, made use of the holy spirit." Rabbi Chacham printed this letter in his collection of Responsa. Another of Rabbi Loew's descendants, Yair Bacharach, claimed that he owned one of the Maharal's amulets. But this time, says Thieberger, "reports about the cabbalistic activity of the Great Rabbi were freely circulated, although the Golem does not seem to have been included in them."

In the eighteenth century, Prague became a center for kabbalistic study. Chayon, Jonathan Eibenschütz, and Naftali Kohen were but three of the leading Kabbalists living there. Thieberger remarks that "between 1710 and 1730 the Great Rabbi Loew became more and more a central figure of Cabbalistic legend, but his connection with the legends of the Golem cannot be dated earlier than 1730"; the earliest legends about Rabbi Loew "are probably those connected with definite places in Prague." For example, the only hint of the supernatural in the family chronicles is the story Perles tells about the death of the rabbi's favorite grandson, Samuel, in 1666. According to this story, the Maharal had promised this grandson a place next to his own grave. When the dying Samuel called the wardens of the burial society to inform them of his promise, they argued that the space was too narrow. Upon Samuel's death, however, the wardens reinspected the spot and discovered that the tomb had moved to make room for the new grave. After Samuel's burial in the desired spot, the space grew smaller again. Until 1847, "this legend of Rabbi Loew is the only one which we find in writing. The stories were only transmitted orally, and many must have been lost or been changed from their original form in the process."

Gradually some of the material from the oral sources found its way into print, such as new editions of the Perles family chronicles and collections of tales and stories by Slavic and other writers. The most important of these collections was *Sippurim*, a book of popular tales about the ghetto brought out in 1847 by Wolf Pascheles, a Prague publisher. This collection includes C. Ludwig Kapper's "Great Rabbi Loew and the Count," which combines incidents from legends by Weisel and others and shows how they developed almost 250 years after the rabbi's death. Most important to this study, the legend of the Golem of Prague appeared for the first time in print in this collection.

Since Thieberger thinks that the golem legend, the most famous of all those about Rabbi Loew, arose only after most of the others about the Maharal, it seems fitting to review the others first. Kapper's tale in *Sippurim* is a good place to begin, since it illustrates the fascination with alchemy, astrology, and the Kabbalah. According to this legend, a Bohemian aristocrat who loved alchemy and astrology often visited Rabbi Loew to discuss secret sciences. When the count expressed surprise at the rabbi's apparent ability to accommodate 400 disciples in a small house, Rabbi Loew invited him and his many friends and attendants to a lavish dinner. The count was stunned by the discrepancy between the outside of the rabbi's home and the opulent interior. During the sumptuous banquet, the count signaled to one of his attendants, who then stole a gold cup before the guests left. Shortly after the visit, the count heard of the strange story of a castle two hundred miles from Prague which had suddenly vanished, only to reappear intact the next day with all of its valuables accounted for but one gold cup.

Convinced that Rabbi Loew had used magic despite his frequent denials, the count insisted that the rabbi teach him the secrets of the Kabbalah. Rabbi Loew at first refused, but upon the threat of death for him and his family, he asked permission to send for his friend from Spain, Don Abraham, to instruct the count. To Rabbi Loew's surprise, his friend arrived that very Friday without having been sent for, because he had had a dream revealing the Maharal's plight. As the lessons were about to begin in the count's black-draped room, Don Abraham explained that only completely innocent people can be initiated into the mysteries of Kabbalah. When he asked the count if he met these qualifications and the count lied in the affirmative, Don Abraham ordered the nobleman to look behind him, where he recognized his dead sister with her child in her arms. The apparitions disappeared as suddenly as they had appeared, and Don Abraham revealed, " 'That was your sister and her—your—child. You yourself have destroyed them.' " The count, overwhelmed with guilt, confessed his crime, asked the two men to keep his secret, and allowed Rabbi Loew and his friend to return to Prague. (In Bloch's retelling of this legend, he bowdlerizes the obvious reference to incest and makes the count guilty only of the pair's murder.)

Variations of this legend appear in *Sippurim,* one of which tells how the emperor, with Tycho Brahe, visited Rabbi Loew in the ghetto. In this version, the rabbi conjured up the castle of Hradschin. In *Pictures of My Boyhood* (1872), L. Kalisch says that his grandmother told him a similar story in which Rabbi Loew conjured up a summer garden for the emperor even though it was winter. (Thieberger points out that similar legends were told about the great Christian theologian Albertus Magnus in the thirteenth century.) In the sixteenth century, such legends expressed "the longing of an age in which the practical application of the Cabbala was rampant."

In another legend about Rabbi Loew found in *Sippurim* and also mentioned by Alois Jirásek in his *Old Bohemian Tales* (1914), the emperor asked the Maharal to conjure up the Patriarchs and sons of Jacob so that he could see what they looked like. Rabbi Loew was reluctant to do so but consented on the condition that the emperor not laugh no matter what he saw. On the day of the magic show, the emperor was awed by the apparitions before him. Unfortunately, when Jacob's sons appeared, and Naphtali, " 'the hind let loose', as he is called in Jacob's blessing, jumped across the ears of corn and flax stalks in order to catch up with the others, the Emperor forgot his promise and started to laugh." Suddenly the apparitions faded and the ceiling of the emperor's apartment began to collapse. Only a command from the Maharal saved the day. According to Thieberger, "Even today there is a room in the castle closed to the public because the ceiling has given away." (In the 1920 silent German film *Der Golem: Wie er in die Welt Kam*, Paul Wegener directed this scene with stunning visual effects. The golem does not appear in Jirásek's tale or the one in *Sippurim*.)

Jirásek tells another legend which testifies to the great impression made on the Jewish community by Emperor Rudolf's one audience with Rabbi Loew in "How the Great Rabbi Loew Met King Rudolf for the First Time." In this legend, Rabbi Loew forced himself on the king, who had ordered the expulsion of the Jews from Prague. While the rabbi was waiting for the king's carriage to pass on a stone bridge, the people threw stones and dirt at him, but the missiles turned to flowers. When the carriage with the royal procession arrived, the horses stopped of their own volition and would not run over the Maharal. Only then did the flower-bedecked rabbi bare his head, kneel before the king, and ask for mercy for the Jews. Favorably impressed, Rudolf invited Rabbi Loew to his castle, rescinded his decree, and thereafter invited the Maharal to visit him often. This legend never appears in Rosenberg or Bloch, but it does appear in Byron L. Sherwin's article, "Rabbi Loew and the Golem." He simply calls it "a Bohemian legend," never mentioning Jirásek. Rosenberg probably omitted it because it had nothing to do with the golem; Bloch may never have heard or read it.

One of the most interesting of the tales in *Sippurim*, which Thieberger includes in the last section of his book, "The Beleles Lane," does not appear in Rosenberg or Bloch. Again, Rosenberg may have omitted it because it does not involve the golem. Bloch, on the other hand, may have excluded it because of its sexual implications. The story tells how a plague broke out among the Jews of Prague during the reign of Rudolf II. Only very young children were its victims. As the corpses piled up, it was assumed that God was punishing the Jewish community for some transgression. Special prayers, fasts, and learned discussions were to no avail. One night one of the rabbis, "on account of his great wisdom and his knowledge of the Talmud, the Cabbala, Astronomy, and Astrology," was given a clue in a dream. This man, of course, was the Maharal, and in his dream Elijah led him to the cemetery, where he saw the children's corpses rise from their graves. The next day the rabbi sent for one of his bravest disciples and told him to go to the cemetery at midnight, pull off one of the children's shrouds, and bring it to him. When the clock struck twelve and the children's spirits began doing their strange dances, the terrified disciple followed his instructions and ran back to the rabbi. At this point, Rabbi Loew saw outside the window the "phantom of a naked child floating rapidly towards him." The narrator then explains that when the clock struck one and the specters finished their dance, one child noticed that his shroud was missing and he could not return to the grave. He pleaded with Rabbi Loew to give back his shroud, but the Maharal refused until the phantom revealed the cause of the plague. "In a street not far from the Rabbi, it said, there lived two married couples, who led an immoral life with their wives. This made God so angry that He had launched this plague on the Jewish settlement. The Rabbi then returned the shroud to the child." The legend ends with the rabbi's punishing the two couples, whose specific behavior is never disclosed, and the plague ceases. The last line is a belated attempt to add a little verbal comic relief to this sombre tale. It explains that "the lane where the two couples lived was given by the people the name of 'Beleles' Lane, derived from the names of the two wives, Bella and Ella."

The last two legends to be mentioned here, not involving the golem, concern the death of Rabbi Loew. Both, according to Thieberger, antedate the golem legend and "aje of a purely cabbalistic-mystical character." The first, based on an oral tradition in Poland, appears in *Sagen und Erzählungen aus der Provinz Posen* (1893), by the Christian scholar Koop, and in Juda Bergmann's *Legenden der Juden* (1919). It tells how Rabbi Loew went to the synagogue in Posen one night before the Jewish New Year to investigate a light he had seen from his house. In the synagogue he discovered a strange being sharpening his knife before a long list of names. The frightened rabbi ran away at first, but then realized that this stranger was the Angel of Death contemplating the list of those about to die from the plague. He quickly returned to the synagogue and tore the list from his hands. When he got home and read the list, he discovered the names of Posen's most eminent Jews, but the fragment that remained in the angel's hands contained the name of Rabbi Loew. After the High Holy Days, the Maharal died.

The second legend, which originated in Prague, was told by Jirásek and retold by Israel Günzig in *Die Wundermänner im Jüdischen Volk* (1921). It was about the difficulty the Angel of Death had in catching up with the Great Rabbi Loew. The angel succeeded only when he hid himself in the fragrance of a rose brought to the Maharal by his favorite granddaughter. It is this legend which inspired the sculptor Ladislaus Saloun to create the monument to Rabbi Loew which can be seen in Prague in front of the new town hall. (In Jirásek's version it is the rabbi's wife who brings him the rose "to remind him of his youthful happiness.")

As popular as were all of these legends about Rabbi Loew, the most famous of all was the one about the golem, which, as Thieberger has explained, seems to have come after most of the others were well known. No other legend was

> so intimately connected in the popular mind with the person of the Great Rabbi Loew as the one about the Golem, and all later legends would not have omitted to use this *motif* whenever it was possible. There are Golem legends about other miracle workers, before and after Rabbi Loew, but none became so widely spread as that of the Golem of Prague.

In his prefatory note to the first printed version of the Golem of Prague legend in *Sippurim* in 1847, L. Weisel explains, "All the following legends I heard from the old people, and I pass them on to the kind reader as I have received them." With admirable economy and no attempt at artistic embellishment, Weisel tells the story of the creation and removal of the golem in a little over 350 words. Of considerable importance is the fact that he never mentions the Blood Libel, the false accusation brought against the Jews, usually claiming that they have killed a Christian child and drained his blood for use in their baking their unleavened bread *(matzot)* at the time of Passover. Weisel's omission of this accusation supports Gershom Scholem's contention that this motif is a modern invention.

Despite his economy of words, Weisel could not resist a little wistful editorializing. After telling how his knowledge of Kabbalah enabled Rabbi Loew to make a golem, Weisel adds,

> Thanks to this art he was able to put life into figures formed from clay and wood, and to make them perform whatever they were told to do, just as if they were real beings. Such self-created servants are worth a great deal; they neither eat nor drink, nor do they require any wages. They work patiently, one can scold them and they do not answer back.

In Weisel's version, Rabbi Loew put the Shem (God's name) into the golem's mouth and removed it every Sabbath, which was the golem's one day of rest. When he forgot to remove it one Friday, "the magic servant went wild, he pulled down houses, threw about lumps of rock, tore out trees by the roots, and played havoc in the streets." A little suspense is added by the narrator, who asks how the golem was to be stopped, since the Sabbath had supposedly begun, with its prohibition against all work, "whether constructive or destructive." The problem was easily solved, however, since "the Sabbath had not yet been sanctified" in the Altneu Synagogue, which was "the official guide on such matters." Rabbi Loew ran outside, pulled the Shem from the golem's mouth, and "the lump of clay fell down and broke into pieces. The Rabbi was greatly upset by this occurrence and was unwilling to create another such dangerous servant." (Apparently it is still a tradition in the Altneu Synagogue to repeat the Sabbath psalm twice. There is no mention of this custom in *Sippurim.* Though the origin of the tradition remains unknown, some attribute it to this legend.)

It is not difficult to understand how the subject matter of all these legends fascinated one generation after the next. People have always been intrigued by the occult. But the Jewish people in particular have longed incessantly for a miraculous deliverance from the hostile world in which they have been forced to wander. Sometimes, as after the Thirty Years' War, the persecution of the Jews in Eastern Europe drove them, as Thieberger has pointed out, "to an increased secret reliance on exorcisms and amulets. At the same time, the belief in spirits and supernatural acts had to be subject to the belief in God's will." Since Jewish lore insisted that only God can give select individuals the power to perform miracles such as creating life from inanimate matter, "religious purity, high erudition, and an intimate knowledge of the divine world are presuppositions of such magical and legendary powers." The man preeminently qualified to handle this role was Rabbi Loew of Prague.

Chapter Two

Yudl Rosenberg's Golem Manuscript: Literary Hoax or Eyewitness Report?

IN 1909 a literary hoax may have been perpetrated on the Jewish reading public by a Yiddish author named Yudl Rosenberg (1860–1935). In that year he published in Warsaw a Yiddish pamphlet titled *Nifla'ot Maharal im ha-Golem* (called *The Golem or The Miraculous Deeds of Rabbi Liva* in Joachim Neugroschel's English translation). Beneath the title was the inscription, "An historical description of the great wonders that the world-renowned *gaon*, Rabbi Liva of Prague, performed with the golem, which he created to wage war against the Blood Libel." Rosenberg, according to Gershon Winkler in *The Golem of Prague* (1980), was a respected rabbi, "a renowned master of Torah, a consultant in Jewish legal problems, and a prolific author of a number of important scholarly works," including a "widely used annotated Hebrew translation of . . . the *Zohar.*" Born in 1860 in Skaraschev, Poland, he was recognized as a halakic authority even in his teens. He emigrated to Canada just before World War I, going first to Toronto and then to Montreal, where "he became one of the most prominent members of the presidium of the Montreal Rabbinate." He died in 1935. It is inconceivable to Winkler that such a venerable scholar could have been the author of a literary forgery.

In any case, like Nathaniel Hawthorne fifty-nine years earlier, Rosenberg addressed his readers in a foreword and claimed to share with them the excitement of discovering a rare manuscript with the true story it contained. Hawthorne carefully explained how he had found the manuscript and small red letter *A* in the attic of the Salem Custom House; Rosenberg reported that the manuscript, the publication rights to which he had bought from one Chayim Scharfstein for

800 kronen, "lay hidden for . . . many years in the great library of Mainz where so many of Rabbi Liva's [Loew's] writings can be found." To help authenticate his find, Rosenberg scoffed at the many disbelievers in Rabbi Liva's golem and told how the great Rabbi Ezekiel Landau, when he was rabbi of Prague, "did, in fact, confirm that the golem was lying in the attic of the old great synagogue." To impress his readers further with the truth of the stories he was about to present, he told how the day Rabbi Landau found the remains of the golem he "fasted and took his ablutions in the ritual bath. Then, donning his prayer shawl and phylacteries, he asked ten of his disciples to recite psalms for him in the synagogue, whereupon he mounted to the attic." When Rabbi Landau returned in terror after a long absence, he said that hereafter he would reinstitute Rabbi Liva's decree forbidding anyone from going there. "Thus it once again became known that the story of the golem is true." Of course, Rosenberg added, there have been disbelievers for decades after Rabbi Landau's experience, and, admittedly, "there is no precise account of the whole story [of the creation of the golem] in Jewish history books." But how can anyone deny the authenticity of the manuscript when "you see that the entire story was written down by Rabbi Liva's son-in-law, that great scholar Rabbi Isaac [Yitzchak Kohen] (a true priest, blessed be the memory of that righteous man)"? His was an eyewitness report that confirmed the story's credibility.

Rosenberg ended his foreword with an appeal to the reader's appreciation for what he had done. "I had to devote a great deal of labor and expense to having the manuscript printed. And thus I hope that every intelligent person will be grateful to me for my work, and I am certain that every Jew will soon give this valuable treasure a place on his bookshelf." Obviously Rosenberg had hopes of recovering his expenses and perhaps making a profit, but he also had a more altruistic and noble objective which today's reader must respect. Blood Libels against the Jews were becoming increasingly common in late nineteenth- and early twentieth-century Europe (for example, the Hilsner case in Polna, Czechoslovakia, in 1899 and the Mendel Beilis case in Russia, from 1911 to 1913, shortly after the publication of Rosenberg's pamphlet), and Rosenberg was trying to boost the morale of European Jewry with the tales of a miraculous redeemer who had saved them from waves of anti-Semitism in the past. Gershom Scholem's contention that the connection between the golem and the Blood Libel is a modern literary invention should again be noted, however.

According to Frederic Thieberger, Rosenberg's work "shows knowledge of Rabbi Liva's family affairs, but none of the position of the Jews of Prague at the time, nor of Prague's topography." For one thing, "just the time of Rudolf II, which is the period of the stories, was a favourable one for the Jews," and there was no evidence of the Blood Libel in Bohemia. Not only is the historical background of the stories inaccurate, but so is the topography, ignorance of which "would have been impossible for anyone living in Prague." For example, the author of the tales calls the very wide river on which Prague is located "Moldavka," whereas "in Czech the river was then already called Vltava, or in German, Moldau. The addition of the Slav diminutive," argues Thieberger, "sounds very strange." Moreover, Rothberg claims he bought an original letter of Rabbi Liva's about both the creation of the golem and the rabbi's famous audience with the emperor, which he says took place in 1573, at the same time he purchased the publishing rights to the golem manuscript. But 1573 was nineteen years before the actual occurrence, before Rudolf was even emperor. It is possible that the idea of attributing the authorship of his manuscript to Rabbi Liva's son-in-law came to Rosenberg as a result of the publication in *Hamagid* in 1872 of Kohen's eyewitness report of his accompanying his father-in-law to the palace. Perhaps Rosenberg really believed that Scharfstein had sold him an authentic manuscript.

Whether Rosenberg's *Nifla'ot Maharal im ha-Golem* is a forgery may never be known. What is evident is that his manuscript is in the tradition of Hasidic hagiography, modern variations of which are Martin Buber's *Tales of the Hasidim: The Early Masters* (1947) and Elie Wiesel's *Souls on Fire* (1972). These works all celebrate the remarkable personalities and miraculous feats of the great "wonder rabbis," the Hasidic *rebbes* of the eighteenth century, and their eminent disciples. In his brief commentary following his English translation of Rosenberg's work, Joachim Neugroschel harshly calls the collection "a journalistic chronicle of adventures; primitive, schematic, and tendentious." Admitting that the pamphlet was an important influence on certain literary works that followed, he nevertheless sees it as "a striking example of Jewish pulp-writing for the masses. . . . The one-dimensional pop quality of the writing, the intrusive journalism, the linear optimism contrast with more complex literary treatments of Jewish life in Eastern Europe." Where historians and literary critics tend to ignore "conventions of pop and pulp . . . such grade B Gothic is always widely disseminated, and captures a much greater segment of the popular imagination." Thieberger seems basically to agree with Neugroschel in his evaluation of Rosenberg's tales, feeling that the "emotional and often dramatic manner" in which he told the legends made Rosenberg's book very popular. For example, "Micha ben Gorion selected a number of the stories for his *Fountain of Judah*, and Leivick based on them his drama *The Golem*, which the Habimah presented to the whole world. However," Thieberger concludes, "as old legendary material, Rosenberg's stories are of no value." What Thieberger evidently means by this last statement is that since the author is Yudl Rosenberg, not Rabbi Liva's son-in-law, not the eyewitness from the sixteenth century who has recorded these amazing tales, the manuscript is unauthentic and thus unimportant. But Thieberger and Neugroschel are too harsh in their treatment of Rosenberg, whose collection of tales has considerable merit even though it may not be what it pretends to be.

The Organization of Rosenberg's Tales

To facilitate an analysis of Rosenberg's contribution to the golem legends, it is convenient to divide his book into six sections. The first five chapters following the foreword and a bill of sale serve as an introduction to Rabbi Liva, describing the strange circumstances at his birth during the Blood Libel plot against his father (entirely fictitious), his thirty-day disputation with three hundred priests led by Cardinal Jan Sylvester, and his audience with Emperor Rudolf (called King Rudolph by Rosenberg). After the disputation, worried about the continuing Blood Libel and persecution of the Jews of Prague despite the king's new decree, Rabbi Liva decides to create a golem to protect his people. The second section consists of three chapters, the first briefly but vividly detailing the ritual followed in the creation of the golem, and the next two supplying humorous episodes describing the golem as a domestic android whose programming needs fine tuning. Chapter 11, the third section, consists of only three short paragraphs and can be seen as a transition to the next section, which is the heart of the work—ten tales telling the remarkable feats of this duo in their successful effort to make life more secure for the Jews of Prague in the late sixteenth century. In the transitional section, Rabbi Liva decides to use the golem "only for saving Jews from misfortune" and puts him on street patrol, especially around Passover. (Four of these tales involve the Blood Libel.) Aiding the homunculus in this work is a special amulet which can make him invisible. After the main body of tales, the fifth section of this arbitrary division consists of only chapter 22, in which Rabbi Liva takes away the golem's life in the year 1590 because he is no longer needed following King Rudolph's new law ending the Blood Libel in Bohemia. The sixth and final section consists of miscellania: chapter 23, which tells about Judah's engagement to Perl; chapter 24, which lists his children; and chapter 25, which is the Table of Contents.

To introduce his central theme, Rabbi Liva's proclaiming that "he would struggle with all his might against the Blood Libel and rid the Jews forever of that foul accusation," Rosenberg begins his tales with an exciting story about the rabbi's birth. An Isaac Bashevis Singer or a Bernard Malamud would have been delighted with this seriocomic story that takes place in Posen, Poland, on the first night of Passover in 1512. On this night a hired Christian is carrying a dead child in a sack for the purpose of throwing it into Rabbi Bezalel's basement. The plot is familiar: the Christian is going to accuse the Jews of Posen of having killed the child to drain his blood for the baking of the Passover *matzot*. The body will be discovered in Rabbi Bezalel's home, the Christian community will be aroused to get revenge, and a pogrom will start, giving the anti-Semites opportunity to attack, kill, rape, loot, and burn. Fortunately, the plot is revealed quite unexpectedly by the following sequence of events. The rebbetsin is in only her seventh month of pregnancy, but when her labor pains suddenly begin, members of the household run into the streets crying for a midwife. Seeing these people running towards him, the Christian carrying the dead child in the sack turns and runs. Unfortunately for him, he runs right by the police station. The officers, seeing the crowd chasing a man with a sack, join in the pursuit and catch the culprit, who then names the people who hired him to plant the corpse in Rabbi Bezalel's home. As a result of this miraculous turn of events, the Jews of Posen are saved. Rabbi Bezalel sees in the exciting events of this evening a propitious sign and prophesies supernatural powers for his son, saying, " 'This child will comfort us and ward off the Blood Libel.' And he was named Judah Liva, the Lion, for he would be like a lion who does not permit his cubs to be mangled."

To complete the introduction of Rabbi Liva and to enhance his stature before the creation of the golem, Rosenberg tells the stories of his thirty-day disputation with the three hundred Catholic priests and his audience with Rudolph II. Rosenberg lists the five major questions which were debated. They concern the use of Christian blood for Passover, the Jewish role in the murder of Christ, Jewish law supposedly requiring Jews to hate Christians, Jewish hatred of converts from Judaism, and the Jewish belief that the Torah makes them greater than other people. Cleverly using parables to defend his people against slander and ignorance of their beliefs, Rabbi Liva so pleases King Rudolph that he is invited to visit the king's palace. According to Rosenberg, "The audience lasted a full hour, and no one knows what they spoke there." As a result of Rabbi Liva's success, a royal decree is issued stating that from then on, "in a trial concerning a Blood Accusation, the tribunal was not to prosecute any outside person, but only those parties whose culpability in the murder could be adduced by proper evidence." In a second decree, Rudolph declares that "the rabbi of the city was to be present at any trial concerning a Blood Accusation. And the tribunal's judgment was subsequently to be submitted to the king for his signature."

At the end of the chapter on the disputation with the Catholic church, Rosenberg briefly introduces a priest named Tadeus (Thaddeus in other sources), who is to become the rabbi's bitter enemy. "But most of all, Rabbi Liva feared the priest Tadeus, who was a terrible anti-Semite and a magician as well and who was bent on waging war against Rabbi Liva and driving him out altogether." Seeing himself as a King David in conflict with the Philistine in Nob, "the rabbi decided to put all his efforts into battling against the priest, his antagonist." This personal antagonism becomes a major plot development, appearing in six of the tales, and figures prominently in the subsequent works of Bloch, Leivick, and Rothberg.

The Golem and His Mission

Readers of monster literature and science fiction have always been fascinated by detailed descriptions of sorcerers and scientists attempting to animate the dead, discover the elixir of life, or create human beings out of inanimate matter. Rosenberg does not disappoint his readers in chapter 8, "How Rabbi Liva Created the Golem." Rabbi Kohen explains that when his father-in-law was uncertain how to combat Tadeus, he "directed a dream question" to God. The answer comes back "alphabetically in Hebrew: 'Ah, By Clay Destroy Evil Forces, Golem, Help Israel: Justice!' " Rabbi Liva understands at once that he can create a golem with the magic power inherent in the combination of these ten words. (Emanuel bin Gorion, the editor of *Mimekor Yisrael: Classical Jewish Folktales,* in retelling the same legend, supplies a different example of Heaven's alphabetical answer to Rabbi Liva: " 'And Be Creating, Dedicate Earth Fittingly, Golem Handles Israel's Jew-hating Knife-bearers.' " According to bin Gorion, the literal translation of the Hebrew is "You create a golem of adhesive material that shall cut off strangers, the horde who rend Israel.") For the difficult task ahead, Rabbi Liva selects two assistants, his son-in-law and Jacob ben Khaim-Sassoon Ha-Levi, his leading student. (In kabbalistic tradition, more than one mind is usually required in the study of sacred texts.) Rabbi Liva swears them to secrecy and explains that he chose them because Isaac had been born under the sign of fire, and Jacob under the sign of water. Rabbi Liva himself had been born under the sign of air, so with the earth used to form the golem, all four required elements would be present.

In the month of Adar in the year 5340 (1580), the three men very early one morning walk to the Moldau River. There they shape a man of clay, three cubits long, lying on his back. Isaac gives his eyewitness report:

> Then, all three of us stood at the feet of the reclining golem, with our faces to his face, and the rabbi commanded me to circle the golem seven times from the right side to the head, from the head to the left side, and then back to the feet, and he told me the formula to speak as I circled the golem seven times. And when I had done the rabbi's bidding, the golem turned as red as fire. Next the rabbi commanded his pupil Jacob Sassoon to do the same as I had done, but he revealed different formulas to him. This time, the fiery redness was extinguished, and a vapor arose from the supine figure, which had grown nails and hair. Now, the rabbi walked around the golem seven times with the Torah scrolls, like the circular procession in synagogue at New Year's, and then, in conclusion, all three of us together recited the verse: "And the Lord God formed man of the dust of the ground, and breathed into his nostrils the breath of life; and man became a living soul."

At this moment the golem's eyes open and Rabbi Liva commands him to stand. The three men dress him in the clothes of a beadle and return home by six the same morning. Rabbi Liva names the golem Joseph because, as he explains to his companions, "he had given him the spirit of Joseph Sheday, who was half man and half demon, and who had helped the Talmudic sages in times of great trouble." Rabbi Liva explains to Joseph that he must obey his every command, " 'even if it means jumping into fire or water.' " The golem cannot speak but has remarkably acute hearing. At home, the rabbi informs his family that he found the poor mute simpleton in the street and has decided to employ him as another beadle. He "strictly forbade anyone else from ever giving him any orders."

The next two stories complete this section and provide the only comic interlude in the remainder of the collection. They lower the tension after the awesome details just recorded and relax the reader in preparation for the Blood Libels, intrigue, Gothicism, supernaturalism, and violence to come. Chapter 9, "The Golem Carries Water at Passover," is a Jewish version of Goethe's "Sorcerer's Apprentice." The narrator tells how Perl disobeys the rabbi and commands the golem to fetch water from the river to fill two buckets for the Passover holiday. Because no one supervises his work, Joseph keeps filling the buckets to overflowing, flooding the house until Rabbi Liva arrives to stop him. In "Joseph the Golem Goes Fishing at New Year's," the narrator tells how Joseph is sent to catch fish for Rosh Hashanah when "there wasn't even a minnow in all Prague." Again Joseph is forgotten until the other beadle, Abraham-Khaym, is sent to fetch him home. As the beadle conveys the rabbi's orders for him to come right away, the obedient Joseph takes his almost filled sack and empties it into the river. Everyone in Rabbi Liva's household is greatly amused by the simplemindedness of this strange fellow, and the rabbi realizes that the golem was made for loftier purposes.

After the three-paragraph transition to the serious tales, Rosenberg groups three of the four stories directly involving the Blood Libel. The first (chapter 12) is about Joseph's saving the moneylender Mordecai Mayzel (named after the Prague merchant who in real life was a dear friend of Rabbi Loew). Joseph intercepts the Christian butcher who is planning to plant the body of a dead child in Mayzel's house so that he will not have to pay a debt of five thousand crowns. Despite the happy outcome, this tale ends on an ominous note of suspense, as Father Tadeus realizes who controls Joseph and "ben[ds] his entire heart and soul on a war against Rabbi Liva and all the Jews of Prague."

The second of these tales (chapter 13) is the longest and most ambitious so far. It tries to combine two subplots, one involving a licentious fifteen-year-old Jewess who seeks out Father Tadeus for conversion; the other involves a Christian woman from the country who lights the stoves for the urban Jews on the Sabbath but suddenly runs away from her main employer before Passover. Tadeus gets the Jewish apostate to start the Blood Libel against Rabbi Liva and his two beadles. He makes her claim that the missing Christian heating woman supplied the blood which they needed, but the cardinal secretly informs the rabbi of the plot against him, giving him a month before the trial to find the evidence needed to prove his innocence. First he hides Joseph and substitutes another bearded mute to be arrested in his place. Then he sends several messengers to different villages to search for the missing girl, but after twelve days they return empty-handed. In desperation Rabbi Liva turns to Joseph, who knows the girl, and sends him to find her, with money and a letter pleading with her to return and tell the truth. Two weeks later, with Joseph still gone, the trial begins and a threatening mob gathers outside the courthouse. As both the prosecution and the defense have difficulty questioning the mute, who does not understand what is happening, the convert is asked to testify, and she incriminates Rabbi Liva, her own father who had left Prague two weeks earlier, and the two beadles, even suggesting that they killed the missing heating woman also. As in the typical melodrama, just when things are looking blackest for the side of good and innocence, a commotion is heard outside the courthouse as Joseph miraculously arrives with the missing woman, whose testimony defeats Father Tadeus and the frightened convert. All ends happily in fairy-tale fashion. "The presiding judge kissed Rabbi Liva on the forehead and thanked him for his energetic labor and great wisdom, which had prevented the judge from falsely convicting pure souls."

Chapter 14, which has nothing to do with the Blood Libel, is an even longer, more complicated story involving Father Tadeus's secret attempt to convert the lovely and learned daughter of a Jewish wine merchant. The plot, which is too complicated for a tale under ten pages, involves intrigue, matchmaking, secret identities, a young duke who falls in love with the girl, and a reluctant Rabbi Liva, who at first does not want to get involved with Tadeus. The golem is sent into action when Rabbi Liva makes him invisible and has him deliver a note to the girl while pretending he is the spirit of her grandfather, prior to his rescuing her from the churchyard where Tadeus has been hiding her. The focus of the tale shifts from the wine merchant's daughter to the young duke, who converts to Judaism. The locale shifts from Prague to Venice to Amsterdam, until the young couple are finally united and their true identities revealed in the conventional happy ending.

The next story, "A Very Wondrous Tale About a Blood Libel Which Spelled Defeat for Father Tadeus," is especially important to the student of the Golem of Prague legend, not only because of its intrinsic merit but also because it provided much of the inspiration for Leivick's remarkable verse drama twelve years later. The Gothic setting, which apparently fascinated the poet, is a large haunted house, known as the Five-Sided Palace because it had five walls facing five streets; in front of each wall there were five columns; and in between the columns there were five windows. On top of the mansion there were five large towers with ancient figures, which were obviously from the days when men worshipped the sun.

Beneath this ancient ruin is a haunted cellar connected to an underground cavern leading to the cellar of a church. At the time of the story, this ancient ruin is inhabited only by Jewish beggars. With this mysterious setting, the Gothic machinery of the story is set into motion. In the great synagogue next to the palace, Rabbi Liva is puzzled when the candle goes out before he can "pronounce the Annulment of Leaven for the First Day of Deliverance." Each time the beadle relights the candle, it goes out again. As the badly frightened beadle begins to recite the annulment, he unconsciously substitutes the word "five" for "have" and then repeats this strange error. Rabbi Liva immediately recognizes the omen and can interpret the nightmare he had the night of the Great Sabbath before Passover. In the nightmare, the Five-Sided Palace was on fire and the flames were threatening the Jews crowded into the synagogue. The rabbi had awakened screaming. The dream message has revealed that an enemy of the Jews is preparing a Blood Libel in the ruined mansion. When the beadle suddenly remembers that the underground cavern leads to Father Tadeus's church, the enemy is evident.

The narrator then explains how Tadeus, frustrated by Rabbi Liva's having defeated his attempt to convert the Jewess in the last tale, killed the child of one of his servants, poured its blood into small vials marked with Jewish names (including those of the rabbi and his family), and hid them in the cellar under the palace. Meanwhile, the police have been tipped off to search the Jewish quarter. At this point, Rosenberg has the narrator intrude with the pious optimism that colors so many of these tales. The message for the troubled Jews of Eastern Europe in the first decade of the twentieth century is unmistakable: though things look black, "it is written in Psalms: 'Behold, he that keepeth Israel shall neither slumber nor sleep.' This means that the Good Lord never sleeps, He watches over His nation, the Jews."

That very night, after the Inspection for Leaven and midnight prayers, Rabbi Liva, Joseph, and the beadle stealthily enter the Five-Sided Palace. Only the recitation of special prayers protects them from barking dogs and a sudden wind that blows out their candles. Because of stones falling from the ceiling, Rabbi Liva has to send the golem on alone to search for suspicious objects. Before long, Joseph returns with the body of the dead child wrapped in a prayer shawl and with a basket containing thirty vials of blood labeled with Hebrew letters. Rabbi Liva instructs Joseph to hide the body in Tadeus's wine cellar and to smash the vials and bury them there also. When the police arrive to search the Jewish quarter on the day before Passover, accompanied by Father Tadeus and many soldiers, they can find nothing. In a few days, as Easter approaches, the servant of Father Tadeus, annoyed by a foul smell, discovers the body of his murdered child in the wine cellar. The police recognize at once the villainy of Father Tadeus, who tries in vain to deny the whole story. He finally confesses, is arrested, tried, convicted, and banished forever.

With the villainous Tadeus removed from the scene, the reader might expect a letdown, with six stories still to come to complete the long fourth section. This is not the case, as the golem performs many wondrous feats. In chapter 16, his supernatural ability to converse with the dead enables him to stop a wedding, preventing a brother from marrying his sister. The golem even brings to the rabbinical court the spirit of the key witness, the long-dead midwife, Esther, who is placed behind a screen to testify that she switched two babies at birth out of compassion for one of two sisters-in-law who had only girls, some of whom failed to survive. Esther pleads from the grave for forgiveness after twelve years of regret. Even this story has a happy ending, as Rabbi Liva gets the fathers-in-law to agree to a new wedding with the same bride. Once again the fairy tale ends conventionally: "The young couple lived to a ripe old age in Prague, and their life together was very happy."

In one of the shortest but most interesting tales, Joseph is able to interpret a puzzling answer from Heaven to one of Rabbi Liva's dream questions. When a congregant drops the Torah scrolls on Yom Kippur, the rabbi is sure that this is an ill omen. Unable to understand the message in Hebrew which he receives from Heaven, he writes out the letters of the reply on separate pieces of paper and the golem instinctively places them correctly to reveal the first letter of each word from the Torah passage read that morning in the synagogue. The passage is a prohibition against committing adultery with one's neighbor's wife, and Rabbi Liva knows immediately that this is his congregant's sin and punishes him accordingly.

Chapter 18 is one of the most unusual in that Joseph is attacked by a group of men who throw him down a well and stone him. The leader of these men had received a public whipping at Rabbi Liva's command because he had violated the rabbi's edict against slandering certain Jewish families for not having a pure Jewish bloodline. Even a golem can be bruised to the extent that it takes him three days to recuperate. Rabbi Liva refuses to allow Joseph to get revenge on his attacker, who soon after dies a horrible death from black mange.

In the three stories which end the fifth section, Rabbi Liva takes on a therapist's role and cures a man from barking like a dog in his sleep after he has been chased by a huge black dog near a haunted house; Joseph is made invisible to pretend to be the spirit of a dead father writing to his anti-Semitic son, a duke, revealing to him his Jewish heritage; and, in a complicated story on the Blood Libel theme, Joseph's preternatural ability to discern spirits of the dead hovering over their graves the first year after burial enables him to save an innocent, wealthy Jew accused of murdering a former employee, and thus saves the whole Jewish community from a pogrom. It is at the end of this chapter (21) that Rabbi Liva revisits King Rudolph and pleads with him to end the Blood Libel once and for all. Again the reader is not told Rudolph's words, but the imperial decree is issued.

The Death of the Golem

The last chapter of Neugroschel's translation of Rosenberg's little book tells "How Rabbi Liva Removed Joseph the Golem" on the night of Lag b'Omer in the year 5350 (1590). In this version, the golem is no longer needed; his mission is completed. Rosenberg ignores earlier versions of golem legends in which the clay creature becomes a threat to his creator. If Joseph the Golem is intended to boost the morale of European Jewry still facing the daily threat of persecution, it will not do to have him go dangerously berserk and threaten the Jewish community, as he does in the stories by Bloch, Leivick, and Rothberg.

The death of Rosenberg's golem is treated as briefly as his creation. Isaac and Jacob accompany Rabbi Liva to the attic of the Altneu Synagogue, where the rabbi has told Joseph to take his bed this night. Rosenberg seems to have forgotten that this is a first-person narration and assumes the role of the omniscient author. (If Isaac is the narrator, it seems unlikely that he would refer to himself as "the *gaon,*" which he does!) At first Rabbi Liva is troubled by the violation of Jewish law in having a Kohen present in the same room as a corpse, "since such a thing was forbidden to a descendant of priests," but then he decides "that such a corpse is not really a defilement." The rabbi makes another exception and allows the faithful beadle, Abraham-Khayam, to witness the scene. In the attic Rabbi Liva, Isaac, and Jacob take "positions opposite to the ones they had taken when creating the golem." This time they face his feet and then circle to the left. They recite words which they have to repeat seven times. "After the seven encirclements, the golem was dead." There is no need to remove an aleph from his forehead or the name of God from his mouth, as in other versions of this tale, because they had never been there in the first place. Then the men remove the golem's clothes, leaving only his shirt, and cover him with old prayer shawls. "Next they shoved him under a mountain of stray leaves from holy books so that he was fully hidden." Abraham-Khaym is instructed to burn Joseph's bed and clothes secretly. A week later Rabbi Liva issues a ban on anyone's going up to the attic. No longer can loose pages of prayer books be stored there, it is said, because of the danger of fire. Only a few wise men in the Jewish quarter know the real reason.

It is hard to defend Yudl Rosenberg against criticism that his writing in *Nifla'ot Maharal im ha-Golem* is too journalistic, too matter-of-fact and uninspired in the handling of some details, too tendentious in stating others. The "one-dimensional pop quality of the writing" which Neugroschel complained of is a fair objection, what with Rosenberg's preference for stock character types (for example, the Jewess, a Christian butcher, the healer and the healer's daughter, the porter, the courier); his minimal use of dialogue and strong preference for indirect discourse; and his silly inventions, such as the judge's kissing Rabbi Liva at the end of "The Wondrous Tale of the Healer's Daughter." Nevertheless, there is something to be said in Rosenberg's favor. In retelling and recording many popular legends, he resurrected for twentieth-century readers a new folk hero, organized his incredible adventures in such a way as to enhance the Maharal's reputation as religious scholar, mystical miracle worker, and elder statesman who won the respect of the imperial court. To European Jewry, soon to be faced by a madman far more dangerous than any Father Tadeus, Yudl Rosenberg gave hope for a redeemer, sent by God, to lead them out of the Holocaust.

Chapter Three

Yudl Rosenberg's and Chayim Bloch's Twice-Told Tales

IN May of 1916, Dr. Sándor Várhely, a well-known European author who was recovering from a serious battle wound, recorded a strange meeting he had one night at a prisoner-of-war camp in Hungary. As Lieutenant Várhely made the rounds of his new post late one evening, he and his guide stopped in front of one of the guards' barracks and observed a man sitting on the floor, weeping over a book which he was reading by candlelight. The guide mistakenly explained that the dark figure, whose name he did not know, was a rabbi saying his prayers. The guide further explained "how the man, even in the strait-jacket of military service, strictly observed all the ritual prescriptions, how he fasted when he could not get Kosher food, how he had wept before the camp commander to be excused from writing on the Sabbath, to which incidentally, the latter, a splendid chap in every way, agreed." Várhely at first thought that this almost anemic, nearsighted man must be a Hasid, but, upon entering the room and engaging him in conversation, discovered that the stranger was not a rabbi but "an expert Kabbalist, a man thoroughly versed in Jewish literature, [though] as a soldier he was a terrible Schlemihl. He had not even mastered the art of saluting." This man, Chayim Bloch (1881–), was soon to become the most famous teller of the tales of the golem.

When Várhely asked why he was weeping, Bloch explained how grateful he was that the commandant had granted him many privileges, one of which was this private room in which he could continue his studies when not on duty. " 'My weeping . . . ,' " he explained, " 'has nothing to do with my military service but my nocturnal lamentations are over the destruction of our Temple, and only the Psalms which I was reading mowed [*sic*] me to tears.' " It was this Jewish businessman's love for his people and their religion that led him to his studies of the history and traditions of Hasidism and his subsequent articles in the *Oesterreichischen Wochenschrift*. Even after having been drafted into the Austrian army, he continued to write for the Viennese Jewish press. After sickness and discharge from the front, he was assigned to the prisoner-of-war camp, where he wrote the book which made him famous, *The Golem: Legends of the Ghetto of Prague*.

In "The War Diary of a Jew," Bloch wrote the following poem, which he titled "October 15 (About to leave for the front)."

I

I am not the same as I was;
    Then, I knew only praying
And now I stand at hell's door,—
    They wish to send me to kill human beings.

II

I know not if mine is the guilt;
    Must my hands with blood be stained?
Must my mind on murder be bent?
    For this, God, did'st thou give strength to my limbs?

III

O God, is it Thy decree?
    Then do I Thy will without murmur;
Yet forgive a heart full of repentance
    And I go to my death unafraid!

In this private lament, Bloch expressed a theme close to the heart of many Jews, especially in the twentieth century: the conflict between the Jewish belief in nonviolence and the demands of self-preservation. Though this theme was to be only vaguely hinted at in Bloch's treatment of the golem stories, it was to reappear in the works of Leivick and Rothberg. To Várhely, Bloch's poem and the diary in which it appeared " 'were prophecies . . . and cries of protest against the Godlessness of Europe.' " Despite the horrors of World War I, which Bloch had seen firsthand, he maintained a steady " 'faith in the goodness of Divine Providence' " and believed " 'that all these things which we have lived through are only the birthpangs of a new humanity.' " It is this same optimism that Bloch expresses in his tales of the golem, where divine providence appears miraculously in the guise of Rabbi Judah Loew.

In his own introduction to his book, Bloch acknowledges having read "a manuscript in the Hebrew language and script, which bears the title 'Nifloet Mhrl'," but, surprisingly, he refers to it later as the work of an "unknown compiler." Either he did not want to admit his large debt to Yudl Rosenberg, allegedly the translator, or the copy he used omitted Rosenberg's name. Bloch's introduction indicates that he accepted Rosenberg's work, "rich in tragic episodes and enchanting tales," as having been "redacted about three hundred years ago." Thus he accepted Rabbi Loew's son-in-law as the author of these "unostentatious words" which tell "with impressive naiveté" the story of the career of the Maharal. Bloch admits imitating the original manuscript, "this unadorned recital which I, substantially retaining the naiveté and the childishly awkward presentation of the unknown compiler, transmit to the reader."

Though he never names Rosenberg, Bloch does mention Gustav Meyrink's famous novel *Der Golem,* published in 1915, four years before Bloch's own book. Meyrink's novel, as chapter 5 will show, makes very little use of the many details in Rosenberg, but Bloch quotes Meyrink's statement about Prague: even though he did not know the origin of the golem legend, " 'somewhere, something which cannot die haunts this quarter of the city and is somehow connected with the legend, of that I am sure.' " Bloch thinks that those who take the golem stories literally are the mystics who actually believe that the correct knowledge of the Kabbalah and the proper use of the *Shem ha-meforash* can endow a clay figure with life.

> Those, however, who do not believe in and deny any justification for the mystical and the occult, aver that we have here to deal with a symbol, the allegorical meaning of which was eventually forgotten, because of the clearness and vividness of the symbol itself, which has consequently come down through the centuries with a sort of independent life of its own in the shape of a legend.

Bloch sees it as his mission to help perpetuate the legend of the golem. In his stories, an element appears that was not evident in Rosenberg's: the increasing wildness of the robot and its potential destructiveness, an additional threat to the very Jewish community it was meant to serve. Traditionally, Bloch observes, the golem was "utilized for the protection of persecuted Jews, at such junctures when mere human strength and wisdom are no longer effectual." Was the golem "a symbol of God's help, which always comes in due season, although frequently (like the Golem) at the last, most anxious moment?" If so, how does one account for the golem's going mad and becoming a threat to his master? Bloch sees two possible answers to this seeming contradiction in the symbol's meaning. First, "the ultimate madness of the Golem, this so startling denouement of all the legends. . . . may simply be a foreign *motif* which, because of external similarity, became amalgamated with these legends." Bloch's alternative is a theological explanation of this development, more in keeping with traditional Jewish thought. "The help of God upon which man ultimately comes to depend supinely and thoughtlessly, brings about his ruin, because the 'Holy One' comes to spurn such spiritless men." Here is the traditional Jewish emphasis on free will and individual responsibility. Whatever the explanation, Bloch hopes that his reader will find in his book "significant tales which may inspire a more profound interpretation of these unusually noteworthy legends."

Bloch's Revisions and Additions

The question which this chapter sets out to answer is how does Bloch's version of the golem stories differ from Rosenberg's? No attempt will be made at linguistic or stylistic analysis since both works are in translation, and it will be up to future specialists to study the original works in Yiddish and German to evaluate the quality of the language and the success or failure of the translators. What this chapter will do is focus on the structure of Bloch's book, differences in technique and detail between Bloch's and Rosenberg's stories, the new stories Bloch has added about the golem and Rabbi Loew, and the strengths and weaknesses of each collection.

The most obvious difference is that Bloch's *Golem* is considerably longer than Rosenberg's booklet. Whereas Rosenberg divided his collection into twenty-five chapters, including his brief foreword and the alleged bill of sale, the English translation of Bloch's book has thirty-three chapters and three introductions: one by Hans Ludwig Held, who published in Munich an article on the golem; one by Harry Schneiderman, Bloch's main translator (four of the stories were translated by an Englishwoman, Mrs. Loneck-Winterbotham); and one by the author himself. Furthermore, Bloch's book is enhanced by the inclusion of some interesting photographs, showing such things as a memorial statue of Rabbi Loew, the inside and outside of the famous Altneu Synagogue, and the graves of the rabbi and his disciples.

In some ways Bloch improves on Rosenberg's work, but he loses something also. First, Bloch sensibly combines in his third chapter Rosenberg's extremely short third and fourth chapters, which tell how Rabbi Liva, now famous throughout the world, is determined to fight the Blood Libel in Prague and therefore arranges to debate the three hundred priests. Rosenberg forgets to explain Rabbi Liva's move from Posen to Prague; Bloch is more careful in accounting for the change, but he distorts history by having Rabbi Loew chosen as chief rabbi of Prague many years before he actually was honored with that position. Also interesting is Bloch's introduction early in this chapter of Father Thaddeus, the rabbi's old nemesis. In this casual way, Bloch reinforces Rabbi Loew's motivation for arranging the disputation. Rosenberg saves the introduction of Tadeus for the end of the next chapter, effectively setting up an ominous undercurrent immediately after Rabbi Liva's success in the disputation. The Jewish community cannot let down its guard.

Bloch wisely drops Rosenberg's sixth chapter, "Rabbi Liva Is Presented at the Court of King Rudolph," and saves this private audience for a much later date. Rosenberg's introducing it so early makes no sense, and the king's issuing a decree helping the Jews against the Blood Libel becomes expendable since this imperial edict will be repeated more effectively much later in both works, coming as a climax after the successful efforts of Rabbi Loew and the golem to save the Jewish community. On the other hand, Bloch adds five golem chapters which do not appear in Rosenberg. The first three (chapters 14, 17, and 25) are stories in which the golem plays an active role. The other two (chapters 27 and 28) occur after his death. Chapter 27 concerns the location of his remains; chapter 28 is a collection of miscellaneous unconnected statements which Bloch calls "Rabbi Loew's Utterances on the Golem."

Chapter 14, the first of the new golem stories, is "A Passower [sic] Miracle." It is another Blood Libel plot and the setting is the first evening of Passover, 5344 (1584). While leading the prayers, instead of *umahalif es hazmanim* ("and He changes the seasons"), Rabbi Loew reads *umahamitz es hazmanim* ("and He sours the seasons"). Immediately the rabbi stops, instructs the congregation to continue praying, and sends word to the other congregations in Prague not to leave their synagogues until he gives permission. Then he sends Joseph the Golem home to bring him both an ordinary matzo and a special one (for the Seder ceremony). Ordered to taste both, Joseph becomes "deathly pale, and indicate[s] that he [feels] pain." Rabbi Loew relieves the pain by touching the golem's body with his hand, and then sends a warning to all the synagogues that no one is to touch matzot baked in Prague because they were "chometz (leavened, ritually unfit . . .)." Everyone in the community is told to share the good matzot.

As in several of the stories of both Rosenberg and Bloch, Rabbi Loew assumes the role of Sherlock Holmes. His investigation reveals that two red-bearded Gentile apprentice bakers were hired the day before to do the rolling (that is, to make lines in the matzot). With a special amulet to make him invisible, Joseph is sent to search the red-beards' home, where he finds the poison powder. Rabbi Loew, certain now of the nefarious plot, goes to the police. The red-beards resist arrest and at first refuse to confess, but one finally breaks down and implicates Father Thaddeus, who is behind the whole plot. The police chief has all the poisoned matzot collected, Thaddeus denies the whole story and is released, and the two red-beards are given five years in prison. On the seventh day of Passover, in "a sermon on the wonderful redemption of the Israelites from Egypt through the miraculous parting of the Red Sea," Rabbi Loew tells his congregation of God's latest miracle in saving the Jewish community of Prague.

Bloch adds chapter 17, "The Golem Fetches Fish and Apples," for needed comic relief. This new fish story is strategically placed after five consecutive stories on the Blood Libel and Father Thaddeus. In this amusing tale the rabbi's wife, Pearl, has forgotten her earlier unpleasant experience when she disobeyed her husband and gave the golem domestic chores. She rationalizes her new disobedience because of the *mitzvah* ("good deed") she and the rabbi are doing in preparing a wedding feast for a poor orphaned girl, and thus the use of the golem to catch a fish "would not be considered a private service." Joseph catches a large fish which he puts, tail up, underneath his shirt. When the still living fish slaps him across the face with its tail, the angry golem races back to the river and throws it into the water so hard that it sinks to the bottom. Joseph's other domestic errand in this story is to buy some apples. When the female fruit vendor insists on placing Joseph's purchase in a bag, the angry golem picks up both the screaming woman and her whole fruit stand and places them on his shoulders as he swiftly runs though the city, depositing his burden in Rabbi

Loew's courtyard. The rabbi is amused by this farcical incident, but he warns Pearl not to use the golem as a servant again. "Since then it is said even to this day in Prague, when one speaks of something that is not right, that is topsy-turvy: 'It is like the Golem with the fish.' "

Far more serious and significant is chapter 25, "The Golem Runs Amuck." The golem's going berserk had been hinted at in comic interludes such as the above, but the concept of his being a threat to the entire Jewish community is new to the recorded Prague legends, this motif having been previously dominant in the Chelm legends clustered around Rabbi Elijah. Bloch's adding this story greatly strengthens Rabbi Loew's motivation for taking away Joseph's life. The story is surprisingly short and simple. Every Friday afternoon, before the Sabbath, Rabbi Loew gives Joseph his instructions for the next twenty-four hours, "for on the Sabbath he spoke to him only in extremely urgent cases. Generally Rabbi Loew used to order him to do nothing else on Sabbath but be on guard and serve as watchman." However, one Friday the rabbi forgets to give the golem his instructions. Joseph, "like one mad, began running about the Jewish section of the city, threatening to destroy everything. The want of employment made him awkward and wild." Since the Sabbath service has already begun, Rabbi Loew has a dilemma: should he desecrate the Sabbath or allow the rampaging golem to go uncontrolled? He forgets momentarily that in questions of danger to human life, Jewish law allows, if not actually insists on, profanation of the Sabbath. Rushing out of the synagogue into the street, the rabbi orders Joseph, wherever he is, to stop. The golem obeys immediately and stands "like a post. In a single instant, he had overcome the violence of his fury." Rabbi Loew orders him home to bed and never again forgets to give him instructions on Friday afternoon. "To his confidential friends he [says]: 'The Golem could have laid waste all Prague, if I had not calmed him down in time.' "

Chapter 27, "Where Lie the Remains of the Golem?," is the first of many legends which have continued to this day concerning attempts to find the golem's lifeless clay. (Post-World War II versions tell of Nazi soldiers climbing to the attic of the Altneu Synagogue and never returning.) In Bloch's tale, which he claims was "almost unknown" until his retelling, the beadle, Abraham Chayim, sets out to imitate Rabbi Loew and create his own golem. According to this legend, Chayim was present at the original act of creation at the Moldau and is reasonably sure he can duplicate the feat. Fearful of climbing up to the attic alone, he secures the secret assistance of his brother-in-law,

Abraham ben Secharja, and the beadles of the Pinkas Synagogue; together they enter the garret, find the mound of clay, and bring it to the synagogue, where they hide it behind the reading desk. Next they solicit the help of Ascher Balbierer, Abraham Chayim's son-in-law, a Kabbalist who claims he has discovered "the mystic alphabetical formula in the *Sefer Jezirah*" needed to create a golem. Late at night, the three men carry Joseph's remains through the streets and alleys of Prague to the cellar of Balbierer's house, where they try in vain night after night to resurrect him.

The story reaches its climax when an epidemic breaks out in Prague, killing hundreds of people, including two of Balbierer's five children, though there are no other victims on his street. The mother had pleaded with her husband not to bring the remains of the golem home because of the risk if they should be caught. Her anxiety apparently convinces Balbierer that he is being punished for violating Rabbi Loew's edict. Therefore he places the corpses of his two children in one coffin and the remains of the golem in the emptied one. The coffins are then taken at night to a special cemetery outside the city for victims of the epidemic. The legend ends with the kind of specific detail that often teases the reader of such tales to suspend disbelief: the men carried the golem's coffin "up to the Gallows Hill which lies one mile and two hundred yards from the Neistaedter Gate on the Vienna state road, and placed it on that side of the hill which is turned toward the city. That was on the evening of the 5th day of Adar."

Although Bloch's collection has nine more chapters, the twenty-eighth is the last one that has anything to do with the golem, a rather strange fact considering the book's title. It is as though Bloch takes all of the remaining statements about the golem which he could not incorporate into the stories and catalogues them in an appendix which he calls chapter 28. Since an appendix is not usually found with eight chapters yet to come, the aesthetic effect is devastating. The effect is not unlike having Dostoevsky decide to add a short sequel having nothing to do with Raskolnikov to *Crime and Punishment*. Rosenberg's work has much better unity, ending when the life of the golem does.

Separating the fifteen paragraphs of chapter 28 are rows of three asterisks. The paragraphs range from one to eighteen lines. The shortest explains that "the Golem could not be counted in a Minyan" (the minimum number of ten adult Jewish males required for public prayer services). The longest discusses the golem's exemption from any illness because of his supernatural ability to comprehend the new medicinal odor released each of the twenty-four hours in the Garden of

Eden. Two sections earlier, Bloch had strangely claimed, with no attempt to show the logical connection between morality and physiology, that "the Golem was never ill, for he was immune from every impulse to do evil." (Here Bloch seems to have overlooked a contradiction with the chapter in which the golem is poisoned and feels pain until Rabbi Loew heals him.) Two of the paragraphs discuss Jewish demonology and explain why Rabbi Loew chose the name Joseph over Jonathan, an explanation that Rosenberg works effectively into his story of the creation of the golem. Three brief sections echo the discussions of sixteenth-century Kabbalists like Moses Cordovero, who debated whether the golem has any kind of soul. Bloch opposes Cordovero's view, declaring that the golem is mute "because as an incomplete creation, he was unworthy that the *Neshama*, the light of God, dwell within him. He was inhabited only by *Nefesh* (sensory being) and *Ruach* (spirit)." *Daat* ("knowledge") the golem could have only in a small amount. "The other two intelligences, *Cochmah* (wisdom) and *Bina* (judgment), he could not be supplied with at all, because . . . there was no *Neshamah* dwelling in his being." On the subject of the golem's sexual instinct, which played no part in the earlier legends of the golem, but which would become important in the works of Leivick and Rothberg, Bloch dogmatically insists that the creature has none, "for if he had had that instinct, no woman would have been safe from him." On the subject of free will, Bloch argues that since the golem, "like the animals and birds, demons and spirits," is able to see things hidden to man, he cannot be said to have free will, which allows man to choose between his good and evil impulses without any supernatural knowledge. And finally, claims Bloch, the golem will be resurrected in some different form "at the end of all human existence."

Before the analysis of the eight new stories Bloch adds after he is finished with the golem, another change should be pointed out. Bloch takes the ending of Rosenberg's chapter 20, "The Last Blood Libel in Prague During Rabbi Liva's Lifetime," the longest story in his little book, and turns it into a short new chapter which becomes chapter 24 of his collection. Rosenberg effectively ends his story with a three-paragraph denouement after Rabbi Liva, through the supernatural senses of the golem, has proved the innocence of Aaron Ginz, who had been imprisoned with his family because of the Blood Libel. After the rabbi sends an official report of the case to King Rudolph with a request for an audience at court, he successfully pleads the case for his people and wins a promise that no more such accusations could be made in his kingdom. Bloch gives Rabbi Loew's audience with Kaiser Rudolf much greater prominence, separating it from the story proper and making it the climax of all the stories to that point. If Rabbi Loew's objective was to end the Blood Libel against the Jews of Prague in his lifetime, he succeeded, and this great victory, Bloch obviously feels, demands more than three short paragraphs ending a ten-page story. However, since Bloch continues the rabbi's adventures for twelve more chapters, this climax comes in the wrong place and loses the special impact Bloch tried to give it.

In expanding Rosenberg's three short paragraphs to two and one-half pages, Bloch enhances the details and adds some of his own. Whereas Rabbi Liva simply reports to King Rudolph on the last case, Rabbi Loew includes a report on all the Blood Libels for the last ten years. Bloch adds a memorable descriptive sentence which both understates the anti-Semitism of generations and acknowledges the liberalism of the emperor: "Although he had been brought up by Jesuits in the country of ever-smoking funeral pyres, the Kaiser was nevertheless not without feeling of justice towards the Jews, so he granted the request in a most gracious manner." Another interesting difference is seen when Rosenberg's journalistic, matter-of-fact report ("The king had a long conversation with him. Rabbi Liva never cared to reveal what was said.") is compared to Bloch's more intimate record of this same information, dramatically placed in quotation marks as a happy Rabbi Loew reports to his friends,

> "I thank the Lord, praised be His name, that I have succeeded in removing from this earth the wrong of blood-accusations. The Kaiser spoke to me about a half hour and gave me his royal word that from now on he would not only root out blood-accusations in his country, but would also treat the Jews the same as other subjects of his Kingdom, and would protect their rights."

Bloch then summarizes the highlights of the kaiser's proclamation, adding one not found in Rosenberg, that in any Christian accusation of a Jew, "the fact must be established by four incontestable witnesses."

Bloch's Eight New Stories about the Maharal

Whether Yudl Rosenberg was familiar with some version of the last eight stories that Bloch recorded in his collection is unknown. If he were and he elected to omit them, his reason probably was that they did not refer to the golem. However, because they give the student of the golem legends more insight into anti-Semitism in the late sixteenth century and into the uncanny attributes of the Maharal acting on behalf of the persecuted Jews, these stories merit mention. At the end of the third one, "Kaiser Rudolf in Captivity" (chapter 31), Bloch explains that Rabbi Loew kept a secret book in which he recorded these events. "Only after his death—the Kaiser, too, had already departed—was the secret book discovered." Since the only posthumous book of Rabbi Loew's available to Bloch was *Hidushe Gur Arye* (1837), a commentary on some talmudic tractates, Bloch simply pretends to have seen the manuscript. He then adds the moral underlying his book as well as Rosenberg's: he retells the stories so that "future generations might know that God does not desert His people, Israel, and that, just when their misery is at its worst, help is at hand."

In each of the stories that follow, Rabbi Loew's reputation is enhanced by his magical powers, his "Solomonic Wisdom," and his devotion to his disciples. Only once, in "The 'Kabbala,' " does he require outside help, as he does in most of the golem stories. Sometimes Bloch supplies two versions of the same story, the basic plot being given a different twist, as so often happens to stories passed down orally from one generation to the next.

Two of the first three stories (chapters 29 and 31) deal with the rabbi's friendship with the kaiser. In both cases Rabbi Loew's magical ability to control another person's dreams saves the day. In "The Expulsion of the Jews" (chapter 29), as a result of the kaiser's edict expelling the Jews from his country on penalty of death and confiscation of all property, troubled Jews "from far and wide . . . came to Prague, to Rabbi Loew, who was considered among the Jews at the time as the Head of the Diaspora." The rabbi assures them that the whole matter will be resolved in their favor on the morrow. That night, Rabbi Loew's magic works. The kaiser has a strange dream in which he becomes separated from his retinue while swimming in a river. The naked kaiser gets lost in the forest, is threatened by some rough woodcutters, and is finally led back to the city by a beggar who supplies him with rags. The city people do not recognize their kaiser in this attire, and he ends up wandering to Prague, where he enters the ghetto. The Hasidic love of parables is evident in the kaiser's reflection: " 'The fate of this people, with their great past and their present low state, is the semblance of my own. This people, too, was great once, and yet, it is not recognized now." An old Jew finally believes the beggarly stranger and takes him to Rabbi Loew, who cuts the kaiser's beard, trims his nails, anoints his body with fragrant oils, and gives him more appropriate clothing. The only condition Rabbi Loew imposes on his monarch is his signature on two copies of a document to revoke the edict expelling the Jews. This the kaiser gives willingly and then wakes up. Has he dreamed the whole thing or has it actually happened? The narrator of this folktale turns fantasy into reality with the perfect final touch—on the table is a copy of the newly signed document and, in a golden tray, the kaiser's recently trimmed whiskers and nails.

"Kaiser Rudolf in Captivity" (chapter 31) is a variant of the same plot. This time a troubled Kaiser Rudolf sends for Rabbi Loew and explains that he must reluctantly sign an anti-Semitic bill submitted to him by his ministers. The rabbi tries in vain to change his mind. When the kaiser falls asleep in the rabbi's garden, he dreams that one of his rebellious princes has defeated him in battle and imprisoned him for eleven years. One day he suddenly sees Rabbi Loew, who promises to free him on the condition that he destroy the edict against the Jews. In this version, the sleepwalking kaiser gives Rabbi Loew the key to his cabinet holding the papers and returns with him to the castle, where he wakes up and expresses eternal gratitude to his Jewish friend for having saved him.

In "Solomonic Wisdom" (chapter 30), the kaiser invites Rabbi Loew to help judge a difficult case involving a Gentile pork butcher who, after spying on his neighbor, a Jewish secondhand clothes dealer, and observing him counting some coins, reports to the police that the same number of coins had been stolen from him. When the Jew is arrested, it is his word against the butcher's. Rabbi Loew solves the case in a manner that would have pleased Arthur Conan Doyle. Pointing out that coins handled by a butcher would have fat on them, he suggests that these disputed coins be thrown into a kettle of boiling water. If fat comes to the surface, the coins belong to the butcher. Of course the water remains clean, and the clothes dealer is declared the rightful owner.

Chapters 32, 33, and 34 have their source in *Sippurim* or in Jirásek's *Old Bohemian Tales*. Chapter 32 is the tale in which Rabbi Loew conjures up the great Jewish leaders of the past for the entertainment of the kaiser and his court, with the warning that there is to be no laughter. Chapters 33 and 34 are variations of the legend about the disappearing palace brought about by the rabbi's magic. In Chapter 34, the guest being entertained is a count who steals a gold saltshaker.

The purpose of these last eight stories can only be to enhance the reputation of the Great Rabbi Loew, but they are ultimately disappointing. In most of them, he is reduced to necromancy, to the kind of wizardry expected from a Merlin. Missing is the lofty motivation of the golem stories, that of saving the Jews from the terrors of the Blood Libel and the threat of a pogrom; instead there is the petty vanity of the kaiser satisfied by the court magician. Hans Ludwig Held's claim that in Bloch's collection the legends of the golem are closer to the spiritual and mystical than to the magical is contradicted by these last tales. Held may have had in mind a story like "The 'Kabbala' " (chapter 35), which Bloch probably got from C. Ludwig Kapper's tale, "The Great Rabbi Loew and the Count," in Pascheles's *Sippurim*. (This is the story in which Rabbi Loew is assisted by his colleague from Spain when a count orders them to teach him the secrets of the Kabbalah.) Held must also have been thinking of Bloch's several allusions to the *Sefer Yezirah* and its Zurifim (formulas).

The final story in Bloch's collection, "Death," is one of the best. Rabbi Loew wins his final victory but loses his life in the effort. After explaining how the rabbi, after the midnight lamentation, spends the next hour every night speaking with the souls of the dead in the Altneu Synagogue, Bloch tells how this nocturnal routine is followed by a terrifying nightmare on the eleventh day of Elul, 5369. Rabbi Loew sees himself before a great court with an open gate. Inside is an altar at which stands a threatening figure, eyes blazing lightning, with a bloody knife in his right hand. Before him stands a long line of the rabbi's pupils, whom he is killing one after the other. Both the rabbi's son-in-law, Rabbi Yitzchak, and Jacob ben Chayim Sasson, his favorite disciple, are awaiting their turn, but he tears the knife from the grasp of the assassin and commands him to stop. Aware that the dream message is another warning, he wonders what he must do to save his students. At this moment he sees a strange light in the synagogue across the street and runs inside. (Bloch takes what follows from Koop's *Sagen und Erzählungen aus der Provinz Posen* [1893]; it is also found in Juda Bergmann's *Legenden der Juden* [1919].) He finds the stranger of his dream reading from the scroll in his left hand and calling out the blood-written names of those he is going to kill. "The last name he heard was his own,—it was at the foot of the list of death."

Recognizing the Angel of Death, Rabbi Loew springs at him and tears the scroll from his hand. Safely back in his house, the rabbi repeatedly reads the list of names, recognizing not only those of his students but those of all the members of his congregation. He is overjoyed with the realization that he has saved their lives. Suddenly he notices that the corner of the scroll is missing. No matter how hard he tries, he cannot figure out whose name is on it. When a week passes with no deaths, a joyous Rabbi Loew holds a thanksgiving feast at which he tells his followers what has happened.

> But soon after the feast Rabbi Loew caught a violent cold, and on the 18th of Elul 5369, his noble soul departed from its earthly tenement. *On the piece of paper which had remained in the hand of the Angel of Death was his name.* The noble teacher in looking over the scroll for the missing name had entirely forgotten to look for his own. He whose name had been the last one on the sheet was the first to fall.

Rosenberg's and Bloch's Tales Compared

When Joachim Neugroschel spoke of the "one-dimensional pop quality" and "intrusive journalese" of Yudl Rosenberg's book, he could also have mentioned other flaws which become more noticeable when Rosenberg's and Bloch's versions of the same stories are compared. To Rosenberg's credit, of course, is his greater success in unifying his collection of tales and sticking more closely to his title character. However, Bloch is the more sophisticated storyteller.

A representative story which reveals interesting differences between the two writers is "The Wondrous Tale of the Healer's Daughter," by Rosenberg, and Bloch's version, "The Renegade." Characteristically, Bloch changes much of the indirect discourse in Rosenberg's story to direct quotation. This way he reduces the amount of explication and narration and makes the scene more dramatic. A good example is Bloch's dialogue between the Jewish apostate Dinah and the cardinal: " 'How do you know'—the Cardinal spoke the words with sharp, penetrating look—'that the Jews slaughter a Christian?' " Rosenberg's narration is flat: "At the baptism the cardinal did ask the expected question, and the girl answered just as the priest had instructed her." Another example is Rosenberg's summary of the content of the false letter supposedly written by the employer who wants Dinah to come back to work for him versus Bloch's version, which supplies the exact letter in quotation marks. Bloch's method is more immediate as well as more dramatic. Less effective is Bloch's sentimental indulgence in the pathetic fallacy when he adds, "The day of the trial was a cloudy one, as if nature wished to show that it felt pity for the Jewish community in its time of trouble." Rosenberg avoids this kind of romantic sentimentality, but, in all fairness to Bloch, it should be pointed out that he does not use it very often.

As Father Thaddeus arrives at the trial of Rabbi Loew and the other Jews accused of the Blood Libel, there is a striking difference in the details in each version. Rosenberg simply reports that "Father Tadeus and the convert arrived in a closed carriage." Bloch enhances the drama by adding the crowd's reaction to the sight of one of their heroes. "As Thaddeus, accompanied by the state witness, rode up, he was hailed by the populace with strong acclamations." Thus the hostile atmosphere bodes poorly for the Jewish defendants. Rosenberg continues his restrained report ("Next, Rabbi Liva drove up, accompanied by Mordecai Meyzel, a leader of the Jewish community in Prague"), while Bloch fleshes out this scene dramatically ("A few minutes later, Rabbi Loew accompanied by Mordecai Meisel, the president of the community appeared. They were received with cat-calls and whistling and cries of 'Christ-killers!' It was only thanks to the precautions of the authorities that they were not trampled underfoot by the mob"). When Rosenberg adds a ludicrous description of the presiding judge kissing Rabbi Liva and thanking him "for his energetic labor and great wisdom, which had prevented the judges from falsely convicting pure souls," Bloch simply states that "Rabbi Loew related what steps he had taken to clear the matter up, and his report was received by the populace and the judges with the greatest attention." Finally, Rosenberg ends his story with a statement comparing Tadeus with Haman, the well-known anti-Semite, adding that all Prague rejoiced in Rabbi Liva's victory, as did Esther's city of Shushan. Block ignores this colorful allusion to Jewish history and simply brings down his curtain with "The Jews of Prague celebrated Shevuoth which came three days after the trial with an enthusiasm they had never felt before."

"Caught in His Own Net," Bloch's version of Rosenberg's "Very Wondrous Tale About Blood Libel Which Spelled Final Defeat for Father Tadeus," has more swiftly moving action and better special effects. Bloch effectively creates an eerie atmosphere with the silence of the city at midnight. As Rabbi Loew, the beadle, and Joseph head quietly for the black and neglected ruins of the Five-Sided Palace, "a rainy damp blew in their faces." The gothic effect is reinforced by lines not found in Rosenberg's tale, such as "The pillars of the court in the endless row, as they emerged from the darkness in the light of the torches, and again disappeared, aroused weird feelings." With their burning Havdalah candles the three men enter the building, "with its doorless and windowless openings. The roof also had partly collapsed, so that the cloud covered sky looked down into the dreary ruins." When the intruders step inside, Rosenberg simply writes that "at once a wind arose and dust whirled about, and they heard the barking of dogs as the wind tried to blow out the candles." Bloch's description of the same moment is more suspenseful and exciting. As the three men enter the dilapidated building, "the odor of the tomb permeated the place and a plaintive whining was audible. The Rabbi listened and caught the sound distinctly. It sounded now like the whimpering of a child, now the whining of a dog, now it would rise in volume until it finally resembled the roaring of a lion."

Later in the same story, Rosenberg's description of the servant's discovery of the body of his missing child in Father Tadeus's wine cellar is much too matter-of-fact. "The lackey realized something was wrong, and he hunted carefully until he came upon the dead child, who he recognized at once." Bloch's description of this macabre scene, though also brief, is much more dramatic and fulfills the reader's expectations of the father's horrified reaction, which Rosenberg strangely omits. While Wachlaw was taking inventory of the priest's wine, "he came upon the corpse of a child. . . . Upon examining it, he was horror stricken and almost swooned, for he recognized his missing child." Rosenberg informs his reader in the denouement that "the priest was arrested at once, and he was tried and banished forever." Bloch's more specific and moralistic version reads, "The monk was sentenced to ten years imprisonment and was unfrocked as one unworthy to continue his sacred office." To this Bloch adds a characteristically personal aside: "May a similar fate overtake all Thine enemies, O Lord!"

The endings of these two versions of the same story also differ in a way that illustrates Bloch's superior artistry. Bloch's simple one-sentence paragraph ends on just the right note of lighthearted commentary. "Who had cleaned out from the *Funfer Palast* the *chometz* which might have soured the lives of the Jews of Prague, only Rabbi Loew and his confidents knew." Rosenberg is much more heavy-handed and cumbersome in his attempt at erudition.

> In regard to these events, Rabbi Liva repeated the Hebrew: "He wanted to protect the worthy woman," by which he meant that God wanted to protect the holy Shekhina, the divine emanation, "and her children as well,"—the Jews. And the holy Shekhinah had sent the word "five" to his lips so that he would know enough to search the Five-Sided Palace.

The differences between Rosenberg's and Bloch's portraits of the golem seem to be slight. In both works the golem is presented basically as an unfeeling simpleton, a powerful robot whose only function is to carry out the commands of his creator. At the conclusion of "How Rabbi Liva Created the Golem," Rosenberg describes the homunculus as always sitting in the corner of the rabbi's courtroom, "with his hands folded behind his head, just like a golem, who thinks about nothing at all, and so people started calling him 'Joseph the Golem,' and a few nicknamed him 'Joseph the Mute.' " Bloch adds a similar touch to this picture of the uncomplicated automaton when in "The Golem as Fisherman" he explains how the golem was told to come home "soon," but "as to the meaning of the word 'soon' he had not the slightest idea."

In both works this simpleton, dressed in the humble clothes of a beadle, is capable of great strength. Rosenberg emphasizes this point more explicitly than Bloch. For example, in "The Tale of the Torah That Fell to the Ground," Rabbi Liva sends Joseph with a note asking the sinner in his congregation to come to him immediately. Rosenberg then adds,

> And when Joseph the Golem went for someone, that person, that person knew he had to come, for if not, it had often happened that Joseph the Golem would take the unwilling man and throw him over his back like a sheep, and then carry him back to the rabbi through the streets.

In Bloch's "Attack on the Golem," Joseph carries the porter "like a slaughtered little lamb, through the city to Rabbi Loew's house." In the earlier version, Rosenberg not only says that Joseph carries him "through the streets like a sheep," but adds, "The porter was no weakling, everyone was afraid of him. But there was nothing he could do against Joseph the Golem." On the occasion when Joseph is attacked and pushed into the well, Bloch writes,

> It was a freezing, cold night. If the Golem had been an ordinary human being, he would have met death instantly. But to him it did not mean much. He dived several times in the ice cold water and attempted to climb up on the walls.

As long as this superhuman strength is put to good use under the control of the rabbi, all goes well. There is only the barest hint in Rosenberg that it can run amuck. This is seen in the story mentioned above, when Rabbi Liva has a few strong men administer a lashing to the porter as his punishment for violating the rabbi's edict. In Rosenberg's version the men carry out the lashing at the rabbi's command, "and Joseph the Golem went to work with a vengeance, like a slaughterer with a bull"; the words hint more at cruelty and brutality than at anger. But what is only an undercurrent in Rosenberg's tale comes to the surface in that of Bloch, who gives the golem a whole new dimension. Whereas Rosenberg simply states that the golem cannot speak, Bloch, in "The Making of the Golem," adds, "And that was really an advantage. God knows what could have happened if a Golem had been given the faculty of speech also!" Bloch's golem is capable of flaring anger and goes somewhat wild in the scenes involving fishing in the Moldau and picking up the fruit peddler and her cart. Though comic moments, these interludes foreshadow Bloch's chapter "The Golem Runs Amuck." One of Bloch's most seminal suggestions, however, appears in a two-sentence paragraph at the end of "The Golem Is Given Work." After explaining how Joseph was put on night patrol in the ghetto, Bloch says, "In this way the Golem became the terror of the enemy of the Jews. Some regarded him as a spectre of Rabbi Loew." The psychological implications of this last concept, the golem as doppelgänger, fascinated Meyrink, Leivick, and Rothberg, and will be discussed in later chapters.

The differences in the portraits of the rabbi in the two collections are small. Rosenberg characterizes him somewhat indirectly, mainly through his actions; Bloch uses more direct statement, more authorial comment. For example, at the end of "Purim Joy and Tragedy," Bloch says that his success in proving the innocence of Reb Aaron and his family "attracted extraordinary attention in Prague and in the entire country, and increased the great respect in which Rabbi Loew was held." Rosenberg simply says that *"the city of Prague rejoiced and was glad."* Bloch goes one step further, ending his epilogue to "The Audience with the Kaiser" with a quotation from Proverbs 22:29, " 'Seest thou a man diligent in his business? He shall stand before Kings.' "

Both Rosenberg and Bloch contribute their bit to hagiography in their glorification of the great rabbi. In "The Betrothal," Bloch says that Pearl's father, Reb Schmelke Reich, asked his future son-in-law to go to Lublin to study under Rabbi Solomon Luria, who "at that time was the star of the greatest magnitude in the heavens of Jewish learning, the supreme head of the Diaspora." In the same story, a Russian cavalry officer pays Pearl for some bread by throwing his extra saddle at her feet. This saddle, it turns out, has a fortune hidden in it. Reb Reich insists that the officer is actually the prophet Elijah, whose appearance attests to the greatness of his future son-in-law.

Sometimes the differences in characterization of the rabbi are more subtle. In "Caught in His Own Net," Bloch (as does Rosenberg in his version) mentions the rabbi's custom of reading prayers from the book rather than reciting them from memory, but Bloch adds, "He used to say that he could tell from the characters what was the mood of Heaven, whether mercy or severity,—if the latter, he understood how to temper it." The addition of this comment disrupts the narrative, but it enhances the characterization of Rabbi Loew as a kabbalistic scholar and wonder rabbi capable of amazing feats.

Only a few final miscellaneous differences between the Bloch and Rosenberg collections of golem legends need to be pointed out. Although both men lace their stories with quotations from Jewish sources, Bloch is the more scholarly of the two, as he quotes from the Torah, other biblical sources, and the Talmud. Rosenberg's occasional quotations are undocumented, but Bloch usually informs the reader whether the passage just quoted is from, for example, Sanhedrin 58b or Beracoth 19b (see "The Disputation"), or he explains certain Jewish religious observances with supporting quotations from Exodus and Genesis (as in "The Making of the Golem"). Whereas Rosenberg will simply mention that a family held a Purim celebration, Bloch will supply loving details. In "Purim Joy and Tragedy," he writes, "With great glee and spirit the company sang the beautiful melody Shoschenot Yaakov"; in "The Birth of Judah Loew," he warmly describes the details of Rabbi Bezalel's Seder. In various stories Bloch alludes to the *Sefer Yezirah* and its Zurifim, whereas Rosenberg never mentions this classic of Jewish mysticism. In "The Disputation," the scholarly Bloch explains that Christ's crucifixion was carried out by Romans. "This is shown by the manner of execution because crucifixion was a form not known to the Talmud and, what is more, was introduced by the Romans." After shortening Rosenberg's version of the parable Rabbi Loew uses in answering the fifth question in the debate with the three hundred priests, Bloch adds three pages of commentary on and analysis of the Jewish position on the concept of the Chosen People and the Jewish attitude toward non-Jews. Bloch's quotations range from Amos and Jeremiah to Maimonides. Rosenberg usually supplies only a translation of the Hebrew; Bloch supplies both the original and a translation, as in the case of the dream message from Heaven which provides Rabbi Loew with the mystical formula for creating the golem. That Rosenberg, however, is also well versed in Jewish lore can be seen in "The Dreadful Tale about the Deserted House near Prague," in which Rabbi Liva discovers that the courier's mysterious nighttime barking is caused by his blemished undergarment and phylacteries.

"For it is written that 'every Jew is accompanied by angels who guard him on every road,' and the angels are created by his fulfilling the commandments of the phylacteries and the fringes." Bloch omits this explanation but has Rabbi Loew give the man a special amulet with the protective inscription, " 'But against any of the children of Israel shall not a dog whet his tongue' (Exodus, ix, i)."

Both writers are somewhat Victorian in their treatment of sex, but Rosenberg is more so. Bloch begins "An Attack on the Golem" with an anecdote involving incest, insisting that fatalism, not the couple, is to blame. Rosenberg omits the story completely. In "The Wondrous Tale That Was Widely Known as the Sorrows of a Daughter," Rosenberg has Tadeus shake the girl's hand; Bloch, in "The Romance of Rahle and Ladislaus," has him also lay his hand on her shoulder. As the Jewess (never named by Rosenberg, as he frequently prefers to treat the characters as stock types) becomes infatuated with the priest, Rosenberg primly records her behavior, "She began secretly corresponding with the priest and would sometimes visit him alone late at night, until one night she didn't even come home to sleep. She vanished like a stone in water." Bloch much more effectively dramatizes for two pages the change that takes place in Rahel Berger. One hot afternoon in July, after work, Rahel "left the store and, seized with a wild impulse, whose origin she could not explain, and did not wish to fathom, she went out toward this promenade." Bloch explains,

> Her soul became more and more lonely, and more dismal. Well she knew that the next few hours would open a deep chasm between her and her father's house. But she was already too tightly caught in the mesh of Thaddeus' net to tear herself free. She wished to remain, but her feet carried her along as if she had lost all control over them.

She knocks at the gate of the monastery. "It had already been dark a long time. Rahel did not return to her home that night."

Sometimes the differences between Rosenberg and Bloch involve their handling of a particular technical problem. For example, in "The Disputation," where Rosenberg lists all five of the priests' main questions consecutively, giving the answers afterwards, Bloch takes them one at a time, with Rabbi Loew's answers interspersed. The result is that Bloch's content is easier to concentrate on, though the differences are minimal. Another example is Rosenberg's taking one long paragraph to describe the making of the golem, while Bloch intensifies the suspense by breaking the narration into eight short dramatic paragraphs. This time Bloch's technique is the more journalistic, but interest runs high in both cases.

Of course, there are also many little differences in detail in the stories in both collections. For instance, in "The Making of the Golem," Bloch has Rabbi Loew place a piece of parchment with the Shem in the prostrate golem's mouth. This traditional detail is omitted by Rosenberg, as is the moment that the three men bow to all four directions of the compass. In "The Wondrous Tale That Was Widely Known as the Sorrows of a Daughter," Rosenberg has the young duke study conversion under the famous scholar Jacob Gintzberg. However, because Rabbi Gintzberg was so busy, he sent the young man to the yeshivah in Amsterdam. In Bloch's version, "The Romance of Rahle and Ladislaus," the rabbi's motivation is more complicated and historically more interesting: worried about the danger to the Jews because of the conversion of a Christian to Judaism, he sends the young count "to Amsterdam where religious freedom prevailed and where no persecution was to be feared." In Bloch's version of "The Dropped Torah Scroll," Rabbi Loew makes the adulterer divorce his wife in keeping with Jewish law, a punishment which Rosenberg never mentions. And finally, as was mentioned above, Rosenberg gives 5350 (1590) as the year Rabbi Liva takes away the golem's life; Bloch records it as 5353 (1593). Since one should always look for symbolic or mystical significance in the use of numbers in Jewish literature, especially when the author is familiar with kabbalistic volumes like the *Sefer Yezirah*, it seems more than accidental that Bloch chooses to have the golem removed from earth in his thirteenth year. Perhaps, as Robert Plank suggests in "The Golem and the Robot" (unaware of the golem as conceived by Leivick and Rothberg), "the golem is destroyed before he reaches sexual maturity." There is, however, a more positive possibility. In Jewish tradition, the Jewish male enters adulthood in his thirteenth year. The golem's work is done, and one hopes that a new era in the lives of the Jews may begin.

Both Yudl Rosenberg and Chayim Bloch must figure prominently in any study of the legend of the Golem of Prague and his alleged creator, Rabbi Judah Loew. Whether Rosenberg was a literary forger and Bloch a plagiarist is, in the long run, of secondary importance. Both men gave shape, form, and continuity to legends that had a long oral tradition in Eastern Europe and had just begun to appear in print in the last half of the nineteenth century. Twentieth-century lovers of short stories, plays, novels, poems, folklore, ballet, opera, and movies may not recognize the names of Rosenberg and Bloch as they read a story or watch a film about the golem, but they owe a debt of gratitude to both writers for helping keep the legends alive and influencing new generations of writers and readers.

Chapter Four

The Golem as False Messiah: H. Leivick's Verse Drama

A contemporary of Yudl Rosenberg and Chayim Bloch who was equally fascinated with the legends of Rabbi Loew and his creation of the Golem of Prague was a Yiddish poet, Leivick Halper (1888-1962), who wrote under the name H. Leivick. (The pen name resulted from a complaint by the established Yiddish writer Moyshe Leyb Halpern, who argued that readers would be apt to confuse the two authors.) Leivick started work on *The Golem: A Dramatic Poem in Eight Scenes* in his late twenties and produced a remarkable, sometimes brilliant, play which combines impassioned poetry, folk legends, biblical allusions, and surrealism with philosophical and religious probing, all infused with stunning imagination. Any reader of this play must marvel at the challenges facing the director, designer, and cast. Published in 1921 and first performed in Hebrew by the famous Habima ensemble in Moscow in 1925, it has since been performed in many other countries and is considered a classic of the Yiddish theatre. Joseph Landis has called Leivick the "greatest poet" in Yiddish literature.

H. Leivick, Radical Thinker and Playwright

At the conclusion of an address Leivick gave at a conference of writers and other intellectuals in Jerusalem in 1957, the celebrated author reminisced about one particular day when he was seven. Two of the experiences of this day had a marked bearing on many of his literary works, especially the play he was to begin writing some twenty years later. In the first of these experiences, Leivick was on his way to heder when he passed a Polish church. There he was suddenly

73

attacked by a tall Pole who struck him across the head, knocked off his hat, and threw him to the ground, warning the young Jew to take off his hat the next time he passed a church. The second experience took place in school, when the distraught child listened to the story of Abraham and Isaac and was frightened once again, this time for the bound Isaac, waiting to be slaughtered on the altar. When the Hebrew teacher asked him why he was crying when he knew that Isaac would be saved by an angel, Leivick remembered asking, " 'But what would have happened had the angel *come one moment too late?*' " The reality of violence in the life of a Jew and the need of a reliable savior were themes that were to remain with Leivick for the rest of his life. In 1957, he reminded his audience that for " 'six million Isaacs lying under knives, under axes, in fires, and in gas chambers. . . . The angel of God did come too late.' "

Young Leivick, a quiet, sensitive boy, experienced great poverty. At five he began heder, and at ten he began a five-year period of study at a yeshivah, sometimes going without food. According to Charles A. Madison, Hebrew books "undermined his piety," and the yeshivah in Minsk opened his eyes to the secular world. After being caught reading a Hebrew novel of the Enlightenment, Abraham Mapu's *Love of Zion*, Leivick was expelled from the yeshivah and changed his mind about becoming a rabbi. In 1905, he joined the Minsk Bund and was soon arrested for having participated in demonstrations against the czar. After being kept in prison for two years, he refused to be defended in court, boasted of his radical ideology to the judge, and was sentenced to four years of hard labor followed by permanent exile to Siberia. Somehow he survived the months of forced marches through the Siberian steppes and wild forests and arrived at a village on the Lena River. Even though the nearest railroad was over a thousand miles away and the days provided only a few hours of light, he succeeded in escaping by horse and sled. With the help of a friend who sent him money from America, he managed to get out of Russia and arrived in the United States in 1913. In America, he worked as a paperhanger and garment cutter while he continued to write poetry about his years in Russia.

The influence of Leivick's prison experiences on his literary career is great. According to Sol Liptzin,

> The longing for a messianic liberator who would burst all bonds and break all bars grew in these years of living entombment to such intensity that it remained with him ever thereafter and

became a main theme of his later works. Leivick noticed that each prisoner who was locked in a cell was waiting for a miracle, for a redeemer who would suddenly open all gates, unshackle all chains, and lead the jailed out to freedom, past forests and seas, on to a distant land.

Madison quotes Leivick himself as saying, "I wrote *The Golem* out of my own direct jail experience. If I had not been in prison, if I had not *lain* stretched out on a stone floor in an ever-dark cell, and if I had not seen others lie similarly, I am not sure I would have written *The Golem*. Certainly I would not have written as I did."

Before analyzing *The Golem* to see how Leivick imaginatively expanded one of the legends which appears in both Rosenberg ("A Very Wondrous Tale about a Blood Libel Which Spelled Final Defeat for Father Tadeus") and Bloch ("Caught in His Own Net"), it would be helpful to review briefly the poet-dramatist's many volumes and favorite themes. One fact which will become immediately obvious is the importance in Leivick's writing of his knowledge of Jewish legends and the religious beliefs of his people. Figures like Isaac, Elijah, and Job appear repeatedly in his work. Steeped in an ethical tradition over three millenia old, Leivick joined the three modern founders of Yiddish literature—Mendele Mocher Seforim (Sholem Jacob Abramovich), Sholem Aleichem (Sholem Rabinowitz), and Yitskhok Leybush Peretz—in their celebration of a moral code noted for its reverence for man, love of God, and insistence on ideal conduct in a not-so-ideal world. Though Jewish tradition has always been aware of evil's destructive force, it has also always been, as Landis observes, "convinced of man's ultimate superiority over evil, of the ultimate victory of man's yearning for good." The Ashkenazic Jew was not so naive as to expect cannons and pistols to be melted into plowshares during his lifetime. "Indeed," says Landis, "his sense of reality was expressed in his use of the phrase 'when the Messiah comes' to indicate the remote and improbable, but he was convinced of the ever-present possibility of man's faithfulness to his mentshlekhkayt" (that is, his humane, compassionate, gentle qualities). Rejection of violence as a solution to man's problems was not based on any idealistic belief in the efficacy of passive resistance, "any sentimental exaltation of weakness or 'the power of powerlessness,' but on a principled repudiation of force as bestializing and on a faith in the ultimate victory of reason and morality." To Landis, "The perspective of a millenial history had brought the conviction not only that force proves nothing but that it is ultimately doomed to failure because of its violation of man's mentshlekhkayt."

While he was in prison, Leivick began *The Messiah in Chains* (completed in 1908), the first of his dramatic works dealing with the theme of the messiah, which continued to fascinate him for many years. Madison believes that this theme "took concrete form after the pogroms in the early 1900's, when it seemed that salvation by a messiah was the only solution to Jewish persecution." In fact, according to Liptzin, Leivick saw messianism as "inseparable from Judaism," and he believed that "the vision of an ultimate redeemer accompanied Jews throughout their long historic experience and made their reality tolerable." Thus Leivick found himself faced with a conflict between his religious dream of redemption and his radical disbelief. *The Messiah in Chains* combines known legend with his own improvised myth. It tells how on the third day after the destruction of Jerusalem by Titus, angels are sent into the wilderness to forge a chain to bind the young messiah. The angel Azriel rebels against his assigned role in the punishment of Israel: " 'the world can't wait, the destruction is too great.' " When he tries to break the chain, lightning strikes his wings and a voice dooms him until the end of time. Satan now arrives on his new mission, to guard the messiah who is brought in by a weeping Elijah. The prophet counsels the youthful messiah to be patient while waiting to be called to a world that is not yet ready for him. After this advice the messiah cries out, " 'People of Israel, do not keep quiet, do not wait, call me as I do—call me; come break my chains, come, liberate me.' " But Satan prevents any such action. Madison sees the angel Azriel as the spokesman for the young Leivick, the rebel against tradition and conformity, "the visionary who risks his own doom in the effort to redeem suffering humanity, the prophet who chides his fellow angels 'who love only themselves and Paradise.' " Elijah weeps as he obeys God, but he promises the messiah that he will go to earth to tell people where he is.

Six of Leivick's plays were produced in the 1920s in addition to *The Golem*. All six of these realistic dramas, beginning with the very successful *Rags* (1921) and including *Hirsch Leckert* (1927), deal with a nonconformist and idealist in conflict with materialistic society. *Hirsch Leckert*, for example, is about a radical shoemaker who refuses to reveal his associates in the wounding of the governor of Vilna, and thus is unwilling to have his death sentence commuted to life imprisonment. "In verse that sings and shouts and takes wing," says Madison, "Leivick glorifies the idealistic individual in opposition to a brutal bureaucracy." At first the Communists welcomed Leivick as a fellow traveler after the production of this play, but, as Liptzin explains,

> they were soon disillusioned . . . when he broke with them in 1929. They were justifying the Arab massacres of Hebron's defenseless Jews in that year as a revolutionary act of liberation from colonialism and imperialism. Thereupon Leivick denounced these heartless admirers of his genius and refused to let them publish his poems in their organs. They reacted by labelling him a traitor to the cause of the proletariat.

In 1932, Leivick suffered a relapse in his battle with tuberculosis and had to spend three years in a sanitorium in Denver, Colorado, where he continued his writing. In this decade he wrote many more poems as well as four plays, one of which, *The Sacrifice* (1933), returns to the story of Abraham and Isaac and adds a startling new twist. An angry and impassioned Isaac, aged overnight by his traumatic experience, threatens to kill Abraham, but then releases him with the bold declaration, " 'This will be my pact with God, with you and the world. And this shall be a reminder to all who raise a hand against a living being: a sign for all generations that none may raise a hand against a living being.' "

During World War II, Leivick suffered guilt feelings because he was safe in New York while millions of Eastern European Jews were being murdered by the Nazis. The setting of some of his dramas of the forties is contemporary Europe; in one play, for example, a rabbi helps the Jews prepare for armed resistance in Warsaw (*The Miracle of the Ghetto,* 1941); in another, *The Wedding in Fernwald* (1949), Elijah appears at the wedding of two survivors of a concentration camp whose spouses had been killed. In *Maharam of Rothenburg* (completed in 1944), Leivick imaginatively blends the modern with the historical, drawing a parallel between the persecution of the Jews in the thirteenth century and in the twentieth. The play opens in Dachau, where a prisoner named Daniel is transported by the Wandering Jew, Ahasver, to medieval Germany. The Maharam of Rothenburg, a leading rabbinical scholar and head of a yeshivah, has suddenly been imprisoned. The authorities demand a large ransom for his release, and even though the Jewish community is prepared to pay it, the Maharam refuses to give permission, warning that complying with the demands of the extortionists would set a dangerous precedent. As a result, he dies in prison seven years later. "In the meeting of the tortured contemporary prisoner and the Maharam," explains Liptzin, "the continuity of Jewish martyrdom and Jewish self-sacrificing resistance was stressed. When the Maharam was asked what status should be assigned to teachers who taught Jewish children swordsmanship, he replied: 'The same status as those who teach them Torah.' " Thus the experience of the Holocaust changed the attitude of the gentle Leivick, who reversed the condemnation of violent self-defense which he had dramatized previously in *The Golem*.

Leivick's last drama, *In the Days of Job* (completed in 1953), combines the suffering of Job and Isaac as the poet tries to understand the suffering of the postwar world. Liptzin calls this final work "the apex of his creative career." In this drama the writer "fought his way out from the darkness of doubt to a reinvigorated faith. He saw that after the deluge of blood a rainbow was appearing in the heavens" in the creation of the state of Israel.

Many survivors of the Holocaust remember vividly Leivick's visits to the refugee camps in the American section of Bavaria with other representatives of the Jewish World Congress invited by the United Nations Relief and Rehabilitation Administration in 1946. Leivick proved to be a sympathetic listener to the countless tales of life in and escape from the inferno, read from his works, and offered whatever comfort and reassurance he could. In 1957, he made his third trip to Israel and addressed the conference mentioned earlier; in Jerusalem he spoke in support of Yiddish "as the language of the intimate folk spirit." One year later Leivick suffered from a paralytic stroke which left him helpless and speechless for the next four years, though his mind remained intact. He died in 1962.

The Golem: A Dramatic Poem in Eight Scenes

In his late twenties when he was working on his verse drama about Rabbi Loew, whom he calls Levi, Leivick became disillusioned with the events of the Russian Revolution. According to Madison, "The woeful years 1914–1920 turned Leivick from his agonized personal memories to the immediately tragic suffering of the Jews in Eastern Europe, which galvanized his thoughts of salvation and stirred his vision of the legendary golem as a mythical redeemer." Liptzin sees the same development. "The bloody deeds of the revolutionary and post-revolutionary years, the degradation of his socialist ideal by the Bolsheviks' use of brutal means, filled the poet's heart with sadness. Messiah obviously had not yet come; the world was in the grip of a Golem."

For those unfamiliar with Leivick's first verse drama on the golem, which, unfortunately, is his only play translated into English, a summary of the plot and a commentary on some of the themes being developed should prove helpful. For some unknown reason, Leivick changed the date given by Rosenberg and Bloch from the late sixteenth to the seventeenth century. Rabbi Levi Bar Bezalel, the Maharal, having heard rumors of an impending Blood Libel against the Jewish community of Prague, has been shaping in secret the giant form of a man from clay with the assistance of the shammes Abraham. Immediately Leivick thickens the characterization found in earlier versions of the legend and has the rabbi correct himself after describing "this great frame / That has been shaped and kneaded by my hands." Looking up to heaven, he quickly adds:

> But who am I to say: "My hands have shaped?"
> Blind was I until You gave me sight—
> A puff from heaven's height upon my brows—
> And showed me where the slumbering body lay.

With these words, Leivick introduces the theme of pride to complicate the character of Rabbi Levi. Has the great scholar undertaken this mission for his own self-aggrandizement, or is he an instrument in the hands of God? "Perhaps," he wonders, "I was ambitious, proud, / Too eager to descry what no man yet / Has seen before." There is a fine line here not found in Rosenberg's and Bloch's retelling of the legends. Leivick will return to this possible flaw in Rabbi Levi's character in subsequent scenes involving Elijah and the messiah, whom he drives away, and in the climax when he accepts the blame for the spilling of Jewish blood.

A second theme Leivick introduces almost immediately is the golem's ominous reluctance to be born. As the stars are going out, a dark figure, the golem's spirit, suddenly strides across the river and warns Rabbi Levi not to proceed with his creation. He warns that he will bring death, blight, and destruction, and wishes that he were lifeless clay again. Liptzin is correct in observing that "to animate the Golem meant to unleash brute force." Though Rabbi Levi naively thought he could control this force and direct it to good ends, "the moment a robot was granted a soul, it could not be prevented from developing a will of its own or from experiencing sadness, restlessness, loneliness, and yearning for love." The determined rabbi ignores the golem's threatening statement as his antagonist, the priest Thaddeus, approaches. He detects a look of murderous hate in the Maharal's eyes, saying, "They seem the eyes of some Golem run wild." Here Leivick picks up Bloch's hint that the dark specter may be the rabbi's alter ego. Such a force, ostensibly created for good, may prove to be evil. Scene 1 ends with the arrival of Isaac, the Kohen, and Jacob, the Levite, to assist the rabbi in the conclusion of the ritual, the details of which are apparently unimportant to the author, who never provides them.

In scene 2, Leivick introduces another element carefully avoided by Rosenberg and Bloch—the golem's sexual desire—thus attempting to humanize Rabbi Levi's android and hinting at future plot complications. Leivick also suggests some important philosophical questions with this sensational development. Can there be life without love? Is life without love worth living? These important questions had been raised by Mary Shelley in the early nineteenth century with the creation of Victor Frankenstein's monster, but, until now, they had been avoided by the Yiddish writers dealing with the legend of the golem. This scene also shows the golem's growing awareness of his great natural strength and his resentment of confinement indoors. He threatens the rabbi ("My hands—how easily they seize your throat / And carry you away" [p. 237]) and vents his frustration by smashing his fist against the wall of the study. The trembling Maharal commands the golem, whom he names Joseph, to speak only when spoken to. (Here is another startling departure from Rosenberg and Bloch, but Leivick realized the serious limitations of having a mute as the central figure of a drama.) Devorale, Rabbi Liva's granddaughter, and the rebbitsin are awakened by the noise the golem is making and are frightened by the huge stranger who, they are told, is a guest in their house. Devorale is compassionate but alarmed. "He looks unfortunate. . . . See how he stares at me! / What does he want, Grandfather? . . . He stares at me. He frightens me." The Maharal lies and tells Joseph that Devorale is his daughter, warning him never to speak to or even look at her. But the golem is smitten by her long hair and says to the worried rabbi, "I felt so good each time she looked at me." The scene ends with the golem asleep and the Maharal wondering, "Is this he? The man I dreamt into existence? / The champion? The hero? He? Such hands, / Such shoulders, legs. So much body? / So much still sorrow?"

In scene 3, the rabbi is visited by some Jews worried about rumors of impending violence in the community. One strange figure, the grief-stricken Reb Tankhum, still in mourning for a son who died a violent death a considerable time ago, represents madness as a crippling reaction to unbearable suffering in a hostile world. Tankhum raves about the five-towered building which the Maharal has also seen in recent nightmares. A more immediate problem is the behavior of Joseph, who complains about the taunts of local boys and men who watch him splitting logs. Putting a curse on the ax, the Maharal makes it such a heavy burden that lightness of arm will never tempt the golem to hurt anyone. Because Joseph also expresses hatred of his creator, the rabbi places a charm around his neck to make him more friendly in the eyes of other men. But the golem's interest in Devorale is not so easily cured. He has prevented the girl from going to the well, grabbing and kissing her. A nervous Rabbi Levi chastises the golem with the remark that here he is, only one day old, and "how soon the man in you / Has hurried to reveal himself / In hatred, passion, and misfortune." Rabbi Levi threatens to hit the golem and then sends him to the Fifth Tower where he will now have to stay with the beggars and other misfits.

Scene 4 shifts to Tower Five, an ancient ruin also known as the Five-Sided Palace. The various misfits, identified only as the Hunchback, Peg Leg, the Sick Man, and so forth, discuss the golem, who forbids them to mention his name. A prediction is made that the Jews of Prague will soon be driven to the Fifth Tower. Suddenly, two new beggars arrive, the Old Beggar (the prophet Elijah) and the Young Beggar in his charge, complaining of sore feet (the messiah). The angry Maharal makes them leave, refusing to let the golem join them. "Their time / Has not yet come. This is *your* time." Rabbi Levi commands the golem to become invisible as Thaddeus and the Monk enter.

In the dialogue that ensues, Leivick goes beyond the personal anti-Semitism of the earlier versions of Thaddeus and makes some perceptive observations on the psychology of religious persecution. According to Thaddeus, Christians are weary of their hatred of the Jews, weary of their own cruelty and anger. In a sense, Leivick is suggesting that the Jew might be seen as the alter ego of the Christian, the good and righteous man the latter would like to be. The Christian craves virtue, peace, and quiet, but the very presence of the Jew continues to goad him. Thaddeus says, "only in your blood will that desire be settled." He is frustrated by the Jews' stubborn endurance. "You smash our dreams of peace, / And all the more, you stoke in us the fires of hate." Anti-Semitism as manifested in the Blood Libel will never disappear "until you free us from yourselves!" Thaddeus and the church he represents cannot understand why the Jews refuse to fight back. He challenges the beggars and other misfits in Tower Five to attack the Christians, beginning with an assault on him.

> Where is there one among you with the courage
> To step forward, seize my staff,
> And break it on my skull. You say nothing.
> Already you await my shout: Get out!
> Always, always you are ready to depart—
> Then go!

The passive inhabitants of the Fifth Tower file out, but the Jewish audience in Moscow in 1925 must have laughed with nervous approval as the invisible golem rains blows on the startled priest and monk, bloodies their noses, and hurls them out the window. The scene ends with the Maharal's instructing the golem to go to sleep.

The Gothic setting and violence of scene 4 are in sharp contrast with the simple setting and meditative conversation in scene 5. The place is a field at night outside of Prague. Elijah and the messiah sit by the road and talk. As Madison has pointed out, Leivick had been attracted to the messiah legends for a long time and "conceived of the golem as the precursor of the messiah, the son of Joseph who is to serve as the temporary redeemer at a critical juncture and use force as necessary, which the real messiah—the son of David—must not employ." Leivick portrays the real messiah in this scene as disappointed in his reception. He bemoans the fact that he cannot die with his fellow Jews in Prague and fears a pogrom at the beginning of Passover. When the angry Maharal arrives, he again orders them to leave.

> The world has not exhausted yet
> Its store of cruelty, on us.
> Has *each* of us in every land felt
> The butcher's knife against his throat?
> Has he yet heard the final groan?
> Or seen the last of lifted swords?

The messiah cannot fight violence with violence. He "must be *the last. . . . / And woe to him if he should try / To intercede for us against our will.*" The Maharal explains that it is another savior who is permitted to do evil, to kill. The messiah, not knowing whether he has arrived a moment too soon or too late, is depressed because he must leave. The scene ends with a despondent Rabbi Levi watching a storm brewing.

The title of scene 6, "Revelation," is Leivick's pun. This is not Saint John's Revelation of the Apocalypse. It is, however, the first time that the golem reveals his true identity to humans other than those present at his creation. Disobeying the Maharal's instructions that he remain mute, Joseph, surrounded by a luminous glow in Tower Five, talks to the madman Tankhum, who claims that all the Jews in Prague are now dead. In this setting, reminiscent of the heath scene in *King Lear*, with its thunder and lightning and various kinds of madness in a world that has gone insane, the golem tells Tankhum, "I am the secret, not of darkness, but of light, / Not always, but now." A frightened Devorale enters with her grandmother looking for the Maharal, since all the Jews of Prague are hiding behind locked doors. The title "Revelation" is seen once again as Joseph tries to comfort the terrified women with his glow of invisibility hovering over him. Disobeying the Maharal again, he says that this is the first and only time that he will reveal himself. Promising not to harm them, he boasts that he is more luminous than the rabbi and messiah. Mixing sexual threats and boasts of his tremendous power with promises of safety, Joseph leads them out of the Fifth Tower. Feeling terrible loneliness upon his return to the ruins amidst the thunder and lightning, his love unrequited by the people he wants to help, the golem falls asleep on the ground, where the Maharal finds him and explains that he has only been dreaming the events of the last two days. Now the time has finally come for him to act. Once again Leivick plays with the word "Revelation." The true revelation comes as Rabbi Levi reveals the word "blood" to the golem and starts him on the sacred mission for which he was created. As the scene ends, the insane Tankhum crosses the stage, asking who can rescue the Jews. (Mendel Kohansky, in *The Hebrew Theatre: Its First Fifty Years*, says that it is reported that at one performance some young Communists in the audience stood up at this point, shouted "We will!" and sang "The Internationale.")

In the penultimate scene, Leivick pulls out all the stops and lets his imagination soar. The setting is a cave in a subterranean area of Tower Five. Mimetic representation is quickly replaced with surrealistic effect. The Blood Libel plot so familiar to modern readers of the legends of the golem is the core situation, but the supernatural effects, the dancing shadows of the torchlight underground, the lyric verse, the allegorical figures—all combine to make this one of the drama's most memorable scenes, even though the meaning is sometimes murky.

As the scene begins, the monk explains to Thaddeus how he has carried out the priest's orders, cutting the throat of the victim and bottling his blood. Both men flee as the Maharal and golem enter. Rabbi Levi is prevented by evil spirits from following the path to the hidden bottles. Only the golem can proceed and overcome such obstacles as a rock slide, barking hounds, and a fire which chars his clothing but not his body. The frightened golem calls for the Maharal as the spirits of the cave dance and spin around him, dimming his luminosity. What appears as the Maharal's figure (but probably is not) threatens him with his staff and commands him to obey.

> I am master. I
> Can do with you whatever I please to do.
> I do not harm you because I toy with you,
> With you and your fears and with your sorrows.
> Beyond that, I have no need of you.
> Stop staring, golem, dimwit, hunk of meat!
> Shut tight your gaping eyes,
> Fall to the ground and lie there. Fall, I say.

(The Golem sinks to the ground.)

> Well done. Your head down. Lower, lower.

The terribly confused golem suddenly is guided by a force identified only as "the Invisible" (perhaps Rabbi Levi who is using his kabbalistic lore, but more likely God Himself), who shakes him, reveals himself this one time, and then shows him a bundle hidden at his feet which contains two bottles of blood. A joyous dance of the dead, who have been waiting for redemption, now takes place around the bottles as the golem watches in terror.

The awakened dead welcome the expected arrival of the three redeemers—the golem, already present, the messiah, and Jesus Christ—and predict the approaching death of Joseph. He sits down inside a prescribed circle just before the messiah, enchained, is pushed hard by an invisible hand into the cave. The Young Beggar accepts his destiny to remain there with the other two redeemers while "the world goes its way" and the three "shape a peace, a peace, a peace / Forever from today." To emphasize their shared identity as saviors, the golem and the messiah repeat each others' words. When the messiah complains of thirst, the golem offers him the blood in the two bottles, but the Young Beggar is repelled and calls out in alarm. At this point the Man with the Cross is pushed into the cave. He complains of his loneliness, pain, and rejection, though he praises and forgives God, his master. The golem welcomes Christ into the sacred circle and offers him a drink from the bottles to quench his thirst, but he gets the same horrified reaction he got from the messiah. The Cave Spirits now return and do a lively dance around the three redeemers, promising to protect them and be their loyal subjects, *their* redeemers. When the Cave Spirits depart, the dead reappear with their song of eternal nothingness.

> There is nothing more to sing.
> There's the cross—but not to carry;
> There's the chain—but not to ring;
> There's the axe—but not to harry.
> So we sing the song of nothing.

Christ need no longer feel the weight of the cross, the messiah need not feel the restraint of the chain, and the golem need no longer wield his heavy ax. As the dead finish their "song of madness," they return to the grave, the candles in their hands going out.

After a few moments of total darkness, the Maharal appears and chastises the golem, who is sitting in silence, gaping like a madman. Joseph at first does not recognize his master and wants to be left alone, far removed from the blood. But Rabbi Levi tells him he cannot remain. "Your life is now at stake. Your mission still / Is not fulfilled." He pities the terrified golem but insists that he leave the darkness and be restored to his former brightness. This scene parallels and reinforces the opening one, when the golem pleaded in vain not to come into this world. Now Joseph embraces the Maharal and welcomes him.

The final scene, "The Last Mission," takes place in the anteroom of the old synagogue on a Friday evening. The unkempt golem is testy and slams the door behind the gathering worshipers. He argues with the shammes and refuses to put on his other shoe, complaining all the while that the rabbi has not visited him in a week. Leivick makes no attempt to bridge the gap and explain what has happened since the last scene. The audience must make some remarkable assumptions—that the Blood Libel has been proved false with the revelation of Thaddeus' plot, the false accusers punished, and the Jewish community saved (Tower Five need no longer be a refuge). Leivick shows no interest in such routine details already known by those familiar with the legends. He is far more interested in the personality of the golem, the conscience of the Maharal, and the theme of the brutality of force, the insatiable appetite of violence. The shammes is unaware of these larger, deeper implications and can only support the rigidity of the Law. "It is forbidden to walk barefoot / In a synagogue," he says, and he calls Joseph a "savage" and a "Madman," a "riddle" he cannot understand. Apparently Joseph has not been able to sleep for three nights, and he claims that he is unaware of "the Miracle" the shammes refers to (probably the defeat of Thaddeus). Joseph has felt cast aside ever since the strange adventure in the cave.

When two of the inhabitants of Tower Five come in, they recognize Joseph and discuss his past erratic behavior. There is some momentary comic relief as the Redhead says, "You mark my words: there's something curious / In this, more than meets the eye," and his companion, the Tall Man, replies, "No mystery at all. A clod, a golem." (Here Leivick cannot resist punning on the word, using it in its vernacular sense.) The Redhead recollects how the golem beat up Thaddeus the night they were forced to abandon Tower Five, but the events of that memorable night remain a mystery to them.

The golem becomes aroused as he hears these men describe the boarding up of the windows and doors of Tower Five. He wants to return, screaming for the rabbi and banging on the wall. As he rushes at the men threateningly, the Maharal enters and subdues him with a stern look and a single command. Joseph claims that Rabbi Levi has deserted him now that his mission has been fulfilled, and he begs the rabbi to stay with him. In a new twist to the legend, the Maharal reveals that he gave Joseph the freedom to go wherever he desired, but Joseph "chose to stay." Joseph confesses that he now knows that the Maharal controls his life. He pleads with the rabbi to abandon the world and stay with him forever in the anteroom. The compassionate rabbi sympathizes with this tortured creature.

> So much unrest in your heart and so much hate;
> So much dark passion and cold anger
> And helplessness flow in your veins.
> How can the fault be yours?

Rabbi Levi explains to Joseph his foolish hope that "you would save yourself, / Find peace and start to live as all live, / As Jews live." But that was his mistake. Force begets force and becomes uncontrolled. When the Maharal refuses to let the golem return to Tower Five, Joseph loses his temper, commands him to stay, and grabs his arm, threatening the unflinching rabbi with his fist. In this war of wills, the Maharal easily wins, and Joseph sinks to the floor in a tantrum as the rabbi enters the synagogue.

Left alone, the frustrated golem grabs his ax, contemplates attacking the Jews at prayer, then shatters the window and rushes out into the street. The Maharal rescues Joseph from the angry crowd, but two Jews have already been struck down. Alone with Joseph in the anteroom, the rabbi asks him if he realizes that he has hurt the people he was created to save. The Maharal accepts the blame himself and asks,

> Are we thus punished for our joy, Oh Lord?
> Are we chastised because we wished to save ourselves?
> Did You not grant approval?
> Was not this done through You?

But then the Maharal sees himself as one of the patriarchs tried by God, or perhaps as another Job.

> Did You reveal to me the more than human,
> Allow me to create, to rule, command,
> Only that I might see at last
> My insignificance, my massive sin?
> And more than that—my sin against all Jews?
> That, in impatience and despair, I wished
> To turn my back on those ways of Your people
> That are eternal, gentle, patient, full of faith?
> My sin in wanting what the foe lays claim to?

The Maharal tells God, "You opened wide my eyes to see that I / Lack wholly any power over fists." The rabbi now realizes that he is the golem's captive; the master has become the slave.

At this climactic moment, Devorale runs in to ask her grandfather to come comfort her crying grandmother. Joseph thinks the girl has come to stay with him also, but she calls him "Murderer!" and struggles to free herself from his grasp. Deaf to the softness of his plea ("How sweet is the aroma of your hair. / How warm your hands. Why do you run from me?"), Devorale struggles helplessly until the Maharal regains his composure and yells at Joseph, who releases the girl. Sending his granddaughter to the congregation to inform them that their rabbi is coming, the Maharal instructs the golem on his final mission.

> The final task. You see, the candles all
> Are dying down. A single light,
> The last, still flickers. Soon it too
> Will die. You must make haste.

Rabbi Levi then commands the reluctant but obedient golem to lie on the ground with outstretched arms and returns him to clay with the simple words,

> I issue this decree: Let hands and feet
> And body with its limbs and sinews
> Return unto their rest.
> Breathe out your final breath. Amen.

With only this prayer and none of the more elaborate kabbalistic ritual mentioned in previous legends of the golem, Leivick has the creature returned to the earth from whence he came. The drama ends on a note of religious affirmation as the Maharal instructs the shammes to call in the Jews to sing again the psalm of Sabbath praise.

The Reception and Meaning of Leivick's Golem

According to Kohansky, Moscow reviews of Leivick's *Golem* in March, 1925, "though not enthusiastic, were good, and the public responded well." Audiences seemed to sense what the censors missed. Leivick's disillusionment with the Bolshevik Revolution and its violent destruction of Jewish cultural and communal life makes it possible to read the play as a parable. Kohansky believes that "the Golem is the revolution, a creature of violence. Like the revolution, he was created with good intentions, but, having found a life of his own, turned away from the intentions of his creator to embark on a rampage of senseless destruction." (Unaware of such a political reading of the play, the Moscow censors insisted on only one deletion, the scene with the ghosts in the cave. This they found "objectionable on the grounds that it fostered superstition.") The role of the golem was played by Aaron Meskin. Judging by the full-page photograph in Kohansky's book, no attempt was made to imitate the monster makeup and mask popularized in the German film versions. According to Kohansky, Meskin's "powerful physique, rough-hewn face and deep voice were ideal for the part, and he invested the inhuman creature with a humanity and warmth that gave the Golem a new dimension not found in the text."

When the Habima company opened its tour in Palestine in April, 1928, with a performance of *The Golem*, the premiere was considered an event of major cultural importance. The reviews appeared the next day on the front page. The Zionist-oriented reviewer of *Ha'aretz* did not like the play, and Kohansky quotes him as writing,

> *The Golem* is not a play of high quality. It has rather cheap moments which probably cause a great deal of enthusiasm among the Jews in the Diaspora and among the Gentiles, but Palestine does not like it. We speak of the excessive exploitation of the synagogue and religion in general. Neither will Palestine accept all that ghost business; we here have conquered many ghosts, or at least make efforts to conquer them.

For a more appreciative understanding of Leivick's drama, the most incisive analysis is that of the play's translator, Joseph C. Landis, who writes,

> Man—suffering, lonely, yearning for redemption, sometimes purified by his sufferings to look with compassion on the suffering of his fellows—man is at the center of his twenty-one plays in prose and verse and his ten volumes of poetry. And man is at the center of *The Golem,* his first published play.

To Landis, *The Golem* is not only a political parable but also a "philosophical morality play"

> in which the Jews become symbolic of a mankind suffering innocently, suffering in spite of its innocence. It is a play about mankind's yearning for redemption; and it is a play in which the Jews, as bearers of redemption in peace and justice, suffer because that vision runs counter to the ways of the world.

Looking at the drama from another, more modern perspective, Landis sees the tragedy of Rabbi Levi as "the tragedy of the creator whose creation does not respond in accordance with his plan; the tragedy of the social dreamer whose dreams are frustrated, who discovers that force contaminates and consumes." *The Golem* is the tragedy of innocent man who, tired of being the eternal victim, "learns that suffering is the inescapable lot of man, that endurance and the wisdom of endurance—compassion for the sufferers—are the only alternatives open to man as Man." Reality is a hard teacher. The Maharal learns "that the traditional wisdom of his people is rooted in the nature of reality, that whatever the temporary effect of the fist, it cannot solve the human condition."

Rabbi Levi is not the only one in Leivick's drama to learn an important lesson; "the Golem learns the pain of the individual's loneliness." Not wanting to be born into this world, once here he discovers that it is the only life possible. The Maharal cannot prevent the inevitable human qualities of fear and sorrow, pity and temptation, from imprinting themselves upon the Golem's heart. When the Golem comes to life, he learns not only to bend his head and chop wood; he learns the sorrow of loneliness, the need for love, the fear of death, the temptation to wield power and destroy. No sooner does he become a man than he begins to long for love—and to dream of his own redemption.

The play is rich in ironies. "The Golem, the principle of Force, yearns for peace and love, and the Maharal, the principle of Peace, creates force. And the Golem, the man that to his creator was a thing, is a thing become a man." It is these very ironies that appealed to the creative imagination of H. Leivick in 1921 and continue to appeal to readers of his powerful drama six decades later.

Chapter Five

Gustav Meyrink and
the Psychological Gothic

IN Gustav Meyrink's novel *The Golem* (1915), an old puppeteer asks a Jewish sage named Schemajah Hillel about the Kabbalah and the *Zohar*. Zwakh, the puppet master, complains that this famous book of the occult can be seen only in a London museum, and that it is written in Chaldean, Aramaic, and Hebrew. He wishes that there were some " 'book containing all the keys to the riddles of the other world instead of just some of them.' " Hillel replies that all of life is made of questions and more questions. " 'Do you suppose that it is only caprice that our Jewish sacred writings are written down in consonants? Every man must find the hidden vowels which determine the meaning destined for him alone. Otherwise the living world would petrify into dogma!' " Like Zwakh, Gustav Meyrink (1868–1932) was fascinated by the occult and, during his adult life, constantly searched for clues to the existence of a life beyond the quotidian. When Zwakh says, " 'I cannot help it. The supernatural is the most fascinating subject in the world,' " he is speaking for the author. It was only natural that Meyrink's obsession would eventually lead him to the Kabbalah and Jewish mysticism; moreover, as a resident of Prague, intimately acquainted with the Jewish ghetto, he could not miss hearing stories about the golem. This legend gave him the title and a motif for, but not the real subject of, his first novel.

Meyrink's Dual Nature

Gustav Meyrink (born Gustav Meyer) was not a Jew. He was born in Vienna on January 19, 1868, the illegitimate son of an actress, Maria

Meyer, and an elderly nobleman, Karl Freiherr Varnbüler von and zu Hemmingen. With a father who rejected him and a mother interested only in her career, the bastard offspring of this relationship had an unhappy childhood. After moving to Prague in 1884, Meyer eventually went to a business college and then worked in the export trade before he and a partner opened their own bank. Yet, according to E. F. Bleiler, "there were at least two other Meyers in habitation within his body." The first of these was

> the aggressive playboy and bohemian, who delighted in using his sharp, sarcastic tongue to annoy the stodgy German patricians of Prague, and wasted no chance to shock them. He was athletic, and won many prizes as a sculler, including championship of the Austro-Hungarian Empire. He was a skilled fencer, a riotous liver who rode about in balloon-decorated carriages with troops of chorus girls, and he affronted the horses by driving the first automobile in Prague.

The other part of Meyrink's personality was "the occultist, dreamer, mystic, and magician." This side of Meyrink could be seen in his bizarre surroundings, such as the tower in which he lived in an old part of the city. His "strangely decorated" room, according to Bleiler, "contained a confessional booth, a terrarium filled with exotic African mice, a large picture of Madame Blavatsky, and a sculpture of a ghost disappearing into a wall." The pivotal incident in the development of this side of his life is like a scene out of one of his own fantasies. About to commit suicide in his early twenties, Meyer was interrupted when a pamphlet advertising a series of occult books was shoved under his door. The young man took this interruption as a sign of the direction in which he should turn and "devoted the remainder of his life to a spiritual quest and praxis that eventually worked through Spiritualism, Theosophy, alchemy, Christian mysticism, Cabbalism, various yogas, Tantrism, Sufism, Far Eastern thought and primitive religions." Intent on exposing fakery, the skeptical Meyer joined various occult groups and, accompanied by magicians, attended numerous séances. Frequently disillusioned, "he came to regard occultism as the 'religion of the stupid,' but he gradually worked out an independent, eclectic position of his own that dominated his later life" and is beyond the scope of this study.

In January, 1902, Meyer suffered a traumatic experience that was to supply him with an important plot development in *The Golem*—he was arrested for bank fraud and jailed for several months during the long

investigation that followed. Though he was charged with embezzle-
ment and misuse of customers' funds, Bleiler thinks that "in all proba-
bility he was innocent and guilty of carelessness only, if even that." It is
possible that he was the scapegoat for the practices of his partner;
possibly he was the victim of some of the many enemies he had made,
especially because of his notoriety in the newspapers, café gossip, and
official affairs. His first marriage, to Hedwig Aloisia Certl, had broken
up, and he could not marry Philomena Bernt, his mistress, until the
divorce was granted seven years later. His second wife was slandered
by a doctor in the army reserve, and Meyer was frustrated and
humiliated when his challenge to duel the offender was at first denied
because of Meyer's illegitimate birth. Meyer's three months in prison
may have saved the doctor, but upon his release in April, 1902, even
though completely cleared, Gustav Meyer was a ruined man. Adding
to his problems was the intense pain from an illness which his doctors
diagnosed as tuberculosis of the spine. As a result, he spent some time
in a sanitarium. Though he recovered, for the rest of his life he suffered
relapses and knew considerable pain.

Even before his arrest, Gustav Meyer had dabbled in writing, but
while he was in the sanitarium he met Oskar Schmitz, an author who,
recognizing his literary interests and penchant for satire, urged him to
write. The immediate result of this advice was Meyer's submission of a
satirical fantasy set in Indochina to one of Germany's finest magazines,
Simplicissimus. This story, "Der heisse Soldat," was published in the
fall of 1901 under the pen name Gustav Meyrink, which he adopted
legally in 1917. For the next ten years Meyrink struggled to make a
living from his writing. William R. van Buskirk sees the satirical thrust
of Meyrink's work as "generally directed against the military, finan-
ciers, Spiessertum [Philistines] and science in its dogmatic sense." Van
Buskirk concludes that the bases of Meyrink's satires can be found in
his life in Prague "and in his reactions as a mystic to a materialistic
society. Moreover, his personality, though paradoxical, expressed a
moral concern for humanity by attacking what he felt to be the false
values of this world in order to make room for the growth of a more real
inner world. In this he was related to the Expressionistic movement."
According to Bleiler, "In bitterness, savagery and verbal brilliance
Meyrink's work is very similar to that of Ambrose Bierce. If Meyrink
was not as prolific or as amusing as Bierce, he was more bizarre and
more profound."

In the first decade of the twentieth century Meyrink's books were
collections of his stories published earlier in magazines like Simplicis-

simus or Herman Hesse's *März*. For a short while he himself edited *Der liebe Augustin*, with such famous contributors as Max Brod, Paul Busson, Stefan Zweig, and Frank Wedekind, but the journal failed because of financial problems. Toward the end of the same period, he began to translate the works of Charles Dickens into German, finishing seven volumes by 1914. He also tried his hand at drama in 1910, collaborating with the Central European writer Alexander Roda Roda (Alexander Rosenfeld), with whom he finished four plays. Bleiler points out that, as part of Meyrink's interest in occult studies, he also "tried to establish a puppet theatre for playing serious, symbolic works (as well as crowd-pleasers). This concept, which was never brought to actuality, finds echoes in *Der Golem*."

Van Buskirk quotes Roda Roda on how Meyrink began work on *The Golem:* "It had been in Meyrink's mind in Prague. He certainly knew of the golem legends while still there and it is almost safe to assume that he had made notes and preliminary sketches of his work while still in the city; that is, prior to 1904." (Bleiler thinks he started it two years later, because it did not appear as a subject in his correspondence with his friend Alfred Kubin, the artist, until January, 1907.) Meyrink originally planned to write a short sketch on the legend, but the golem theme was too big. He decided to collaborate with Kubin, who was to do the illustrations as Meyrink finished new chapters for *März*. This plan failed, according to Kubin, when Meyrink ran dry and was unable to continue. A practical man, Kubin then used the illustrations for his own novel, *Die andere Seite*, in 1908. Whether Meyrink knew Kubin's novel in 1909 is unclear, but there are some interesting similarities between his work and Kubin's, such as the ghetto setting, the moral atmosphere, the fanciful image of the hermaphrodite at the end of both novels, and especially the figure of the alter ego, the split personality.

As Meyrink continued work on his novel, various publishers tried to buy the rights, but he refused and talked of publishing the book first in England. Months and years passed as he put publishers off with promises that the novel would be finished in a matter of weeks. In 1911, a fragment of the work was published in *Pan*, and Meyrink signed a contract with the publisher Kurt Wolff. More years passed. "The truth of the matter," says Bleiler, "was that Meyrink had become lost in his own story. He had too much material, too many ideas, too many characters, and he could not see his way clear to discarding elements and establishing a central line." Apparently Meyrink resorted to all sorts of outside help, drawing up geometric patterns, diagramming characters and plot lines (according to Van Buskirk, even working out the complicated plot on a chessboard with a friend) until finally "discarding about half the material." Bleiler thinks that these pangs of composition perhaps account for the "occasional jerkiness and thinness that do not occur in Meyrink's other novels."

When *Der Golem* was finally published in book form in 1915, it soon became a best-seller (almost a quarter of a million copies), but Meyrink, desperate for cash, sold his work outright to Wolff for two thousand dollars, rather than wait for royalty checks. Over the years the novel has been translated into Swedish, Dutch, Russian, Italian, Spanish, and other languages. Despite the success of this novel, allegedly his best, Meyrink's works have not continued to sell well. They have been more or less neglected by the literary world, except for a special issue of the French magazine *L'Herne*, although Thomas Mann, Franz Kafka, and Herman Hesse all praised them.

Encounters with the Golem of Prague

A brief summary of Meyrink's complicated novel will make the analysis that follows easier to comprehend. The unnamed narrator, living in the ghetto of Prague about 1890, is, through his dreams, reliving the bizarre events in the life of Athanasius Pernath, a gem cutter, whose hat he mistakenly took home one day after mass. Pernath, a bachelor between forty and forty-five, has recovered from a nervous breakdown. His past completely obliterated by hypnosis, he has been able to return to society but is currently undergoing a strange identity crisis. Struggling to suppress his libidinal desires, he has a mystical yearning for an ideal state transcending the actual. Three women are involved in his quest: Rosina, the whore, and Miriam, the mystical Jewess, represent the two extremes; the Countess Angelina, whom he once loved when they were children but who is now an adulteress threatened by blackmail, stands somewhere between the other two and represents a third alternative. Pernath's decision to help Angelina escape from the blackmail attempt of a greedy junk dealer, Aaron Wassertrum, leads him to join forces with the junk dealer's vengeful son, a consumptive medical student named Charousek. Pernath's adventures lead him to a frightening trip underground through secret passageways and trapdoors, a night spent trapped in the golem's room, and a lengthy imprisonment by the local authorities for a murder he never committed. Finally, Pernath, through the guidance of Miriam's father, Schemajah Hillel, and a fellow prisoner, the rapist-murderer Amadeus Laponder, is able to survive the perils of his quest for ideal selfhood and reach that state of eternal union with Miriam in a paradisiacal world which only select individuals are allowed to enter.

Unlike the works discussed in chapters 2 to 4 of this study, Meyrink's novel does not give the golem a central role despite its title. In fact, the legendary figure actually appears in no more than one-fifth of the pages, and Rabbi Loew's name is never even mentioned. (The rabbi does, however, play an important role in two major scenes in Meyrink's last novel, *Engel vom westlichen Fenster*.) It is evident from one of the few existing drafts of Meyrink's *Golem* that he had difficulty deciding how to use the legendary creature. One possibility was to have him appear simply as a ghost. Another plan involved having Charousek disguise himself as the golem in order to drive the villainous junk dealer to suicide. A third plan involved Karlitschek Bum, a character who does not appear in the published novel; he was beaten by an angry mob while dressed in the golem's clothes. Only a variation of this last plan found its way into the plot.

A clue to some of the novel's complexities is provided by Schemajah Hillel, the registrar of the Jewish Council House and also the keeper of the paraphernalia of the Old Synagogue, including the clay image of the golem. He tells the puppet master Zwakh, " 'It is possible for a man to find himself in murky windings underground, from which he may not emerge save by virtue of a talisman that he bears within himself.' " To illustrate his point, Hillel then tells the talmudic story of what happened to three men who descended into the Realm of Darkness. One went mad, one blind, and only Rabbi Akiba returned, explaining " 'that he had met himself.' " It is this dangerous pilgrimage that the protagonist must undertake in his quest for his ideal self. Like Spencer Brydon in Henry James's remarkable ghost story, "The Jolly Corner" (written only a dozen years before Meyrink's), Pernath must undergo an intensely psychological experience in which he confronts his frightening alter ego in order to discover his true identity. In both cases, a middle-aged man meets the trial successfully.

The question which preoccupies Pernath is " 'Who is this "I"?' " Meyrink extends this theme of uncertain identity by introducing the golem as an unexpected visitor to the gem cutter's room. Pernath does not recognize his strange visitor, who never speaks a word but removes a rare, handsomely bound book from his pocket and leafs through the pages until he comes to the chapter entitled "Ibbur, or the Fecundation of the Soul." The initial letter in red and gold has worn away and needs repairing. With only a gesture, the stranger indicates the necessary restoration and leaves. Through such symbolism, Meyrink implies that Pernath's own ego is in disrepair: his own soul needs refurbishing.

Further hints of the nature of Pernath's problem are given as he reads the designated chapter after his visitor's departure and imagines that the words take on erotic shapes. (Meyrink contradicts himself in chapter 13, where the narrator says that the book "was written all in Hebrew, and for that reason quite incomprehensible to me.") First they appear to be gaily dressed female slaves who dance for him. Then they all give way before a gigantic naked female who is dragged into the room, the pulse in her left wrist throbbing "like an earthquake." She is finally replaced by a naked man and woman embracing; they merge and become a hermaphrodite. This figure is soon followed by others "risen from the dead," who stare into his heart and terrify him with beseeching looks. The voice of the book reveals things that had been in him all along, but forgotten "till this day of delivery." The scantily clad female slaves and the archetypal figure of the orgasmic woman all suggest Pernath's subconscious desires, but the figure of the hermaphrodite foreshadows his deliverance from this sensuality to a higher, more etherealized state—in other words, the fecundation of his soul.

Meyrink's use of the mysterious golem to represent Pernath's other self is suggested when the artist, after his guest's departure, tries in vain to remember his visitor's features, until suddenly, "my skin, my muscles, the whole of my body, remembered . . . without telling my brain. They made movements I had neither willed nor desired. It was as though my limbs belonged to me no more." To his amazement, he begins to imitate the stranger perfectly. Even Pernath's appearance changes. "My unfamiliar face was now clean shaven, with prominent cheekbones, my eyes were slanting." As the other figure completely takes over Pernath's being, he is terrified. "I knew now who the stranger was, and that at any moment I could feel his personality within me at my will; yet still was I unable to conjure up his actual presence before me, face to face. I knew I should never be able to." As he places the stranger's book into his iron box for safekeeping, "it was as though my sense of touch needs must flow through a long, dark streak of nothingness before it merged into my conscious self, as though betwixt me and inanimate objects yawned a great gulf of time; as though they belonged to an age past and gone, of which I had once been part."

The bridging of this "gulf of time" and the merging of the conscious and unconscious selves must all take place before Pernath's quest can be completed. Playing a crucial role in this transformation is the golem, who allegedly returns to haunt the ghetto every thirty-three years. (Meyrink's use of Christian symbolism here reinforces his theme of resurrection and redemption, the transcendence of the ideal over the real.) According to the legends Pernath is told, the golem is always identified with destruction and violence. When he reappears, someone is usually murdered. Meyrink implies that Pernath is beginning to identify with this dark force, the subconscious, the irrational, the id. Such doubling of character in novels and drama, according to Robert Rogers in *The Double in Literature* (1970), increases reader identification with the protagonist because of "the displacement of the hero's guilt onto his secret sharer."

Further clarification of the complicated, multifaceted symbolism of the golem is seen in the narrator's description of the Prague ghetto. The golem is identified with the dark underside of the city. The "discoloured buildings" in the rain resemble "derelict, dripping animals," "uncanny and depraved"; they are like "weeds rising from the ground"; "something hostile, something malicious . . . seemed to permeate the very bricks of which they were composed." In the drain of the dirty street, a bridal bouquet is seen, "a bunch of withered myrtle drifting along in the filthy water." The narrator's choice of adjectives and objects loads the description with negative, unpleasant, mysterious, and even threatening implications. One of the most interesting hints is that of sexual depravity. Now that the morning wedding is over, the pure flowers of the bridal bouquet are wilting in the sewer.

As the narrator thinks about the people living in these ancient buildings, he remembers the kabbalistic legend of the golem.

> And, as that same Golem stiffened into clay the instant that mysterious phrase was removed from its lips, so must, I thought, these humans dwindle to soulless entities so soon as was extinguished within them some slightest spark of an idea, some species of dumb striving, however irrelevant, already deteriorated with most of them, from the look of it, into a mere aimless sloth, or a dull waiting for they know not what.

To the narrator (and author), the golem thus comes to symbolize the sick soul of the ghetto. On the margin of Pernath's consciousness flickers the realization that this drabness and animal dullness, this extinguishing of the divine spark, this indefinable and threatening depravity, is what he, a middle-aged bachelor, a stranger among strangers, is drifting into. Even more ominous is the identification of the golem with criminal forces. Pernath agrees with Charousek that the

> intangible spirit of crime walks through these streets day and night in its quest for human lodgment. It floats on the air, and we see it not. Suddenly it swoops on a human soul; yet still we are impervious to its presence, and no sooner have we sensed it than it has flown away again and the moment has passed.

Though Pernath does not consciously realize it, he is being attracted to this "spirit of crime," this "evil, hostile spirit" which he feels staring at him "from the face of each and every house," with their doors looking like "so many black, wide open mouths with cancerous tongues."

The golem is discussed most fully in a scene in the gem cutter's room, where a few of his acquaintances have gathered to drink hot punch. It may be Pernath's birthday, someone suggests. Meyrink prepares the reader for further occult experiences, hinting at Rabbi Loew's animation of the inanimate by having Prokop, a musician, comment on the curtains blowing in the wind. " 'It's almost like a miracle when things that lie without a particle of life in their bodies suddenly start to flutter.' "

From Pernath's description of the stranger who brought him the book, Zwakh is convinced it is the golem. Though he is generally well informed, Zwakh makes an amusing error as he begins to discuss the legend, an error that Rosenberg, Bloch, and Leivick would never have made. " 'The original story harks back, so they say, to the sixteenth century. Using long-lost formulas from the Kabbala, a rabbi is said to have made an artificial man—the so-called Golem—to help ring the bells in the Synagogue and for all kinds of other menial work.' " The Jews, of course, did not have bells in their synagogues, but Meyrink did not know this. Zwakh continues, " 'But he hadn't made a full man, and it was animated by a sort of vegetable half-life.' " This comment is another clue to the golem's role as Pernath's other self, the primitive, natural force in man. Zwakh retells the tale of the golem's going berserk, smashing everything in his way, until the rabbi destroys him. Prokop says he has heard the story of the rabbi's conjuring up the spirits of the dead and making them visible for the emperor. " 'The modern theory is that he used a magic lantern.' " Zwakh laughs at such rational explanations of the supernatural, adding, " 'I don't know how the Golem story originated, but this I know—there is something here in this quarter of the town . . . something that cannot die, and has its being within our midst.' "

The other men urge the puppeteer to tell them more. " 'I hardly know where to begin,' " Zwakh continues. " 'Golem stories are all hard telling.' " He explains that every thirty-three years something odd happens in the streets of Prague, " 'not so out-of-the-way or startling in itself, yet the terror of it is too strong for either explanation or excuse.' " A ghost appears, " 'an utterly strange man, clean shaven, of yellow complexion, Mongolian type, in antiquated clothes of a bygone day; it comes from the direction of the Altschulgasse, stalks through the Ghetto with a queer groping, stumbling kind of gait, as if afraid of falling over, and quite suddenly—is gone.' " The apparition always returns to an old house near the synagogue. Zwakh remembers that when he was a child, sixty-six years ago, the house on the Altschulgasse was searched thoroughly to find the room with no door and the one barred window. " 'They hung washing out of every window, and the room was discovered. As the only means of reaching it, a man let himself down on a rope from the roof, to see in. But no sooner did he get near the window than the rope broke and the poor fellow fractured his skull upon the pavement.' "

The connection between the mysterious, doorless room of the golem and the mental condition of the gem cutter is brought into focus when Pernath begins to understand his

> strange recurring dream of being in a house with a series of rooms sealed off from me . . . the painful inability of my memory to function where associations of my youth were concerned . . . all these problems had suddenly achieved their terrible solution: I had been mad, and treated by *hypnosis*. They [the doctors] had, in short, locked up a room which communicated with certain chambers in my brain; they had made me into an exile in the midst of the life that surrounded me.

Meyrink's intent is clear: if Pernath is to find true mental health, he must disobey his doctor's advice to forget the past; he must break out of the isolated room; he must break down the protective wall shielding him from unhappy memories. Only by reviewing the past and confronting it can he heal what Pernath later calls his "bleeding halves." If Pernath can confront his double and survive the trauma, he may discover his ideal self and find everlasting peace of mind. However, there is always the risk that the rope will break anew as Pernath tries to look through "that barred window of my inner consciousness."

Suspense is slowly built up by various descriptions of the experiences other people have had in encounters with the golem in the past. Each has his or her own explanation of what the golem represents. Zwakh, for example, claims that when he met the golem thirty-three years ago, he suffered a momentary paralytic shock. Everyone on the street was terrified. The only explanation he can offer is that

> "once in every generation a spiritual disturbance zigzags like a flash of lightening, right through the Ghetto, taking possession of the souls of the living to some end we know not of, and rising in the form of a wraith that appears to our senses in the guise of a human entity that once, centuries ago, maybe, lived here, and is craving materialisation."

Zwakh admits the possibility that this strange being may exist within their midst every day, without their realizing it. It may be like the "electric tension" in the air as a storm builds up, culminating in lightning which is needed to clear the stagnant air of the ghetto. Zwakh's next comment shows the growing popularity of Freudian theory in European literary circles at this time.

> "Something forces the dreams of the subconscious up into the light of day—like a lightning stroke—giving rise to an object that, could we but read its riddle, symbolises, both in ways and appearance, the mass-soul, could we but understand and interpret the secret language of forms."

The arrival of the golem is always foreshadowed, continues Zwakh, by some mysterious sign, such as plaster peeling from a wall in the shape of a person or faces seen in the front of a window. Zwakh claims he could feel the phantom's presence as he listened to Pernath describe his meeting with the stranger in his room. He remembers another childhood experience, when his family were amusing themselves by casting lead. Suddenly, as his sister emptied a ladle of molten lead into a bowl of water, the lump assumed the shape and features of the golem's head, frightening everyone present. Zwakh is pleased that his theories have been corroborated by Schemajah Hillel, to whom the apparition that appears in the ghetto is

> "a projection of the thought that had sprung to life in the brain of the old rabbi before he had succeeded in giving it tangible

> form, and . . . it could only appear at stated intervals of time,
> under those astrological conditions in which it had been created;
> that then, and then only, would it come back to the earth on its
> agonized quest for materialisation."

Even Hillel's wife claims to have confronted the golem face to face
and felt a paralysis similar to Zwakh's.

> "She said, too, she was quite positive that what she had seen
> was her own soul divested of its body; that just for a moment it
> had stood opposite to her, and gazed into her face with the
> features of a strange being. In spite of the terrible fear that had
> got her in its grip, the conviction had never left her that this
> thing confronting her was only a part of her innermost self."

Here, presented as the thoughts of a minor character who never
actually appears in the novel, is Meyrink's most overt statement on the
meaning of the golem in this work. When Mrs. Hillel speaks of the
strange apparition being "her own soul divested of its body," being "a
part of her innermost self," that is exactly what it means to Pernath.
The golem is his double, his doppelgänger. To reinforce the connection
between the golem and Pernath, Meyrink has Vrieslander, a guest who
has been carving a puppet all the while, fashion a face that Pernath and
Zwakh suddenly recognize. The wooden eyes seem pleased to have
found Pernath, who realizes that *"It was I myself . . . I and none other
. . . and I lay there on Vrieslander's lap, gaping."* When Zwakh cries out,
" 'God! It's the Golem!' " and tries to grab the newly carved head to
inspect it, Vrieslander opens the window and throws it into the street
below, apologizing for his poor workmanship. The puppet head disappears into the sewers and someone remarks that " 'it's on its way to
Hell.' " In this manner Meyrink foreshadows the underground journey that Pernath will soon have to take on his mysterious quest. The
fog filling the streets of Prague contributes to the eerie feeling of the
occult, and Pernath thinks he hears the sound of a hand banging
against a metal plate when the men place their ears close to the drain in
the cobblestones in search of the puppet. To Pernath, these are "the
sounds of a soul in agony, rising from the earth."

Pernath's own agony as he struggles with the golem within is intensified when he accompanies his friends to Loisitschek's, the local
tavern of ill repute. (In this tavern, Panne Schaffraneck, an aged Jew,
plucks a harp and sings a song about the Blood Libel involving two
rascally bakers, Red Beard and Green Beard, whose attempt to poison

the ghetto Jews is prevented by divine intervention. This is basically the same tale that Chayim Bloch was to tell three years later in "A Passover Miracle," a story not found in Rosenberg but apparently well known in Prague.) Though he is surrounded by companions, Pernath is not really a part of their circle. He continues to be the loner, the alienated man. He is fascinated by the sight of a homosexual dancing with a nobleman, while the captain of the Dragoons dances with the almost naked and drunk Rosina. Pernath describes the scene swimming before his eyes as being "as fantastic as any opium dream." This figure of speech captures the feverish, almost drug-induced atmosphere of much of the novel. Confronted by this scene of sexual depravity, Pernath feels sick to his stomach and wants to cry out, but cold fingers seize his tongue. Just before passing out, he recognizes them as belonging "to that ghostly hand that had presented me, in my room in the Hahnpassgasse, with the book *Ibbur*." The paralyzed Pernath is brought to Schemajah Hillel's room, and Hillel recites a psalm of David and lights one of his seven-branched candelabras in order to exorcise the golem's grip. The Jewish sage explains, " 'It's only the supernatural, the Kischup, that can strike terror into the soul of man.' " Man, he says, is like a burnished mirror. " 'Once its surface is smooth and shining, it reflects all the images that fall upon it, without pain or grief. Blessed is that man,' he added softly, 'who can say to his own self, "I too have been burnished." ' " This is the ultimate state towards which Pernath unconsciously strives. This is that fecundation of the soul which *Ibbur* represents, but Pernath is still a long way from achieving it.

Hillel is one of the mentors who can lead Pernath to this state of perfection. He offers his pupil a more positive interpretation of the golem than that given earlier. " 'The man who sought you out, and whom you call the Golem, signifies the awakening of the dead through the innermost life of the spirit. Each thing that earth contains is nothing more than an everlasting symbol clothed in dust.' " Such transcendental philosophy necessitates learning " 'to think with your eyes.' " In other words, each physical object covers a spiritual truth, which man must learn to intuit. " 'He who is once waked can no longer die. Sleep and death are one and the same thing' "; when Pernath read *Ibbur*, unknowingly he chose the path of life. Hillel advises him, " 'As knowledge comes, so comes recollection. Knowledge and recollection are one and the same thing.' " Thus there is hope that Pernath's memory will return. The implication is that true knowledge of self cannot be attained without awareness of one's past.

Pernath is beginning to feel a peace of mind and clarity of thought that he has never known. He is even able to solve the problem of cutting a gem which had troubled him before, but he still cannot remember his childhood. Nevertheless, he realizes now that "in the scarce visible line engraved upon our being, is to be found the solution of our uttermost secret." Before falling asleep, Pernath sees in his imagination two flaming letters from *Ibbur*, "one signifying the Arch-type Woman with the pulse that beat like an earthquake, the other, at an infinite distance—the hermaphrodite on the pearly throne, with the crown of red wood upon its head." Before his soul can be burnished, before he can achieve this perfect state, Pernath must travel "an infinite distance."

Athanasius Pernath and His Quest for Self

Pernath's symbolic journey in search of himself begins when he discovers a trapdoor in the room in his building where Angelina and her lover had been meeting. The pull of the occult is overpowering. "Something invisible was calling to me, something from the Other Side, and I could not understand it." Meyrink's amalgam of Freudian psychology, occultism, Jewish legend and mysticism, and Gothic romance culminates in this chapter in a scene of terrifying suspense.

Groping his way in the dark, Pernath follows a seemingly endless subterranean passage beneath the ghetto until he ascends a spiral staircase and finds another trapdoor shaped like a Star of David. Pushing it open, he enters a small, dark room, empty except for a rubbish pile in the corner. There is only one window, and it is barred. The room, which is on the third floor, has no conventional door. As Pernath investigates the rubbish with his feet, he discovers a complete deck of seventy-eight tarot cards, which Meyrink introduces as an important clue to the meaning of the quest. The tarot cards have long been considered by those experienced in their use as a valuable tool to probe the hidden meanings of past, present, and future. Insisting that the events in the external world are never capricious or haphazard, the mystic endeavors to interpret the external signs through these cards, which he uses to unlock the mysteries of both his private soul and that of the cosmos. "Thus," according to Stephen A. Hoeller in *The Royal Road: A Manual of Kabbalistic Meditations on the Tarot* (1975), "divination by means of the Tarot may be defined as a practical way in which a bridge is built between the world where physical events take place in time on the one hand, and the timeless world of the archetypes of the collective unconscious on the other." It is such a bridge that Pernath must cross on his psychological pilgrimage.

Pernath first succumbs to fear, screaming futilely for help as he scans the streets below the window. He manages to overcome the coldness permeating his body only after pillaging and putting on the moldy rags from the heap on the floor. Fascinated by the Pagad card from the top of the tarot deck, he can make out the Hebrew letter aleph in the shape of an old-fashioned man with his left arm upraised. (Later Hillel will explain that the aleph has "one hand pointing to heaven, and the other downwards, meaning: 'As it is above, so it is below; as it is below, so it is above.' ") The gem cutter has a strange feeling that the face on the card resembles his own, even to the short pointed beard which the Pagad figure ordinarily does not have. By identifying Pernath with the aleph, Meyrink reinforces his theme of the double and underscores the correspondence between the Other World and this one, as well as the duality of good and evil.

By now Pernath realizes where he is—in the room on Altschulgasse in which the golem materializes every fourth decade. His terror intensifies as the Pagad card seems to inflate until it assumes a human form, and he is looking into his own face. Like Jacob wrestling with the angel, Pernath's soul wrestles with that of the Pagad for his life. Daylight finds Pernath the victor, and he places the Pagad card, now reduced to its normal size, into his pocket.

Exploring the junk in the room, he remembers how he had painted such cards in his childhood. As his childhood memories begin to return, he remembers that the twelfth card is "Le Pendu, the Hanged Man." Any of Meyrink's readers familiar with the symbolism of the tarot deck would immediately recognize the meaning and appropriateness of this figure, suspended between two worlds, hanging upside down, his right ankle tied to a wooden gibbet, his hands apparently tied behind his back. His face registers a calm contentment, and, in some tarot decks, a halo surrounds his head. As Meyrink points out, the Hanged Man card is the twelfth in the pack. According to Alfred Douglas in *The Tarot: The Origins, Meaning and Uses of the Cards* (1973),

> In Arabic numerals it is a combination of the numbers one and two, signifying the interaction of unity with duality which gives birth to a third dimension. The perils of number eleven [the raging lion] have been resolved, therefore it is a symbol of renewal and salvation.

Since Meyrink was assuredly familiar with similar interpretations of the Hanged Man card, it is instructive to look more closely at Douglas's comments to see how appropriate the image of the Hanged Man is as a symbol for the protagonist of Meyrink's novel. According to Douglas, the Hanged Man

> becomes agonizingly aware that he is not one person, the conscious self he identifies with, but only part of a greater whole. He sees two halves which are antagonistic to one another, yet are at the same time complementary. He cannot go back and reclaim the assured selfhood of his youth, yet equally he must not submit to his shadow. His only hope is to become free of both opponents, to step back into a central position in which he is balanced between the two.
>
> In so doing, he realizes that in casting himself off from the solid ground of his past consciousness, he can only trust that a larger power will support him and stop him falling into a psychic void. In order to proceed he must have the courage to let go of all he has learnt, voluntarily release the grip of intellect, and allow the deeper force within to take reins.

The Hanged Man, in this interpretation,

> now has to pass two trials—that of courage, and that of faith. Courage, in that he must sacrifice all that his conscious mind holds dear, and also renounce the instinctual demands of his shadow; faith, in that he must believe in the existence of a higher self which transcends his conscious awareness.

The content expression on the Hanged Man's face is the result of his finding "himself in a blissful state of total freedom from desire"—"balanced equally between the demands of both the conscious mind and its shadow." In this state he has been rewarded with "serenity and inward peace."

Meyrink's protagonist is seeking the same reward; the golem represents the Hanged Man's "shadow," and Pernath can find his higher self, "serenity and inward peace," only with "total freedom from desire." But Meyrink, at this point in his novel, soft-pedals the allusion to the Hanged Man and comes back to the symbolism of Rabbi Loew's homunculus. Returning along the passageway he came, Pernath realizes why people in the street are terrified by his appearance. They think that his strange figure in medieval garments is the golem.

Meyrink's technique throughout his novel is to alternate suspense-ful narrative sections with philosophical discussions in which the characters comment indirectly on the symbolic meaning of the action. One of the most significant of these discussions takes place after Pernath's return from his harrowing experience on the Altschulgasse. In this conversation, Hillel suggests an important new perspective on the meaning of the golem. Up to this point, the golem has been seen primarily as an evil force trying to take possession of a troubled indi-vidual. Hillel, however, denies the existence of the golem as an evil spirit stalking the ghetto. With a knowing glance at Pernath, he scoffs at Zwakh's insistence that the golem's recent reappearance foretells "a weird chain of events" involving additional murders. " 'I shouldn't [believe in him], if I were to see him sitting here in front of me,' " he tells the puppet master. Talking metaphorically, he reminds Zwakh, " 'There's always stirring within the roots of things. Sweet as well as poisonous.' " In other words, since the same life force that reanimates the rosebush in the spring stirs life in the poison oak, Hillel wisely suggests that, if there were such a thing as the golem, it would be subject to a higher power and thus could be a precursor of good as well as of evil. In terms of the protagonist's development, the stirring up of Pernath's natural desires may ultimately be a necessary part of the fertilization of his soul. A subtle duality can also be seen in Hillel's informing Zwakh that as registrar of the Jewish Council House, his job is to " 'manage the Registry of the Living and Dead.' " Meyrink cannot resist teasing his reader at this point with the narrator's thoughts. "I could feel a certain hidden significance in his words." (That is, Per-nath's current state of death-in-life can be transformed, through the agency of the golem, to a life-in-death.)

It is in this same conversation that Zwakh questions Hillel about the Kabbalah and the *Zohar*. Hillel calls for every man to search for "the hidden vowels." For the occultist, this is a call to discover the world beyond the one he knows; for the novelist, this is the challenge to the reader to find what goes on beneath the surface. A riled Zwakh scoffs at Hillel's mere use of words, saying, " 'If I could make sense of such stuff, you could call me the *Pagad ultimo* of the pack.' " Pernath is, of course, stunned by the coincidence of this allusion, and he is fascinated as Hillel explains to Zwakh that when he has the tarot cards in his hands he actually has the whole Kabbalah. The tarot game "contains two and twenty trumps—precisely the same number as the letters of the Hebrew alphabet." The word "tarot," says Hillel, " 'bears the same significance as the Jewish "Tora," that is to say, *"The Law,"* or the old

Egyptian "Tarut," "*Questions asked,*" and the old Zend word "Tarisk," meaning "*I require an answer.*" ' " Hillel explains that " 'just as the Pagad comes first in the game of cards, so is a man the first figure of all in his own picture-book—his own doppelgänger, so to say.' "

Hillel's telling the parable of Rabbi Akiba's return from the Realm of Darkness, where " 'He looked his own self in the face and kept his reason,' " is strikingly relevant to the quest of Pernath, who has just come back from his own sojourn underground. Looking "piercingly" at Pernath, Hillel concludes with a quotation from "our grandmothers."

> " 'He dwells high above ground, in a room with no door, and one window only, through which understanding with mankind is not possible. Whosoever can both banish and *purify* him, that man will be reconciled with his own self.' As for the game of tarot, you know as well as I how each player has his own hand to play, but he who knows how best to use his trumps wins the game!' "

Though the source of Hillel's quotation is vague, the meaning and relevance are clear. Pernath is becoming increasingly aware "of the colossal and utter loneliness" that alienates him from mankind. He remembers how even from childhood "an insatiable longing had obsessed me for the strange and wonderful, for the life other than ours on this globe." This fascination with the occult has led Pernath away from normal human relationships to an isolation similar to the golem's in his room in the ghetto. The lesson for Pernath is slowly coming into focus: he must, through the exertion of free will, rid himself of the golem within (the sensual, self-destructive force and its accompanying alienation), and, in so doing, he might be the golem's redeemer as well.

Pernath's divided self is further seen in the struggle between the antagonistic forces represented by Charousek and Hillel. " 'No one can hate anything as deeply as I do unless it is a part of himself,' " says Charousek, describing his feelings for his own father, the junk dealer, from whom he is alienated. The opposite of this hatred is Hillel's love for his daughter Miriam and all humanity. Whereas the Jewish sage is a saintly altruist who gives his salary away despite his poverty, the materialist junk dealer thinks nothing of ruining lives to satisfy his insatiable greed. Pernath tries to follow in Hillel's footsteps and slips the impoverished Charousek some money. The gem cutter is also learning from the mystic Hillel that "true sight comes only with closed eyelids" and depends on "inner vision."

Just as Charousek and Hillel represent opposites in the development of Pernath's soul, so do the two women, Angelina and Miriam. Miriam begins to model for him as he works on a gem with her image. The more he sees her, the more he confides in her about his mysterious past and his fears that a final revelation might destroy him. Her sweet innocence and preference for the ideal over the real suggest the fair maiden archetype so popular in nineteenth-century fiction, in contrast to the earthy, sensual, flirtatious Angelina, so ironically named. Miriam is saintly like her father and takes as her creed her father's mystical teaching, " 'The world only exists for us to be thought out of existence by us.' " Pernath is strongly attracted to both women; each appeals to a different part of his split personality.

The gem cutter's artistic talent begins to surpass anything he has previously known. "Creative powers had been awakened within me that raised my work on to a completely different level—far, far higher than the average ruck." He feels himself "on the threshold of a new existence," but is troubled by the question, "Must . . . mysticism be synonymous with the suppression of all desire?" The polarity between asceticism and sensuality confuses him. In his dreams and fantasies the figures of Angelina, Miriam, and even the young whore Rosina alternate, sometimes replaced by the naked female "with the pulse like an earthquake." The monastic side of Pernath feels that "this sickly germ of uncertain love was like a cancer eating away my breast."

The conflict in Pernath's subconscious is dramatized when he invites Miriam for a drive in a carriage, but this ethereal creature, more in tune with the spirit than the flesh, refuses him. She tells Pernath how she yearns for " 'the soulless earth [to become] informed with the spirit, and the laws of Nature [to be] set at naught.' " Craving magic over reality, Miriam dreams of a perfect union between two human beings that transcends the flesh. The clue to her dream is her asking Pernath if he is familiar with "the old Egyptian cult of Osiris" and her informing him of her admiration for the symbolism of the hermaphrodite—" 'the beginning of a new way that is eternal.' " Since Meyrink alludes several times in his novel to the symbolism of the hermaphrodite and Osiris, these allusions need clarification.

The source of the myth of the hermaphrodite is Greek mythology. According to legend, the beautiful nymph Salmacis seized the comely Hermaphroditus while he was bathing in her spring. When the young man did not return her caresses, the gods answered her plea to be united forever with the youth by creating a single being combining the physical characteristics of both sexes. In Meyrink's *Golem*, the hermaphrodite symbolizes Miriam's dream of the perfect physical union for all eternity.

The allusion to Osiris comes from Egyptian mythology. Osiris, one of Egypt's major deities, was the son of earth and sky and represented the principles of good in combat with evil, personified in his brother Set. Set dismembered Osiris and scattered the parts throughout Egypt. According to different myths, Isis, the sister-wife of Osiris, collected the pieces and buried them. In one version, she succeeded in making all the pieces come together again, and thus Osiris became the god of resurrection and eternal life. Osiris is a fitting symbol for Athanasius Pernath, who, in trying to resurrect his lost past, wants to reconcile his antagonistic selves and enter that blissful state of higher consciousness. During this struggle between his two halves, Pernath is invited to go on a carriage ride with Angelina, who intoxicates him with her coquettish actions. As they confess having dreamed of each other the previous night, he strips her hand of its glove and, "half crazed with love," bites "the ball of her little thumb." Thus the golem, the id, the dark force in Pernath, surfaces.

The Mystical Transformation of Athanasius Pernath

Even though the golem plays a relatively small part in the totality of his novel, Meyrink's obsession with the supernatural and his febrile imagination give his book its distinctive texture. Pale Miriam and even the more vibrant Angelina are not enough to hold the reader's interest. They have less life than the fabulous apparitions which Meyrink animates with brilliant effect as he portrays Pernath's dream world. In the last half of the novel especially, Meyrink uses the golem only subliminally and introduces "the army of night thoughts that . . . bid fair to overwhelm" Pernath, as the gem cutter fears that he is going mad or has already died. Matching the terror of the scene in the golem's room is the night of "Lelschimurim . . . the Night of Protection." Feeling a tension in the air, an unspecified, formless terror, Pernath tries in vain to kindle a light, but the wick will not burn. Desperately he cries out his challenge to the Other World: " 'CAN'T YOU HEAR ME?' " Eventually an apparition with "a nebulous globe of pale mist" in place of a head appears before him. "My instinct of self-preservation," Pernath reports, "told me I should go mad from fear or horror, once I saw the phantom's face—and yet it drew me like a magnet." The apparition keeps offering him large red seeds, some spotted with black. Pernath has the feeling that he must make a momentous decision. Faces of his ancestors pass before him, culminating in "one hideous countenance—the face of the Golem, and none other!" Strange forms circle around him, some in purple robes, some in reddish black. Some are the creatures of an alien race. Suddenly Pernath strikes the seeds from the outstretched hand. The gray apparition and reddish black forms disappear and are replaced by bluish forms which encircle him. Golden hieroglyphs appear on their chests. Each holds up one of the red seeds he had knocked to the floor. Outside it is thundering and hailstones are falling. A phantom voice tells him not to be afraid, and another enigmatically informs him, " 'He whom you seek is not here.' " After flaming gold letters spell out a strange inscription on his chest, Pernath falls into a dreamless sleep.

Another key example of Meyrink's use of the supernatural and mystical in the second half of the novel to deepen the suspense and enrich the characterization of Pernath in his continual attempt to communicate with the ideal world occurs after the carriage ride with Angelina. Wandering in Prague, he gets lost in the Street of the Alchemists. His way in the mist is blocked by a large, whitewashed house with a lattice gate. Knocking on the window fails to catch the attention of "a veritable old Methuselah of a man" whose sockets "look as empty as the eye-holes of a mummy." When Pernath manages to find his way back to his friends in the tavern, Prokop explains that the house, according to a Prague legend, is visible only in a fog, " 'and then only to those folk born of a Sunday! It goes by the name of "Lost Lamp House." ' " By day, one sees only a huge grey stone with a sheer drop behind it into the river below. " 'You can thank your lucky stars,' " Prokop tells Pernath, that " 'you didn't take one step more.' " This stone, supposedly placed there "by the Asiatic brothers who are said to have founded the city of Prague," is the foundation of a house to be inhabited by a hermaphrodite. " 'It will carry a hare as its coat-of-arms. For the hare was apparently the symbol of Osiris.' " Zwakh is amazed that Pernath had his strange experience on this very spot and remarks, " 'There are hidden linkages, from whose bond certain men apparently cannot free themselves, if their souls have the faculty of seeing forms which are denied to the external senses.' " That Pernath is one of these select beings capable of communicating with the Other World has already been illustrated beyond Zwakh's wildest imagination.

It is in this same chapter that Prokop simplistically announces that the mystery of the golem is now cleared up. Haschile, "the mad Jewish beggar," had been caught the day before walking the streets of Prague in the golem's old rags, which he had found on the doorsteps of some house. Such rational explanations of the supernatural serve in Meyrink's novel only for comic relief, and he quickly returns to the more serious matter at hand. The conflict in Pernath between his earthy desires and his craving for the ideal spirituality represented by Miriam culminates in his succumbing temporarily to Rosina's lures. His lowest descent into sensuality heretofore had been his erotic fantasies and biting the ball of Angelina's thumb, but he can no longer resist the dark, subterranean forces fighting for possession of his psyche. However, the price he pays for the evening's pleasure is a guilty conscience and a depression so severe that he decides to commit suicide.

Meyrink's final step in preparing Pernath for the mystical transformation of his character at the end of the novel is his unexpected arrest and imprisonment before he can kill himself. At the police station he refuses to answer questions about Angelina and her lover. The superintendent of police claims he is an old friend of Pernath's father and urges him to cooperate with the investigation. When Pernath refuses, he is accused of having murdered the man whose damaged watch he had recently accepted as a gift from the junk dealer. Thus Wassertrum succeeds in implicating him in the murder. A handcuffed and angry Pernath is put into a cell. Meyrink's love of satire is seen in the sign over the prison door, "Law Chastises the Guilty and Protects the Innocent." Despairing in his cell, Pernath looks out at an old watch tower with a clock dial, the hands of which are missing. This ominous symbol suggests, not the timelessness of the blissful state he has been seeking, but the fact that for him time has stopped. There is no such thing as protection of the innocent, as Pernath will discover as he rots in jail for months, the victim of a ruthless, indifferent, stupid bureaucracy. In fact, one of Pernath's three cellmates has been accused of murdering the same man the gem cutter is alleged to have killed.

After weeks of poor food, lack of water, and failing health, Pernath receives a long secret message from Charousek with an escape plan, but the stubborn prisoner rejects it, insisting that an innocent man should not need such recourse. The messenger reveals to Pernath that Angelina is now divorced and has left with her child. With Pernath's new awareness of the depth of his love for Miriam, this part of his inner conflict is resolved and Angelina is no longer needed to dramatize his split personality. She never reappears in the novel. The messenger also reveals that the junk dealer is dead, his throat slit by Pernath's former cellmate, who has escaped. (Pernath himself had toyed in prison with the idea of using a file to kill the hated Wassertrum. His fantasy is fulfilled when his cellmate steals this very weapon and commits the murder for him. Meyrink again achieves his purpose of making the protagonist more attractive to the reader through the device of displacement.)

As Pernath peruses Charousek's letter, he discovers how the junk dealer had framed him with the stolen watch because he had helped Angelina. Charousek also explains his feeling of kinship with the gem cutter, a feeling which arose partly because of their mutual interest in the occult, a hint at which was "a certain sign" which he once recognized on Pernath's breast. Now a wealthy man, having been left everything in Aaron Wassertrum's will, Charousek hints at his own suicide. He still wants to punish the junk dealer, even in " 'the Kingdom of Shadow.' " In his own will, Charousek is leaving one-third of his new wealth to Pernath, explaining that years ago the junk dealer had ruined Pernath's family and stolen everything they owned. Pernath is stunned by Charousek's generosity and thinks him a saint like Miriam and Hillel.

To Pernath's list of saints and mentors, one last name has to be added, Amadeus Laponder. This new prisoner, with his "Pagad-like smile" and "smooth-skinned Buddha countenance," represents Meyrink's final use of character doubling to dramatize the inner conflict of his protagonist. Laponder, who has confessed to rape-murder (his victim may have been Miriam—the reader cannot be certain) represents, like the golem and Charousek, the dark side of Pernath's psyche. Pernath's sexual interests are thus displaced on Laponder, who acts out the former's controlled impulses. Somehow, the gem cutter, the medical student, and the murderer are all linked fraternally by their having had some contact with the Other World. Both Charousek and Laponder are familiar with the secret sign they recognize on Pernath's breast, but Laponder goes far beyond Charousek in penetrating Pernath's innermost being. He is, for example, a medium through which Miriam and Hillel are able to contact Pernath. Miriam's voice is transmitted one night through the sleeping Laponder's lips and speaks of the couple's love for one another and " 'the unspeakable happiness we had at last found . . . that could part us nevermore.' " When Pernath asks if she is dead, she says no, only asleep, but the reader must remember Hillel's earlier statement that " 'sleep and death are one and the same thing.' "

Laponder's dreams, which he describes vividly to Pernath, involve a visit to the sleeping Miriam, watched over by her loving father, and a trip underground to the room on the Altschulgasse, where he saw the golem with his slanted eyes and queer clothes. Laponder even confirms that this strange creature was reading a book made of parchment, but the page began with an aleph (the double man representing the oneness of both worlds), not an *I*. Pernath is amazed at his fellow prisoner's ability to duplicate his own experiences. "Obviously, somehow or other Laponder had managed during his sleep to penetrate my subconscious self, and was now reproducing the result at random." But Laponder craves more information about Pernath's past experiences, because they also concern him in some way and will supply him with an essential clue he lacks.

Apparently both Laponder and Pernath were approached by the same headless apparition offering them red and black spotted seeds. Although Pernath struck them to the ground, Laponder accepted them and thus was condemned to death. The seeds, explains Laponder, " 'signify the powers of magic,' " and they will now remain " 'in the custody of your forefathers until the time of their ripening. Then will the faculties still latent within you spring into being.' " Each man has within him " 'the *spiritual vestiges* of thousands of [his] forebears.' " Thus Laponder had to commit the crime he did, as hideous as it was. " 'Something inside of me, of which I had had no previous knowledge, came to life, and was stronger than I was.' " It " 'was but the working out of some dormant principle, long hidden within my being, over which I possessed no power.' " Only with his execution for the crime will he be set free. (Through Laponder's death, the destructive side of Pernath will be overcome symbolically and the spiritual liberated.)

Pernath considers his new mentor another saint, despite the horror of his crime. Laponder explains that the hypnotism which removed Pernath's memory of his childhood is really a " 'holy stigmata,' " the sign

> "of all those bitten by the Snake of the Kingdom of the Spirit. It almost looks as if two lives must be found together in us, like the mistletoe and the oak, before the miracle of awakening can take place. What is usually accomplished by death, the separation of the two selves, has resulted here from extinction of the memory—or sometimes by a sudden internal reversal and upheaval."

Such an upheaval, a complete change of personality, occurred in Laponder when he turned twenty-one. At that time, his dreams became reality to him and vice versa. Every man, if taught, could enter this state.

> "And the key consists in simply and solely this: that a man, during sleep [the state of Meyrink's narrator], shall become conscious of his ego-form, his *skin*, so to say, and aware of that infinitesimal rift through which his conscious self presses in that transition state which lies betwixt waking and deep sleep. . . .
>
> Our struggle to attain immortality is our struggle to gain ascendancy over those unruly ghosts and warring elements innate within our being. We await the crowning of the true I, which is the same as the Messiah."

Here is the key to Meyrink's novel. The golem ultimately symbolizes all those "unruly ghosts and warring elements" deep within each man. They must be overcome, tamed, in the individual's quest for immortality, to attain that perfect state which is the redemption of the soul, that discovery of the ideal self made real. This is the true mystical (some would say religious) experience. When Pernath reaches that state, he will no longer be bound by his own senses and reason. He will have entered a new, mystical dimension, symbolized by the crowning of his doppelgänger, whom Pernath now calls Habal Garmin, giving him the name of a kabbalistic figure who, according to Schemajah Hillel, represents absolute purity and incorruptibility.

With a vivid analogy, Laponder tries to clarify his philosophy.

> "Human beings are like tubes made of glass, through which many coloured balls may roll. Most men are restricted to one colour only. Should the ball be red, the man is branded as 'bad'; if yellow, then he is 'good.' Should two balls pursue their passage through the same tube, one yellow and one red, then that man has 'an unstable character.' But we who have been bitten by the Serpent compress within ourselves the experience of a whole race within an age. Coloured balls rush wildly on their way through the glass tube, and when it ends, then are we 'prophets,' and the mirror of very God himself."

In terms of Laponder's analogy, he himself has reached that stage of stability and inner vision where he has now become a prophet. To use Pernath's earlier phrase, Laponder's soul has been "perfectly burnished" and thus can serve as a mirror of the highest ideality, God

Himself. As for Pernath, he has been passing through the stage of being "an unstable character," but the end is in sight when he too will pass into a new dimension where the ideal becomes the real.

Pernath is overwhelmed by Laponder's insights and considers himself far inferior to the murderer-rapist, but Laponder disagrees and says that he is "infinitely below" the gem cutter. Pernath has supplied him with the key he lacked—a reference to the hermaphrodite. As the jailer comes to execute him, Laponder insists that he is a happy man. " 'This is my bridal day. . . . And with it my crime is closely knit.' "

Upon his release from prison months later, Pernath is a wealthy man, heir to one-third of Charousek's estate because the student took his own life over Aaron Wassertrum's grave in pursuit of his father's evil spirit. In a sense, Charousek carries out the death wish so strong in Pernath. When the latter tries to take a cab to the Hahnspassgasse, he is told that it is impossible since the Jewish quarter is being rebuilt. The drosky lets him off before a heap of ruins; his old house is but a skeleton. The only name the workmen recognize is that of the mute who cuts out silhouettes in the Café Chaos. When he visits this café, Pernath is stunned by his own image in the mirror. He sees a remarkable change, "an entirely unfamiliar face—wrinkled, pasty, grey as putty, with scrubby beard, and long, tangled hair."

Pumping the bewildered mute for information about his friends, Pernath learns that Zwakh, Vrieslander, and Prokop are on tour with the marionettes. Hillel has gone, but no one knows where; Miriam is gone also, and when Pernath asks where, the mute pantomimes sleep. At the Jewish Council House, Pernath is told that Hillel has left, presumably with his daughter. The mystery of Miriam's possible murder is left unanswered. Pernath next rents rooms in the Altschulgasse, the only street in the ghetto not being torn down. "By some curious law of coincidence it turned out to be precisely the same house as that in which the Golem was said to have taken refuge, according to the old legend." Pernath's earlier experience in the golem's room has been wiped from his mind like "a vanished dream."

On Christmas Eve, Pernath brings a little tree and red candles to his room, longing to be a boy again. He plans to start searching for Hillel and Miriam at the beginning of the new year, but for now he has "a feeling of happy contentment—the sweet peace of a man who, after many wanderings, returns to his home, and sees from afar the spires of his native town." Meyrink's imagery of the traveler returning home hints at Pernath's imminent discovery of the details of his boyhood and youth. This implication is reinforced when the gem cutter discovers a street peddler selling the "heartshaped stone strung on a piece of silk" that Angelina gave him as a child in her castle garden when they parted years ago. "In a flash," says Pernath, "my youth stood revealed to me—in miniature, as though I gazed at it through a peep-show on a small scale." However, Meyrink supplies no further details and ignores the reader's expectation of further revelations, presumably because he is more concerned with the nature of the mystical experience than with rational, Freudian explanations.

Alone in his attic room, Pernath sits almost in a trance as the candle burns down. Suddenly he sees his doppelgänger again, and, as Laponder had foretold, there is a crown upon his head. The moment of redemption has arrived with the crowning of Habal Garmin. But at this ecstatic moment, Pernath discovers that the house is on fire. He climbs the roof to safety and uses a chimney sweep's rope to let himself down as he was once taught in school. Passing a window, he looks in and sees Hillel and Miriam. When he drops the rope, he is, like the Hanged Man on the tarot card, momentarily suspended "betwixt heaven and earth" before he falls, unable to grasp the smooth window sill which is "SMOOTH LIKE A LUMP OF FAT!" This odd simile is repeated from a Buddhist parable told in the opening chapter, according to which a crow, thinking he had passed over a delicious lump of fat, flew down for a close inspection, only to realize that he had been deceived. The parable was meant as a warning to Gautama's followers not to be duped by the false pleasures of this world. The full meaning of this lesson cannot be understood until the final chapter, with its revelation of a paradisiacal world beyond this one. Meyrink implies that Pernath must not be deceived into expecting his love for Miriam to be consummated on earth.

In the final chapter, the narrator wakes up in a hotel and wonders if all that has happened to him has been a dream. His name is not Athanasius Pernath. That is the name of the owner of the hat he took by mistake at the cathedral. When he tells the porter he wants to go at once to the old Jewish quarter, he is informed that it is impossible, since it has all been rebuilt long ago. "Obviously," the narrator realizes, "I had experienced within my dream, everything that Athanasius Pernath had lived through. Everything have I witnessed, heard, and felt, within the space of one night, as though I had been he."

Searching for Pernath to exchange hats, the narrator is directed to Loisitschek's. Figuring that Pernath must be ninety now, the narrator looks for someone who might remember him. He asks a waitress when the stone bridge had broken down and is informed that it happened in a winter storm thirty-three years ago, the same evening the golem and other apparitions had appeared to him offering the red seeds. (A footnote from the editor at this point explains this mistake in Meyrink's chronology, since Pernath was supposed to be in his forties when the bridge was damaged in 1890.) Pernath eventually finds two old men, one of whom, the blind Schaffranek, sings the same song he sang in Pernath's time. When the narrator speaks into the old man's ear and asks if he remembers Pernath, the senile Schaffranek asks jokingly if he means " 'Pereles.' " When the narrator shouts, " 'No. *Not* Pereles! Pernath!' " the old man comes back with " 'Pascheles?' " Disappointed, the narrator gives up. How many of Meyrink's readers got this little joke in 1915 is unknowable, but the readers of this study will surely recognize Pereles as the author of *Megillath Yuchasin,* the first family chronicle of Rabbi Judah Loew. Pascheles, of course, was the editor of *Sippurim,* the collection of tales of Prague with the first printed tale of Rabbi Loew's golem.

The other man in the tavern remembers Pernath well. " 'If I'm not mistaken,' " he says, " 'they used to say that he was mad. Pernath once said, yes I believe he once said his name was—let me think—Laponder—and at other times he'd give himself out for a certain . . . Charousek!' " By explicitly identifying the three men with each other in this way, Meyrink clarifies for the last time the function of Laponder and Charousek as Pernath's doubles. The old man adds one last bit of information; he thinks that later in life Pernath " 'married a very beautiful Jewess!' "

The squint-eyed boatman who has been listening to this conversation and denies that Pernath ever existed offers to show the narrator the "Last Lamp House" on his trip down the Moldau. Early in the morning, the narrator excitedly recognizes the house on the Altschulgasse with the iron bars and slippery stone, but in answer to his query, he is told with authority that this house never was on fire. While he is being rowed on the Moldau, the narrator experiences a kind of déjà vu.

> My soul seems possessed with a strange feeling of solemnity. A faint, indefinable feeling rises within me as of something proceeding from another life than this—some previous enchanted existence: the whole world, in fact, seems enchanted, seen through a haze of dreamy recognition, as though I had lived already at many times, and in many places, simultaneously.

Through this "haze of dreamy recognition," Meyrink has created an intricate pattern of doubles, reflections in a row of mirrors: the narrator, the golem, Charousek, and Laponder, all providing glimpses into the mystical transformation of the soul of Athanasius Pernath.

As the narrator proceeds down the Street of the Alchemists, he feels familiar with every inch. However, instead of a "glimmering white house" barring his way, a magnificent gold one stands there now. On the garden wall is a mosaic of "frescoes depicting the Egyptian cult of the god Osiris." On the swinging door is seen once again the god himself: "a hermaphrodite in two halves, the right female, the left male." The figure seated on the throne has a golden head shaped like a hare. The ears stand up like two pages of an open book. When the very old gardener, wearing ruffles on his neck, silver buckles on his shoes, and a curious coat, asks through the bars what the narrator wants, the latter silently hands him the hat of Athanasius Pernath. As the doors of the marble house open, the narrator sees Athanasius Pernath and a young-looking Miriam standing as in a temple. "So like is he to myself," the narrator observes, "it is as though beholding my own face and figure in the glass!"

The old servant, obviously the now redeemed golem, hands the narrator his correct hat, delivering a message "as though proceeding from the bowels of the earth." The message from Herr Athanasius Pernath is a thank-you for the return of the hat and an apology for not being able to invite him in because of the ancient rules of the house. He also explains that his master has never worn the narrator's hat, having immediately discovered the mistake. The last line of the message (and novel) is Meyrink's final joke on the reader. " 'HE ONLY HOPES HIS HAT MAY NOT HAVE GIVEN YOU A HEADACHE.' "

The Rabbi and the Golem, *metal sculpture by Harry Friedman of Oak Park, Michigan.* Photograph by Bernard Brodsky

The old Jewish cemetery in Prague. Courtesy of the Embassy of the Czechoslovak Socialist Republic, Washington, D.C.

Rabbi Judah Loew's grave in the old Jewish cemetery in Prague. Courtesy of the Embassy of the Czechoslovak Socialist Republic, Washington, D.C.

Monument to Rabbi Judah Loew by Ladislaus Šaloun in front of the town hall in Prague. Courtesy of the State Jewish Museum, Prague

Model of the Altneuschul in Prague, the oldest extant European synagogue still in use and the setting for several of the golem legends. Courtesy of Beth Harefutsoth, The Nahum Goldmann Museum of the Jewish Diaspora, Tel Aviv, Israel

The Golem, *illustration by Georg Jilovsky for* The Golem *by Chayim Bloch.*

Baruch Tchemerinsky as Rabbi Levi in The Golem: A Dramatic Poem in Eight Scenes, *performed by the Habima Theatre of Moscow.* Courtesy of the American Jewish Historical Society

Father Thaddeus, Rabbi Levi's antagonist in The Golem: A Dramatic Poem in Eight Scenes, *performed by the Habima Theatre of Moscow during a tour of the United States in 1948.* Courtesy of the New York Public Library

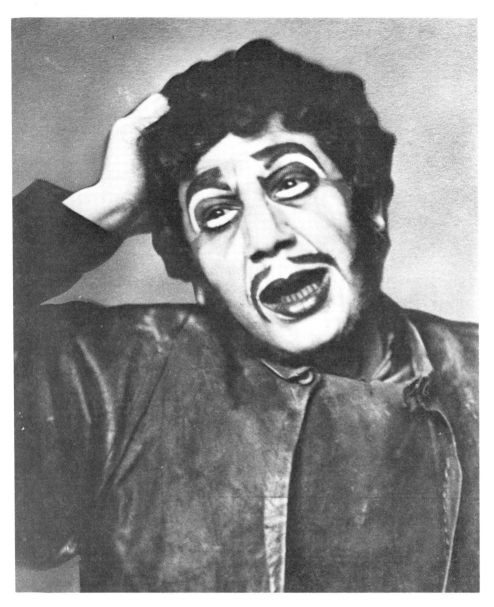

Aaron Meskin as the golem in The Golem: A Dramatic Poem in Eight Scenes, *performed by the Habima Theatre of Moscow during a tour of the United States in 1948.* Courtesy of the New York Public Library

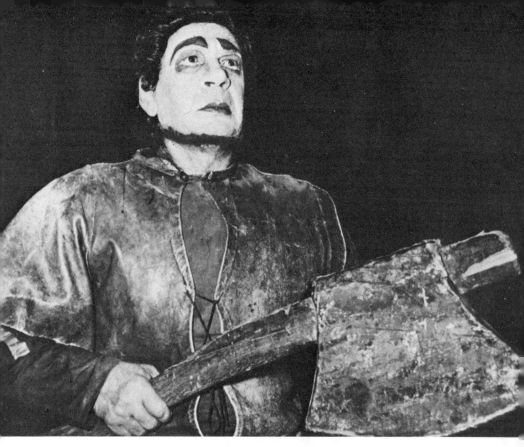

Aaron Meskin as the golem with his broadax in The Golem: A Dramatic Poem in Eight Scenes, *performed by the Habima Theatre of Moscow.* Courtesy of the Keter Publishing House Jerusalem Ltd.

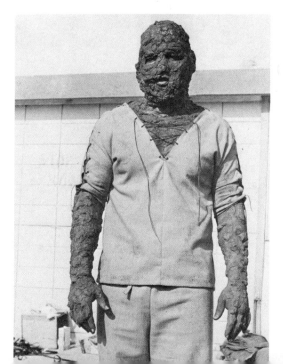

The actor David Gans made up to play the golem in Black Golem. Courtesy Frederick Sweet, American Twist Productions

The golem offering Pernath a book,
illustration by Hugo Steiner-Prag for Der
Golem *by Gustav Meyrink.*

The golem walking the streets, illustration
by Hugo Steiner-Prag for Der Golem *by*
Gustav Meyrink.

Pernath making his way to the hidden room,
illustration by Hugo Steiner-Prag for Der
Golem *by Gustav Meyrink.*

The golem in the streets of the Prague ghetto, scene from Der Golem: Wie er in die Welt Kam. Courtesy Museum of Modern Art / Film Stills Archive, 1 W. 53rd Street, New York City

The golem and Emperor Rudolf's soldiers, scene from Der Golem: Wie er in die Welt Kam. Courtesy Museum of Modern Art / Film Stills Archive, 1 W. 53rd Street, New York City

Rabbi Löw, the golem, and the Jews of Prague, scene from Der Golem: Wie er in die Welt Kam. Courtesy Museum of Modern Art / Film Stills Archive, 1 W. 53rd Street, New York City

The German child offering the golem an apple, scene from Der Golem: Wie er in die Welt Kam. Courtesy Museum of Modern Art / Film Stills Archive, 1 W. 53rd Street, New York City

CONTINUED ON 2ᴺᴰ PAGE FOLLOWING.

Superman meets the Galactic Golem. SUPERMAN is a registered trademark of DC Comics Inc.; illustration © copyright 1972 DC Comics Inc. and used with permission.

Chapter Six

Abraham Rothberg's
Sword of the Golem

THE most significant work of fiction on the Golem of Prague in the last fifty years, and the major American contribution to the literary treatment of the legend, is a novel by Abraham Rothberg (1922–) published in 1970. Titled *The Sword of the Golem*, it is, according to the author, "about peace and violence, about when the sword is to be used, and when it is to be sheathed, if ever." Rothberg's dedication reads, "To all who have searched the past of the Golem and questioned his meaning; but most of all to the great Leivick, who breathed new life into the Golem's clay."

Although Rothberg has written six novels (of which *The Sword of the Golem* is his fifth) and a four-volume *Eyewitness History of World War II*, he is not well known. A native New Yorker, he was a roving correspondent for the *National Observer* and a special correspondent for the *Manchester Guardian* before becoming a professor of English at St. John Fisher College in Rochester, New York. In 1963, remembering early Hebrew legends of the golem taught him by his father and uncle, Rothberg visited the Jewish museum in Prague as well as the old cemetery, the Altneuschul, the grave of Rabbi Loew, and the area of the old ghetto. It was on this visit, he says, that "slowly the book began to jostle the corners of my mind." That Rothberg knew his subject intimately is evidenced on every page of his work. Leivick's verse drama may have been his major source of inspiration, but Rothberg was also familiar with Chayim Bloch's tales and Gustav Meyrink's novel.

Rothberg's ability to reanimate the clay of the golem as if he were bringing this strange creature to life for the first time is no small

120

accomplishment. To this story of sixteenth-century Prague he brings fresh insights and post-Holocaust perspectives. In a prize-winning article, "What Time Is It Now?" (1973), he explains how he came to write *The Sword of the Golem*. "The more I read, the more it seemed to me that sixteenth-century Prague and Bohemia were like our own time and place, a time of terrible transition though from what to what no one knew or could guess. And a place of awful unease." It seemed to Rothberg that the more he learned about the period of Rabbi Loew's life, the better he understood the present. "So when the time came to write, I found myself writing not a historical novel, but in fact a truly contemporary one, a novel not of sixteenth-century Prague but of our own troubled twentieth century." One can detect in this pacifist novel the mood of an America weary of the tragic loss of life in Vietnam. But, more to the point, it reflects the hurt in the memorable statement of Golda Meir, who in 1967 told the Arab world that her country could forgive her old enemies for everything they had done except their turning Israel's sons into killers.

The analysis that follows will demonstrate how Rothberg adapted some of the old tales to his own purposes. The character of Rabbi Loew (spelled Low by Rothberg) and that of the golem take on broad new dimensions. Like Meyrink, Rothberg was fascinated by the psychological implications of the double, but unlike his German predecessor, the American novelist was content to limit himself to the world of the story being told, with no incursions into the realm of the occult beyond the kabbalistic lore involved in the creation of the golem and Rabbi Loew's dream communications with God. Meyrink favored ghostly apparitions, feverish nightmares, dreams within dreams, the transmigration of souls, underground journeys, East Indian mysticism, and the occult world of tarot cards and Egyptian mythology; Rothberg prefers the relatively simple world of the sixteenth-century European ghetto.

New Psychological and Moral Dimensions

Rothberg deliberately changes the date traditionally given for Rabbi Loew's creation of the golem on the banks of the Moldau, moving it from 1580 to 1589, exactly two hundred years after the monstrous pogrom of April 18, 1389, an event still memorialized by Jews every Yom Kippur with an elegy written by Avigedor Karo. The change of date, though slight, does add the weight of history to the events of the novel, and the allusion to the fourteenth-century pogrom foreshadows the horrors described in chapters 24 and 25. Far more significant than moving the date up nine years, however, is Rothberg's characterization of his Rabbi Low. Going far beyond the relatively uncomplicated portrayal found in the tales of Rosenberg and Bloch, Rothberg follows Leivick's lead, adding new elements to deepen and enrich the character of the rabbi. These new complications are extremely important and show how later generations of readers can find fresh meanings in old legends.

The first new element is the theme of doubt. In the simple purity of the earlier tales, the rabbi had no doubts that God had chosen him, the acknowledged spiritual leader of the Jewish community of Prague, and thus of all Bohemia, to protect his people against their enemies. However, in Rothberg's version, as Rabbi Low becomes aware of the golem's obsession with evil and brutality, he begins to question his own motivation, his own capacity for error and sinfulness. "Did I," he asks himself early in the novel, "in my zeal to protect my people, misinterpret the dream the Almighty sent me? Was my own fear of Thaddeus and his accusations of bloodguilt a poison that flawed this creature at birth? In my joy that we had a defender, was there also vengefulness and spite, hatred and malice?" His first inclination is to assume that since God gave him the ability to create a man out of clay, he cannot be a grievous sinner in the eyes of the Omnipotent. But there is always the possibility that God is punishing the Jewish community by allowing him to create not a redeemer, but a scourge.

Rothberg, in another new development, uses the rabbi's wife, Pearl, to probe this whole matter of Judah's possible moral flaw. She does not like the golem and asks her husband to get rid of him after his mission is accomplished at Passover. (Apparently Judah has informed her of Joseph's mysterious origin; Rothberg never makes this clear.) Pearl complains that Rabbi Low acts like a general when Joseph is around. " 'It is as if, suddenly you were David, Josiah, Bar Giora, a commander of armies sending soldiers to their deaths.' " Pearl has to admit that Judah treats the golem like a son, but because she implicates her husband in the death of their own son, Bezalel, the paternal relationship is ominous. (The reader is reminded of this relationship in chapter 16, when the golem, who has run away, returns and saves the rabbi from an angry mob and then disappears. Rabbi Low links his son and the golem, thinking, "That imperfect creature, the creation not of his loins but of his hands, was not Bezalel, yet the Golem was as much of a son as he would now have. A veritable Kaddish.") Pearl compares her husband to Abraham about to sacrifice Isaac and warns him,

"Do not contend with the Lord, Judah. Do not let your pride in being the Höhe Rabbi Low lead you astray. You are not the Messiah. You are an eighty-one-year-old man. Let some other now be a hero, responsible for saving the ghetto."

His conscience pricked by the reference to Bezalel, Judah Low has to ask himself,

Had he, out of ambition and pride, forced Bezalel against his nature to follow in the footsteps of the Höhe Rabbi Low and so led him to his death?

Rothberg is the only author considered in this study to try to use the story of Bezalel Loew, but his attempt is not very successful. The details are murky, only hinted at, never adequately clarified. In real life, of course, Bezalel became a rabbi in Kolín and ran a rabbinical academy until his death in 1600. Judah wanted Bezalel to be appointed his successor, but the old rabbi had made enemies whose opposition thwarted his dream. Just how Judah Low's ambitions for his son caused the latter's death is never clearly explained, but Rothberg conceives the golem as a surrogate son for the bereaved Judah, and thus Judah's role in Bezalel's death foreshadows his having to remove Joseph in the denouement of *The Sword of the Golem*.

Pearl is not the only character in Rothberg's novel who tries to warn Rabbi Low of the dangers of pride. Mordecai Marcus Meisel, the Jewish merchant, financier, and philanthropist, who was Judah Loew's close friend in both real life and fiction, argues strenuously with the rabbi over the best way to try to save the Jewish community. Meisel, who has access to Emperor Rudolf, wants to use some of his vast fortune to buy the Jews' safety. Judah naively insists on the opportunity to debate the Catholic church so as to convince the ecclesiastical authorities once and for all that the Jews are innocent of the Blood Libel. Meisel tells his old friend, " 'Judah, you are carried away with your obsession to be a savior.' " When Judah defends his sincere wish to save his coreligionists, Meisel warns him of the sin of " 'pride that apes humility, the arrogance of one who sets himself in the forefront without remembering that those who remain behind him must pay for his affront. You are not the Messiah nor were meant to be.' " It is Meisel's feeling that Rabbi Low does not have the same compassionate love of men that he had when the merchant brought him to the Klaus Synagogue in Prague some years ago, and he attributes the change to

Judah's anger when " 'the community refused to make Bezalel your successor.' "

That Rothberg had done his homework well, carefully studying the life of Judah Loew before embellishing the known facts with his own imaginative touches, can be seen in Judah's praise of Bezalel, when he tells the financier that his son " 'would have carried on what we had begun, Marcus. He would have stood fast against the discord and the selfishness of the ghetto, against its divisiveness, against the greed and violence of the *goyim* outside.' " Bezalel " 'would have insisted on teaching Bible and Talmud to build character, to preserve our traditions, instead of sending students off on the crooked paths of sterile hairsplitting and useless, showy disputation.' " Apparently the idealistic son was crushed by the community's refusal to allow him to continue his father's crusade, and he would not be comforted by Rabbi Low's telling him of his own years of rejection before being invited to Prague, of his many years as an educator before being given the higher post he wanted. Meisel denies that he had the influence to keep the impatient, bitter, and immature Bezalel in Prague. In fact, the elders overruled him. Judah admits that his son " '*was* too young. . . . That was why I wanted him to be my deputy for a while, to learn, to mature.' " But Meisel tries to ease his friend's guilty conscience and insists that Bezalel, even though he was an excellent teacher, was " 'not man enough to be Rabbi of Prague. You are convinced,' " he tells Judah, " 'that Bezalel died of a broken heart, but I don't believe that people die of broken hearts. Of broken heads, of broken bones, yes; but not of broken hearts.' "

Meisel pleads with Rabbi Low to compromise his principles and lose the public debate with the Catholic church so that the Jews can be saved, even though many of their sacred books will then be burned. Judah sums up the crux of his dilemma, sadly mocking his own title. " 'And now the Höhe Rabbi Low must walk low.' " His friend underscores his problem with the criticism, " 'Pride, Judah, pride. If you persist, the consequence will be blood.' "

Meisel's prediction suggests the second new dimension Rothberg introduces to the legend: the moral debate over the Jews' use of violence in self-defense. If the golem is seen as representing the id, and the Höhe Rabbi Low the superego, then the external struggle of the Jews against the Gentiles can be viewed as the moral confrontation between Jewish idealism and historical necessity. From this perspective, the moral and the psychological come together, with the golem appearing as the rabbi's alter ego. The explicit decomposition of Low's character can be seen, for example, when Rothberg describes the worried rabbi walking the ghetto streets a week before Passover "as if he were himself the Golem." (Usually the identification is more subtle.)

From the opening pages of the novel, Rabbi Low struggles with a dilemma in creating the golem. "Is not he who cuts down with the sword an even greater victim? He who lifts up the sword is worse by far, for he loses his share of the world to come. But he lives, he lives, his heart cried, and he who is cut down is dead." In instructing the clay even as he shapes it, the rabbi emphasizes that the golem is to be " 'one who works the Lord's will.' " He is " 'Israel's defender, a Gideon, a Saul, a David. . . . The Lord's anointed for His holy task.' " When the golem replies, " 'To kill,' " the rabbi corrects him, " 'To save.' "

Rothberg also dramatizes Rabbi Low's internal dilemma by splitting his character into two opposing forces, represented by his disciples, Isaac and Jacob. Isaac Hayyot, his scholarly son-in-law, represents the traditional Jewish abhorrence of violence and the unswerving belief that God will protect the Jews. Jacob Nissan is a fiery radical who argues that Jews must learn to protect themselves. This is the argument that led to the Warsaw ghetto uprising of World War II and to the formation of the Jewish Defense League after the war. Jacob believes that Jews should " 'die like men, not like cattle. We must not become victims. We have been victims long enough. . . . Too long.' " Rabbi Low sides with Isaac, quoting the Talmud in support of pacificism. " 'Whoever raises his hand gainst his neighbor, even if he does not strike him, is an evildoer.' " When Jacob asks what one is to do when his neighbor raises a threatening hand first, Rabbi Low stubbornly insists that Jews " 'do not exalt the sword or the fist. We need not die like cattle, but we must not live like beasts. We can live like men.' " When Jacob cries out against the futility of such idealism, the rabbi confidently points to the golem as the new weapon " 'that God has sent to protect us.' " This last statement is the heart of the matter to him. Though the golem represents force, he is sent as a redeemer by God, and thus whatever violence he is responsible for is sanctified.

The first instance of the golem's awesome power and cruelty is presented in a minor key. Having overheard the plan of a group of students to burn the Altneuschul, he waits for them at night, knocks the heads of two of his victims together, and uses their bodies to put out the flames. The second incident follows shortly thereafter. To foil a plot to desecrate the Jewish cemetery, the golem puts on a white sheet and ancient battle helmet, terrifying the plotters. The comedy of the scene is abruptly terminated when he uses his ax to chop off the finger of one student braver than the rest. Isaac, assigned as the golem's private tutor, complains to his father-in-law about his pupil's fascination with " 'hatred and evil, . . . violence and force.' " The worried Isaac argues that men should not be " 'all *yetzer*, all evil impulse.' " The rabbi defends the golem as a novice at evil, a child, but Isaac sharply disagrees. " 'Rabbi, he is *not* a newborn. He has learned many things that I did not teach him. . . . Everywhere he seeks out murder, war, brutality.' "

With these brush strokes deepening and darkening the portrait of his characters, Rothberg also sharpens the suspense. Isaac wants Rabbi Low to send the golem back, ominously predicting that " 'the Golem will bring disaster on us all,' " but Jacob calls for all able-bodied Jews " 'to fight the Philistines.' " He does not want the residents of the ghetto to rely only on this new David to fight Goliath. When, in a third incident, the golem catches a Christian butcher in the act of hiding a dead Gentile child wrapped in a prayer shawl in Mordecai Meisel's cellar as part of the Blood Libel, the defender of the Jews not only beats up the man but tears his arm from its socket in the process, before delivering him to the bailiffs. "Rabbi Low blessed him for having saved the ghetto, but still the Rabbi's heart was not set at rest."

A third major change that Abraham Rothberg has made in his treatment of the legend of the Golem of Prague is the remarkable transformation in the golem himself. Again Rothberg's debt is to Leivick, rather than to Rosenberg or Bloch; however, one is also strongly reminded of Mary Shelley's monster, who begs his creator, Victor Frankenstein, for love and understanding but is denied the compassion he craves. As Donald Glut has pointed out in his fascinating study, *The Frankenstein Legend: A Tribute to Mary Shelley and Boris Karloff* (1973), the young scientist "never accepted the fact that beneath the shrivelled yellow flesh of his creation lay an emotional being that cried to give as well as receive love. It was for this rejection that the being eventually became a 'monster,' bent upon murderous revenge." Rothberg's golem is more complicated, but the kinship is striking.

From the beginning, Rothberg's golem, like Leivick's, objects to being born. "The very earth resisted his creation and lay limp and diffuse, refusing to be formed out of chaos into that which was human." The "recalcitrant clay" repeatedly strives to be "reabsorbed" into the Moldau riverbank. "An anguish in the clay pulsed to [Rabbi Low's] fingers, speaking without speech, 'Do not rip me from this womb of clay!' " Rabbi Low can sense the clay's silent plea. " 'Did I request you to be my maker? Did I enjoin you to tear me from the bowels of the earth? Leave me embedded in the unfeeling clay, in the silent, peaceful dark.' " The golem even threatens the rabbi. " 'If you bring me to life, my rage shall devour the living, my strength shall lay waste the earth.' " When Rabbi Low explains that neither of them can resist his destiny, the gray corpse laments his fate, which is to be " 'a clenched fist, a hulk, a golem!' " " 'A golem, yes,' " the rabbi answers, " 'but one who works the Lord's will.' "

That Joseph Golem can be a nay-sayer as well as a yea-sayer is seen not only in his objection to being born, but also in his rejection of the yellow hat and armband the Jews are forced to wear in the ghetto. This golem is neither a dumb tellurian force nor just a computer designed to interpret divine codes. He asks to be taught how to put on phylacteries, which the rabbi explains "were meant to connect the arm, heart, and head in the performance of good deeds." He also asks the rabbi to teach him to read and pray.

Whereas Rosenberg and Bloch denied the golem any sexual urges, Rothberg again turns to Leivick and goes far beyond his model. Almost immediately Joseph shows interest in Rabbi Low's serving girl and ward, Kaethe Hoch. The rabbi is uneasy about this development, but he reassures himself that

> a golem lived only to fulfill the will of his creator, an incomplete creation deprived of the light of God within him. A golem was supposed to have neither wisdom nor judgment, nor was he endowed with a will of his own or sexual feelings. Yet . . . the Golem's glances at Kaethe left no doubt that powerful emotions surged within his frame.

Joseph's growing interest in sex, combined with his potential for violence and cruelty, does not ease the rabbi's mind.

When Rabbi Low suspects that the Passover matzot have been poisoned, he commands the golem to taste one, but Joseph at first refuses, afraid to die. His creator has to remind him of his mission, to save the Jews even if it means his own destruction. Only when the rabbi assures him that he will not die at this time does Joseph reluctantly bite a matzo and fall to the ground in convulsions. Using his special healing powers, Rabbi Low puts the golem to sleep and removes the pain. Observing him closely, he wonders if this strange creature has changed recently.

There seemed to be a finer grain in the coarseness of his features, some sensitivity that had not been there before. . . . Had Joseph become less Golem and more human, or was it that he was now more familiar so that his strangeness had been lessened by time and usage?

When he awakens, the golem tells the rabbi, " 'I have felt like a man, for I remember the pain. . . . You have taught me suffering.' "

In subsequent chapters, the golem grows more sullen and angry. When the rabbi awakens him one morning to send him to search in other towns for Jitka Myslikov, the missing witness who can save Mordecai Meisel (under arrest for the Blood Libel), Joseph refuses to be touched after the blessing. He tells Rabbi Low, " 'Command me. Compel me. Send me. Do not speak kindly to me, Rabbi, do not be gentle.' " His explanation of his feelings confirms the change in him the rabbi has observed. " 'If you touch what is man in me, it hurts. If it hurts, it makes me more human. I cannot bear the pain of either.' " Entering a new village, the golem feels like an Ishmael. " 'I am as strange to other men as Jews are. As they are outcasts, so am I an outcast. If nothing else, I am a Jew because of that.' " This kind of feeling makes him sympathize with Jitka, who is "as much an outcast among her own as he was." When he finally finds her, she admires his build and is the first person to treat him as a man, as a human being. She invites him on picnics, makes love to him, and asks why he never laughs. Unlike Jitka, who claims she hates people, Joseph says, " 'Though people spurn me and make me wretched, I would be among them. I would help them.' "

Even though Rabbi Low had commanded Joseph not to tell Jitka why she is needed back in Prague, he disobeys his orders and tells her all, because he is sensitive enough to realize that she will respond favorably to such treatment. In response to her query, he says that he too is a Jew. Their arrival back in Prague during the trial saves Meisel and the Jews temporarily, as it did in the tales of Rosenberg and Bloch. Only Joseph is hurt, as Jitka soon runs off with a Hungarian ostler. " 'She wanted a place she could call her own. A man she could call her own,' " the rabbi explains. When the golem asks if he is not such a man, the rabbi reminds him of his purpose, his mission in life. "A moan escaped the Golem's lips and he sat there rocking his head as if it was too much, too heavy for him to carry on his shoulders."

Rothberg's central irony is an effective strategem to stir reader interest and enrich the texture of his novel. The golem, created originally to use brute strength in defense of the Jews, a creature obsessed with violence and cruelty, becomes more human and sensitive as he lives among people. In a way, the rabbi has become *his* alter ego. When Joseph complains of his loneliness, Rabbi Low explains that that is his fate; he must " 'remain a stranger' " and deny himself " 'the ordinary satisfactions.' " In response to the golem's argument that he did not choose to be what he is, the rabbi admits that this is essentially true of all people. " 'None of us choose to be the creatures we are. We are and we become. We are chosen and then choose to accept what we are.' " With this neat paradox, the rabbi is able to explain away the apparent contradiction of free will in a predestined existence. When Joseph begs the rabbi to set him free, Judah answers that only God can do that. Getting no satisfaction from this conversation, Joseph throws a childish temper tantrum.

> "I shall free myself. If I must be a murderer in defense of your Jews, then I shall be a murderer in my own defense. I will be free. I will kill you first, my jailer, my enemy. I hate you! I hate the sight of your face and the sound of your voice that taunt and pursue me wherever I turn. . . . I shall take your head between my hands and crush it like an egg. I shall smite you into the earth from which you drew me forth."

Rabbi Low does not flinch as the golem springs at him. "Trembling, the Golem stood over him, his great fist raised high, then he turned aside and hurled himself against the walls, striking them with his shoulders, his fists, his head, until the house shook." Joseph pleads in vain with the rabbi to make him an ordinary man, not a hero with a mission. The rabbi feels sorry for the misery he has caused the golem, but he sees himself as standing "like the Lord's flaming sword that turned every way to keep the Golem from returning to . . . Eden, or going forward into the lesser paradise of common life."

Joseph's misery is compounded when Rabbi Low, fearing the golem's growing interest in Kaethe Hoch, decides to find the girl a husband. Pearl selects Jacob Nissan. Again the reader is reminded of Joseph's role as Rabbi Low's surrogate son when the troubled rabbi feels like Abraham about to sacrifice Isaac (a comparison suggested previously by Pearl) when he has to inform the golem of his plan. He wonders whether it is "easier to suppress his compassion because he thought the Golem an incomplete man, not truly a human being; or simply because he had forced himself to concentrate on the Golem only as an instrument of salvation." His task is even more difficult, because "the clay from which the Golem had been formed seemed to have grown daily more sensate, thoughtful, and pained." When the bitter Joseph asks what happened to his free will, the rabbi can only fall back on his faith: " *'Everything is in the hands of God, except the fear of God.'* " Because Joseph refuses to accept this theological answer and threatens to marry Kaethe anyway, Rabbi Low has to use his trump card and reveal that the golem is incapable of having children. It " 'would be a grave sin to inflict such a future on Kaethe.' " The golem is stunned. Before he flees, he curses the rabbi, the Jewish people, and God.

> "Engine of destruction you have made me. Monster misshapen you have created me. Despoiled of God's image and bereaved of man's solace, I shall wreak havoc on this world. From out of this hell you have made within me, I shall make a hell without. Everywhere I shall sow ruin and plant destruction. Whenever I see man, like a wild beast, I shall destroy him. From this day forward it shall be war between me and men, between me and you, between me and God!"

"The Time of the Golem"

That Rothberg has gone far beyond his predecessors, even "the great Leivick," in retelling the famous legend should be evident by now. He has succeeded in making the old new. A talented novelist, he has successfully combined an exciting plot, authentic local color, and complex main characters with layers of psychological implications and moral overtones. It would be a most unusual reader who did not care what happens to the individual characters and the whole community. Disbelief has been effectively suspended, and the reader now wonders how Rothberg will resolve the sociological, psychological, and moral problems he has been developing. Even with the foreknowledge of the previous golem tales, even knowing what will happen to Joseph, the reader is compelled to follow the events to their inevitable conclusion.

Before the public debate with the Catholic church, Rabbi Low is advised by Count Pokorny, the cardinal's emissary, to have Thaddeus killed. Such intrigue runs counter to the rabbi's moral philosophy. "Once the killing began, there was no end. . . . And so man lost his most valuable possession, his *tzelem Elohim*, his Godly image, that within him which distinguished his humanity." Thaddeus is, of course, declared the winner of the debate by the cardinal, who decrees that all copies of the Talmud and other Jewish holy books be burned the next day at noon in the square of the Judenstadt. A terribly depressed Rabbi Low stumbles on the long walk back to the ghetto, but just as a peasant is about to club him, the golem, who had been standing at the back of the hall during the debate, comes to his rescue. Joseph quickly disappears again, but Judah is comforted by even this brief return and thinks of the golem as his son.

The paradox of the golem being both David and Goliath is seen when Isaac reports to his father-in-law that he has observed Kaethe with Joseph in the cemetery. To Isaac, Joseph seems to have grown larger like Goliath. " 'Yet,' " he admits, " 'something more human and gentle also moves in him, something imploring that might burst into tears or change into a caress.' " In this indirect way, Rothberg comments on Rabbi Low's split personality: the golem is both compassionate and vindictive, soft and hard, capable of good and of evil. The rabbi assures Isaac that the golem " 'will be our David, not *their* Goliath,' " but he is biased when it comes to his clay creation, and he blinds himself to the tragic possibilities. He sees only what he wants to see and is naively confident in his ultimate ability to control his automaton, despite mounting evidence of Joseph's disobeying his orders. The golem continues to see Kaethe, even though she is betrothed to Jacob. When Kaethe pleads with her foster father to break her betrothal and let her marry Joseph, Rabbi Low decides to reveal to her that Joseph cannot have children. The hopelessness of their relationship is soon dramatized when Kaethe is attacked by four hooligans attempting to rape her. Joseph rescues her just in time and wants to kill the men after hunting them down, but the rabbi forbids him to seek revenge. The golem calls Rabbi Low a hypocrite—apparently it is good to kill only when the rabbi gives the command. Joseph chooses to disobey and prefers to do evil.

Before the violent climax of his plot, Rothberg probes Judah Low's mind and thus explores the psychological and moral implications of the developing action. As a man grows old, Judah concludes, pride dies along with passion. Yet his own passion to save the Jews of Prague has not diminished. "Age brought the knowledge of how the *yetzer* hid in such ambition to do good, like a worm in a rose, [and] grew swollen from the pride of having done good." Man's propensity for evil can never be completely overcome, he decides; the sages had realized this when they argued that without evil impulse, " 'men would never build a house or take a wife or beget a child or engage in commerce.' " This *yetzer* in man was a driving force subtler than the *serpent*, . . . snared man's most honored intentions, wound itself around his conceit, and provoked his obstinacy until, blinded by the majesty of his motives, man was moved to deception, delusion, evil.

Could this evil propensity have been involved in the creation of the golem? Was this the reason behind the estrangement from God which Judah has recently been experiencing? Why has God not been communicating with him in dreams or visions as in the past? In creating the golem, he "had hoped to profane a single vessel to keep from profaning many men, as Jacob wished to do." Those Jewish youth who, inspired by Jacob, were arming themselves for the coming battle were "prepared to walk in the ways of the nation, to lose their Jewish souls and perhaps their lives." They ignored God's words to Zechariah: *"Not by might, nor by power, but by My spirit."* Was disobeying God and following man a form of idolatry that the Hebrew Bible forbade? "Of one thing he was certain: he had prayed and listened and obeyed the voice of God in creating the Golem. How else would the vessel of clay have risen sensate from the river's bank?" But Judah's attitude toward Joseph is ambivalent. Even though he despairs of Joseph who has fled from him, "a part of him rejoiced in Joseph as well." The rabbi cannot help but admire Joseph's spirit, independence, and feelings as the automaton becomes more human; perhaps God Himself has such ambivalent feelings about Adam's descendants. Judah Low worries that such thoughts are blasphemous.

Rabbi Low's confidence is restored when Joseph suddenly returns on the night of the first Passover Seder and slips into the place traditionally reserved for Elijah. In a silent, mystical exchange of scriptural verses with the golem, the rabbi is convinced that Joseph is answering God's question, " 'Who will go for us?' " It is God Who has succeeded in turning the golem's heart. A silent nod of their heads before the puzzled faces at the table seals the covenant. Listening to his grandson Bezalel ask the Four Questions, Rabbi Low is comforted by his faith in God's always having allowed a remnant to be saved.

Joseph joins fully in the Passover ritual, having been taught well by Isaac, but he does not join in the family conversations and games. Most significantly, when it is time to recite the prayer asking for God's blessing on "the head of the house," Joseph substitutes the words " 'my honored father.' " Only at the conclusion of the Seder, with the singing of the last three stanzas of "Had Gadya," are Rabbi Low and the golem able to foresee what is going to happen.

There was no mistaking the look in the Golem's eyes as they sang the two verses that told that the Angel of Death then came and slew the slaughterer, and that finally came the Most Holy, blessed be He, who slew the Angel of Death. The Golem's lips moved and shaped the words, but no sound emerged, no song. He knew he was the slaughterer to be slaughtered; he knew that Rabbi Low was his Angel of Death.

The rabbi intuitively understands "the gleam of satisfaction, of revenge" on the golem's face, as the song ends with the words describing God's final vengeance when the Angel of Death is destroyed.

In chapter 21, Rothberg takes an old tale that antedates the golem legend and adapts it to his purpose. As was explained in chapter 1 of this study, the tale is based on Polish oral tradition and appeared in both Koop's *Sagen und Erzählungen aus der Provinz Posen* and Bergmann's *Legenden der Juden*. In Rothberg's version, Rabbi Low has a nightmarish vision in which the Angel of Death is killing a long line of Jewish men until the rabbi strikes the knife from his hand. The rabbi then tears the scroll from the slaughterer's hand and flees the synagogue. In his study he reads the names inscribed and is happy because he has saved all these people. But then he notices that one corner is torn off and still in the hands of the Angel of Death. The chapter ends with the question, *"Whose names were they?"* Those familiar with this old legend know that the one name that remained was the rabbi's, but Rothberg uses poetic license and prefers a different ending.

The inevitable violence and tragedy of Rothberg's ending begin after Mordecai Meisel's death from natural causes. As the local authorities try to confiscate his possessions despite the generous bequest left to the emperor and local institutions, Jacob and his men unload the wagons as fast as the bailiffs load them. Isaac, Jacob's alter ego, representing the other side of Rabbi Low's split personality, remains in the synagogue praying. When the rabbi appears, he insists that there be no violence. Pokorny, at the head of his troop of cavalry, scoffs at the rabbi's faith in the Messiah and man's reason. To him, all that counts is "power"; his view is the same as that of the golem, who tells Rabbi Low that Meisel's wife, Frumett, would not have broken under torture the way her two nephews did. " 'She knows the value and power of property,' " he says. When the rabbi compliments Joseph's intelligence, the golem answers, " 'Suffering makes for wisdom, Rabbi.' "

Rothberg interjects another early legend at this point, again using the dream technique. This time Rabbi Low dreams of the story of Rabbi

Rav's sending a golem with a message to his colleague Rabbi Zera, who angrily restored the golem to dust when the messenger was unable to answer any of his questions. Why Rothberg adds this tale from the Sanhedrin tractate of the Babylonian Talmud so late in his novel is hard to determine, but he probably intends it to serve as a foreshadowing of Joseph's death. Whatever the reason, its inclusion here is gratuitous and disruptive.

Just as Joseph feels abandoned by God, Judah feels the distance between God and man to be greater than ever, their two worlds separated by an impenetrable curtain. Man craves to understand the order in God's plan, but all he sees in this life is disorder. " 'Only study of the Law lifts the curtain and permits one to approach God on the other side.' " Judah's explanation of evil in God's universe is that man was purposely created imperfect.

> "He must realize perfection himself. So, too, is his world not created in final perfection; man must realize and create the world's perfection himself. The way of true conduct lies in keeping order in daily life and in recognizing order in the occurrences of the world around us. Sin is disorder. To put order into the world is man's messianic task."

The pogrom finally breaks out in chapter 24, as the Christians re-enact the passion of Christ at Easter. While Isaac spends his time praying in the synagogue, Jacob becomes the golem's teacher and explains the symbolism of the ritual they are watching from a roof. Surprisingly, Joseph says he would rather be with Isaac, but the rabbi sends him out with Jacob. The golem is amazed at the similarity between the Christian prayers and the Hebrew psalms. Jacob scorns the Twenty-second Psalm, which he sees as passive surrender to one's enemies. He points out the contradiction between the Christians' belief in Jesus' teaching to turn the other cheek and their carrying weapons in their religious processional. He knows that when they are inflamed with hatred for the Jews, who they are told killed their god, they will strike out in revenge. Both Jacob and Joseph feel the same *yetzer* in themselves and wonder if Rabbi Low also has it. Although they come to no conclusion, Rothberg's reader knows that the answer is yes—that Judah Low has projected the *yetzer* in him on the golem. Through this decomposition of his character, Rabbi Low's need for ego gratification and his propensity for revenge are sublimated.

At the gate of the ghetto, the marchers claim to see blood pouring from the wounds of Christ—proof to them that the Jews have desecrated the Host. The cry for each man to save his soul by killing a Jew runs through the streets. As Jacob's forces meet the foe in bloody combat, the golem is at first reluctant to fight, the Isaac side of his personality dominating the Jacob. "His arm seemed held back by Isaac's words, by the Rabbi's, by what he had learned himself." Even when he watches Jacob surrounded by three attackers, he hesitates, not just because of the indoctrination of his teachers, but because as a man in love with Kaethe, he sees himself winning her if Jacob is killed. It is greatly to Rothberg's credit that this psychologically complex motivation lifts his plot above two-dimensional cartoon simplicity. But the golem does not hesitate for long and leaps to Jacob's aid, the *yetzer* in him overcoming all other feelings. The fact that his propensity for cruelty and violence is enlisted on the side of the persecuted Jews greatly complicates the moral issue, reinforcing Rothberg's theme of the ambiguity of good and evil.

Chapters 24 and 25 are the goriest and most violent of the novel. Rothberg omits little in his catalogue of atrocities during the pogrom. The Jews are driven back to the three key defense points: the synagogue, town hall, and cemetery. The golem is man's unleashed id, and he kills many Christians. However, Rothberg underscores the duality of this creature when he writes, "His lungs panted with the joy of fighting, but his stomach turned with the nausea of murder." In a plot incident not found in any of the previous sources, the golem singles out Thaddeus as his special victim. Although the friar tries to brain Joseph with the wooden crucifix he is tarrying, Jacob deflects the blow with his sword and kills Thaddeus with his dagger.

The golem discovers Kaethe's naked body in her bedroom, her neck broken. In a rage, he smashes everything within reach before cradling her body tenderly as he cries. Wrapping some of her shorn golden tresses "like a phylactery around his left arm," he goes insane as "a blinding hatred blistered his eyes." Striking out with his ax at everyone in his path, he kills Jews as well as Christians. Count Pokorny tries in vain to stop him, as Jacob explains that the emperor has sent the hussars to help the Jews, to save a remnant. Joseph is unmollified, crying out, " 'I have no people. . . . Neither Jew nor Christian, no father or mother, no wife or children.' " As he knocks Pokorny's sword to the ground and raises his ax over him in triumph, a bleeding Isaac staggers out to tell Joseph how he tried to save Kaethe, tried to reason with the inflamed mob, but was beaten senseless. Taking out all of his frustrations on this man of reason, faith, and nonviolence, the golem blames Isaac for Kaethe's death and splits him "from head to groin" with his ax. Too late, Rabbi Low appears (where he was up to this time the reader is never told) and orders the golem to put down his weapon. He also commands the angry Jews not to touch Joseph in vengeance. When Joseph complains to the rabbi, " 'You called me Golem,' " he replies, " 'When you are a golem . . . there is no Joseph.' " As all of the main characters withdraw to Kaethe's bedroom, they find Pearl crooning over the body. Pearl accuses her husband of being Kaethe's murderer, just as the golem had accused Isaac. In this way Rothberg suggests that passive men of reason and piety are just as guilty in this tragedy as passionate defenders. All are implicated. It is impossible to assign individual blame.

Rabbi Low refuses to condemn God for having forsaken the Jews. " 'It is man, not God, who has forsaken us,' " he says. " 'Even in the millenium we can hope only for the weakening of the evil impulse, not for its extinction.' " Joseph calls such blind faith madness, but the rabbi commands him to be silent. When Joseph tauntingly replies, " 'I shall speak as I will,' " the rabbi replies, " 'You have already spoken as you will,' . . . and he pointed to Isaac's corpse." Rabbi Low knows what he must do but is reluctant to condemn Joseph to death. " 'The Golem is like a son to me, not like Bezalel perhaps, not even like Isaac, but a son nonetheless.' " Pearl reminds him that Joseph's bloody hands widowed their daughter. When Jacob argues that his own hands are bloodier than Joseph's, Pearl underlines the crucial difference.

> "But you killed reluctantly. . . . The Golem killed like one of *them*, with joy. To our people, you are a hero and he is a monster. They will stone him for the Jewish blood he has shed."

Rothberg gives Pearl a larger role, a stronger voice, than any of his predecessors had done. Now that Joseph's mission is ended, a failure, since more than one hundred Jewish fighters are dead, three thousand ghetto Jews killed, and countless others wounded, Pearl wants her husband to get rid of him. When Jacob asks if she wants them to kill Joseph, she answers, " 'He is a golem. A golem is neither murdered nor mourned.' " Jacob continues to defend Joseph, pointing out that he is " 'as much a human being as you are or I am.' " Cutting to the core of the novel, and reminding the reader again of Mary Shelley's monster, he argues, " 'Perhaps we violated his humanity so that he was forced to do what he did.' " Pearl adamantly insists that the golem be returned to dust that very night.

A crestfallen Rabbi Low is mystified by the failure of his plan, but in his prayers he accepts full responsibility.

"On my hands, the blood he shed, O Lord, on my head his transgression, for I created him and thought him your emissary and our defender. Why else did You give me the power to shape his clay and create his strength, unless Your desire was that we should be saved from the sword? Your mystery evades me. Your presence eludes me. Did You not permit me entry into the other realm only so that I might do Your bidding? Did You not endow my hand to shape the clay and my mouth to breathe Your breath into him that he might live?"

Rabbi Low seems completely humbled as he realizes that for all his intelligence he is incapable of pulling aside the curtain that separates man from God. The unfortunate golem was forced to wear God's name,

"a collar on his neck from which he struggled to be freed. He did not covet the role of the redeemer, nor even did he find in his superhuman strength more than a burden. He cried out to be left to follow the way of common man, but I insisted and he yielded to what was my command, and what I thought to be Yours."

The rabbi suddenly remembers the passage in the Hebrew Bible where the woman of Tekoa carries out Joab's plan and convinces King David to allow his son Absalom to return from his banishment. "But what had come of that? Divisiveness, warfare, and death." The Temple of God could not be built until the people were united and rebellion crushed. "Yet, even then, the great King David had been denied the privilege of building God's house because he had shed blood." Through this allusion to King David, Rothberg reinforces the Jewish tradition of nonviolence and subtly suggests that even the seemingly contrite rabbi still suffers from an inflated ego.

The quotation from the talmudic scholar Radak on the King David-woman of Tekoa passage leaves no doubt as to Rabbi Low's conclusion after the horror of the pogrom. " 'Mankind must not increase the spilling of blood.' " Crying out to God, he asks a series of questions.

"Did I have a messianic nightmare that I might make an end to this violence without end? Did I imagine a worldly redemption, which cannot be garnered where there is none? Did You move me, out of my pride and desperation, to spill blood through the

Golem and yet think to keep my hands clean? In my blind desire to do good, did I commit the very sin I sought to avoid for Your people? Did You tempt me with my dream of salvation that I might be the one to shield Your people from the sword, that I might avoid the rule of man's necessity and Your necessity that we must wait, suffer, endure, have faith in Your providence and mercy? Did I walk in the ways of the nations and thereby lead Your people in that very same path—and not Yours?"

Jacob reports that the golem refuses to come at the rabbi's command, that he is afraid of the punishment that awaits him. Jacob had urged Joseph to run away and assimilate with the Gentiles, but the golem had refused, arguing that he could not leave his "father." When he finally reappears, it is Rabbi Low who asks for forgiveness for the life he made him live. Joseph denies it, asking whether he is thus " 'more than human, or less.' " Confessing that he is afraid of death, the golem criticizes Rabbi Low for what he has done to him.

"You brought me out of the darkness; but you would not let me live. You fed and clothed me; sheltered me, you taught me to study and to pray; but you would not let me live. *To be un-married is to live without kindness, without religion, without peace.*"

When the golem tries to justify his actions as Rabbi Low had done before (" 'To kill was my fate. I performed my holy destiny.' "), the rabbi no longer accepts this argument. " 'In that was my error—and my despair.' " Joseph tries to cheer the rabbi, reminding him that his enemy Thaddeus is dead and that the emperor has issued a new " 'proclamation exonerating the Jews from all accusations of blood-guilt. Is that not a great victory?' " With the terrible loss of life, thousands maimed, and all the smoldering ruins, the rabbi cannot see any Jewish victory. Worst of all, the hands of the Jews themselves are " 'covered with blood.' " The golem argues, " 'Had we not shed their blood, more of ours would have been spilled. You think helplessness would have deterred them? No Rabbi, that is a dream.' " Rabbi Low will not be comforted. Even though Joseph was created to kill the enemies of the Jews, " 'Your life was not to be ours, and my purpose was to keep ours from becoming yours. I would have your forgiveness for that.' " But Joseph is as stubborn as the rabbi and refuses again. He cannot leave, he cannot stand the nightmares he is having, he cannot live in peace; yet he is afraid to die. To his surprise, the Höhe Rabbi

Low admits that he too is afraid. " 'I know what must be done and am afraid to do it, because that which I sought to avoid I precipitated.' " The rabbi also asks Joseph's forgiveness for denying him a wife.

> "Children the Lord denied you, not I. I thought it the Almighty's intention that you should defend us against our enemies without distractions so that you might be more stalwart in our defense. . . . How stupid! I forgot that man is more ferocious than any other animal. Yet the more human you became, the gentler you seemed to grow, a reproach to all of us who are merely men."

Joseph does not mention the "Had Gadya," but when he lists the sequence of killings, he tells the rabbi, " 'Now it is your turn to kill. Me. I do not feel guilty.' " That attitude, of course, is what frightens the rabbi. Joseph tells him that " 'the time to have been afraid was at my birth, . . . not now.' " To this the rabbi replies, " 'I was full of fear then, but full of hope. Now, too, I am full of fear, but altogether without hope.' " Joseph is told to appear in the attic of the Altneuschul at midnight, and both he and his creator know what is to be done there.

To Rabbi Low's surprise, Pearl changes her mind and wants the golem to live—" 'Because he, too, is a son,' " she tells him. " 'Your child, not mine, yet a son in the house. He will die like Bezalel who, since he could not be the Höhe Rabbi Low, had to die in Kolín.' " Rothberg thus uses this dialogue with Pearl to dramatize the conflict in Judah's mind. Pearl simply acts out one half of his split personality. When Rabbi Low's authoritarian side (the superego) reminds her that the golem " 'has killed three Jews and wounded six others,' " she defends him, pointing out his complex motivation. What Joseph did to Isaac " 'was in an anguish of love and loss, crazed with the killing you made his trade. He is guilty, but is he not also innocent? Is there no forgiveness for that?' " Like Herman Melville's Captain Vere at the court-martial of Billy Budd, who has killed the ship's master-at-arms, Rabbi Low answers, " 'My forgiveness, Pearl? Joseph has that. But the law and the community require justice. The law stands above man and I must carry it out impartially.' " Pearl is not placated, and warns her husband that for such lack of mercy there will be no forgiveness " 'here or in the world to come.' " She sees the parallel between Bezalel and Joseph, neither one willing to forgive Judah. She serves as a Greek chorus with the remark ending the penultimate chapter: " 'You have succeeded in much with the community Judah, but you have failed with your sons. . . . The Lord, Judah, has had His own ways to punish.' "

At midnight, as he mounts the stairs of the attic of the Altneuschul with Jacob, Judah Low remembers the scroll he tore in his dream from the Angel of Death, "and now he knew that the torn fragment bore both his name and the Golem's." Again he thinks of himself as Abraham about to sacrifice Isaac and feels the need to suppress rebellious thoughts. Joseph is waiting for them in the dark. Whereas the previous legends describing the death of Joseph involve at least three other people, the same number needed at his creation, Rothberg performs the ritual with only two.

Rabbi Low begins with a confession to God. " 'Lord, we have not been pure at heart, nor free of base ambition and sinful thought, and we have therefore used the holy name of the Lord in vain.' " He asks for forgiveness for both himself and Joseph. When the golem says he is afraid, the rabbi takes his hand and comforts him. Just as he did not want to be born, the golem cries out that he does not want to die. As he screams out " 'Death,' " Rabbi Low takes the Shem from his mouth and takes "from beneath the great twisted tongue the parchment with the holiest name of the Lord." Instantaneously, Joseph's hair and beard turn white. "On his forehead, first pale as flesh, then scarlet as blood, the word *Truth* shone. *Emes*. With his forefinger, the Rabbi gently erased the first letter to make it *Mes*—'corpse.' " As the golem's body is reduced to a great gray corpse, the flaming *Mes* is replaced by a shimmering gold shin, "initial of that holiest name of the Almighty, Shaddai." The voice of the golem, borne into the night by the cutting wind, cries out, " 'Do not forget me!' " and fades away with the combined plea and command, " 'Remember me!' " Jacob and Rabbi Low recite the mourner's Kaddish, after which Jacob is instructed to cover the golem's corpse with what is left of discarded prayer books and old prayer shawls. When Jacob asks how he should answer questions about Joseph the next day, the rabbi tells him to announce that no one is to go up to the synagogue loft again. It will no longer be used to store old prayer books or other sacred objects.

Asking Jacob to leave him alone, Judah Low removes the clay from his fingers, tears his vest over his heart, and sits weeping on the floor. But the novel does not end for another page. In a scene reminiscent of Brueghel, Rothberg describes Rabbi Low's early morning walk through the ghetto streets, observing the fishermen, butchers, flower girls, and water carts which in the morning sunshine "transformed the ghetto's winter into spring." W. H. Auden summed it up well, when he wrote in the opening lines of "Musée des Beaux Arts,"

> About suffering they were never wrong,
> The Old Masters: how well they understood
> Its human position; how it takes place
> While someone else is eating or opening a window or just
>   walking dully along.

To Judah Low, the ghetto is different and yet the same this morning. He realizes that "the time of the Golem would remain with them until the coming of the Messiah because everything was fatal propensity and impulse, *yetzer;* in the time of the Golem the brute spirit of man could not be straightened, its crookedness would forever be an afflic-tion." A wiser but saddened man, he laughs at the stone lion above the door, the symbol of his salvation, as he returns home to Pearl.

Thus Rothberg ends his story on a note of ambiguity that is so characteristic of the modern novel. Using the dialectical approach in arguing the case for and against war, understanding the need for violent self-defense but deploring the resulting bloodshed and horror, rejecting the old absolutes of good and evil in a world where the two are so frequently inextricable, Rothberg begrudgingly accepts the im-perfection of man, a condition symbolized so aptly by his phrase, "the time of the Golem."

Chapter Seven

The Golem Remembered in Popular Culture and Poetry

THERE is a golem joke that goes something like this. A wealthy American Jew visiting Prague after World War II wanted to see the remains of the golem in the attic of the Altneuschul. When the shammes explained that it was forbidden for anyone to enter, the American businessman was insistent, opening his wallet and taking out a substantial bill, which he slipped into the shammes's pocket. Fifteen minutes later, the visitor returned and complained angrily that he had wasted his time and money because he found nothing in the attic but old, worn tallisim, torn prayer books, and mounds of dust. When the shammes asked if there were nothing else in the attic, the angry American remembered one other thing—an old mirror on the wall. "Aha," said the shammes, "then you *did* see the golem!"

Golem stories have continued to fascinate readers of all ages from Prague to Buenos Aires. As the twentieth century enters its last two decades, it is safe to predict that this interest will grow. Two world wars, the Great Depression, wars in Korea, Vietnam, and the Middle East, the atom and hydrogen bombs, space exploration, and nuclear energy have intensified man's need for superheroes. The time always seems ripe for a new redeemer. The bigger the problems, the greater the need. Modern man's interest in the occult is insatiable. An Age of Science, which has witnessed man's journey to the moon and back, still enjoys being terrified by Dracula, Frankenstein, and Rosemary's baby. The exorcism of Satan in books and film has created a new generation of believers. *Superman One* breeds *Superman Two,* and the Incredible Hulk joins Mandrake the Magician in the eternal combat against evil. No wonder there was a resurgence of interest in the golem legend in the 1970s, for it is a legend combining all the ingredients of a popular film or television series: violence, the occult, religion, historical roots, supernaturalism, and even sex.

This final chapter surveys the golem legend as it appears in twentieth-century film, comic strips, short stories, children's literature, and poetry. The challenge of portraying this legendary monster on celluloid, in painting, and in poetry, as well as in fiction, has been immense, and artists have responded enthusiastically. The German films and Superman comic strips may have greatly distorted the concept of the golem as he appears in the tales of Rosenberg and Bloch, but Beverly Brodsky McDermott's paintings to accompany her children's books would certainly have appealed to both men, and H. Leivick and Jorge Borges, had they known each other, would have found that they had much in common.

It is not surprising that composers have also been inspired by the legend of the Golem of Prague. This study will not analyze individual musical adaptations, but four should at least be mentioned in passing. Two are operas: one by Eugen d'Albert, *Der Golem* (libretto by F. Lion), which premiered at Frankfurt in 1926 but is no longer performed; the other, *The Golem*, composed by Mr. and Mrs. Abraham Elstein, which had its world premiere at the New York City Center Opera in March, 1962. Gershom Scholem, in *Kabbalah*, mentions a third, a *Golem Suite* for orchestra (1932), composed by Joseph Achron, who was influenced by the Habima production of Leivick's play. According to Scholem, "The last piece of this suite was written as the first movement's exact musical image in reverse to symbolize the disintegration of the homunculus." The fourth musical adaptation, *Der Golem*, a ballet by Francis Burt, choreographed by Erica Hanka, was produced in 1962 in Vienna.

The Movies Discover the Golem

Several movie versions of the Golem of Prague have been made, but the man most frequently mentioned in discussion of these films is Paul Wegener, the great German silent film actor and director. According to Donald F. Glut, in his fascinating study *The Frankenstein Legend: A Tribute to Mary Shelley and Boris Karloff* (1973), Wegener was filming locations in Prague in 1913 for a supernatural horror film when he first heard of and was intrigued by Rabbi Loew's homunculus. Within a year his Bioscop company produced *Der Golem* (renamed *The Monster of Fate* for English viewers), with himself in the title role. In this film, the creature could not possibly have passed as a human being. Wegener's Golem was truly a monster, his face clay-like, his hair seemingly carved from stone, his boots heavy. This was indeed a worthy predecessor to the later Frankenstein Monster of the talkies.

As in Mary Shelley's version,

> An artificially created being was given the gift of life only to eventually turn upon humanity as a violent horror that must be destroyed. The main difference between the Golem and the Frankenstein Monster were the forces that brought them to life—the first magic; the second, science. The results were nevertheless the same.

This first golem movie, directed by Wegener and fellow screenwriter Henrik Galeen, almost suffered the same fate as the silent versions of *Frankenstein*, which were never seen again. Fortunately, however,

> a print was miraculously discovered in 1958 by Paul Sauerlaender, a European film collector. The owner of a toy store in Europe was selling old 35mm movie projectors and giving his customers small lengths (from twelve to fifteen feet) of silent film which turned out to be this original Golem feature. Luckily for the sake of film history Sauerlaender was able to track down the various owners and emerge from the hunt with a complete film of *Der Golem*.

Within a contemporary setting, the film tells how some workers discover the golem's remains in the ruins of an old synagogue. An elderly antique dealer buys them and brings the monster to life through the use of the Kabbalah. As long as the golem serves as a slave things go well, but then he falls in love with the antique dealer's lovely daughter (played by the actress Lyda Salmonova, Wegener's wife). Like Mary Shelley's Frankenstein, the golem develops a soul and suffers terribly when the girl rejects his repulsive form. After going berserk, he falls from a tower and is killed.

The most famous of the early golem films is the one Wegener directed in 1920, *Der Golem: Wie er in die Welt Kam* (*The Golem: How He Came into the World*). This film, set in medieval Prague, attempted to be more faithful to the legend than the earlier ones had been. Why the credits list "adapted from Gustav Meyrink," after "scenario by Henrik Galeen," is a mystery, because the film has no resemblance to the novel. The sets, designed by Professor Hans Poelzig, the noted German architect, and built by Karl Freund, recreated the Jewish ghetto. Captions appear infrequently as the story is told mainly through the images.

The opening caption introduces an important astrological motif not emphasized in the golem stories previously analyzed in this study: "The Learned Rabbi Löw reads in the stars that misfortune threatens the Jews." This astrological motif is reinforced by the image of Rabbi Löw, in what appears to be the pointed hat of a magician, studying the stars through a telescope in his tower. He is also using a book of alchemy, while in his laboratory below, the bubbling beakers introduce a chemical motif completely foreign to Rosenberg, Bloch, Leivick, Meyrink, and Rothberg. (All of the laboratory apparatus, nonexistent in the earlier legends, was to play a major role in the many subsequent Frankenstein films influenced by Wegener's.) The seven haloed stars above the rabbi's tower suddenly "dissolve into a mailed fist" which holds the emperor's decree against the Jews, expelling them from the city because of their allegedly despising Christian ceremonies, endangering the lives and property of their fellow men, and using black magic.

Whereas Rosenberg and Bloch stress the religious ritual and divine inspiration in the creation of the golem, the German film emphasizes magic. Rabbi Löw traces the figure of an artificial man from an alchemist's drawing. Astrological signs and secret writing supply him with instructions for the creation of the huge statue, which he shapes from clay. Astrological signs also indicate that this is an auspicious time to summon the demon Astaroth and make him reveal the secret word which will bring the statue to life. From his book Rabbi Löw learns that the golem was first created "long ago by a magician of Thessaly." According to his instructions, *"If you place the magic word in the amulet on its breast, it will live and breathe as long as it wears it."* Another old book suggests a Jewish source, claiming, *"He who possesses the key of Solomon can force Astaroth to reveal the word, if he observes the due hour of the meeting of the planets."* Taking his Star of David and a piece of paper, wearing his "wizard's hat ornamented with cabbalistic symbols" and a Jewish star, Rabbi Löw draws a magic circle about him with his wand, then waves three times, producing a ring of fire and another Star of David. Suddenly Astaroth's head appears, and when the rabbi commands him to speak the magic word, smoke coming from his mouth spells out

AEMAET, the Hebrew word for "truth" (that is, God). After dazzling special effects of blazing torches and flashing wand, Rabbi Löw removes his wizard's hat and collapses as he tries to step out of the magic circle. When his one assistant, the terrified Famulus, awakens him, Rabbi Löw writes *AEMAET* on a piece of paper, inserts it in a hollow Star of David, and screws it into a socket inside the clay circle on the golem's chest. Immediately the golem comes alive. (Glut explains how the change from statue to man was effected on the screen right before the cameras. According to Carl Boese, an assistant director," Rabbi Löw was to fumble with the paper upon which the magic word was written. His action supposedly attracted the attention of viewers who never saw the four men remove the statue and Wegener take its place.") The golem obeys the rabbi's orders but loses his animation when the Star of David is removed.

As in so many of the earlier stories, the golem is the rabbi's servant. People are amazed at his prodigious strength when they observe him splitting logs and getting water from the well. Adults are terrified by this strange giant of a man, but not the children who, for the first time in the legend, will play a crucial role in the story's denouement.

In Galeen's scenario, the unnamed golem shows signs of having human feelings. When Rabbi Löw takes him to the emperor's Rose Festival, he snaps at a girl who has the audacity to touch his cheek, but he shows appreciation of another's gift of a flower. Because women flee from his touch, the golem's "face is sad as it learns its own horror." The emperor uses the rabbi as a "magician" to entertain his guests. (This is the same story as that found in Pascheles's *Sippurim* and Jirásek's *Old Bohemian Tales* and mentioned in Meyrink's novel.) Rabbi Löw warns the emperor that no one must laugh as he conjures up spectacular scenes of the Exodus, the wandering tribes of Israel, and Moses. However, when the emperor's girl friend giggles at the antics of the court jester and makes the emperor laugh also, an angry Moses threatens the mocking guests. Three huge ceiling beams fall as the golem blocks the exit. One man is crushed to death, but the golem is unscathed as the courtiers panic. A terrified emperor shakes the entranced rabbi and promises to pardon the Jews if he will save him. Rabbi Löw comes out of his trance and orders the golem to hold up the falling beams so that the fleeing guests can escape.

Galeen's scenario also introduces a subplot appealing to a movie audience but not found in any of the previous golem stories. Rabbi Löw's flirtatious daughter, Miriam, has a tryst with Florian, one of the emperor's knights. She fell in love at first sight when she saw him riding by with a rose between his teeth. When the rabbi returns in triumph from the emperor's festival and orders the ghetto watchman to wake the Jews with the "glad sound of Schofa horn," Miriam, afraid of being discovered with Florian, locks her bedroom door. Florian's presence would have gone undetected had not Famulus, who is in love with her, decided to deliver personally the joyous news of her father's success.

Wegener's golem shows increasing dislike of his creator. When Rabbi Löw admiringly puts his hand on the golem's shoulder, the latter stares at him with hatred. Tension builds as the threatening homunculus covers the Star of David, preventing the rabbi from reaching it. The angry golem slowly moves behind the cowering rabbi, who suddenly removes the Star of David just in time to make the rebellious servant freeze. Reading in a German text a warning that at the right conjunction of the planets Astaroth will reclaim the golem, who will destroy his master and all living things, Rabbi Löw decides to smash the clay figure with a wooden mallet. Unfortunately, he is interrupted by the celebration of the Jews below. This interruption gives the jealous Famulus the opportunity to reanimate the golem and order him to seize his rival, Florian.

The destruction wrought by the golem from this point to the conclusion of the film again illustrates Gershom Scholem's observation that a dangerous golem was a profound change from the original conception, in which he was identified with Adam. The enraged automaton breaks down Miriam's door, brushes Famulus aside, and grabs the girl by the braids until she is momentarily rescued by Florian. But then the golem hurls Florian from the tower, knocks down the persevering Famulus, and carries the fainting Miriam to the rabbi's study, where he places her prostrate form on a study table. There this modern Caliban studies the girl intently, tenderly touching her face, throat, breasts, and hip. When he puts his face next to Miriam's, Famulus sneaks back and tries to remove the Star of David, but is prevented by the golem's threatening him with a burning brand. (The Frankenstein monster is usually portrayed on film as fearing fire.) This torch starts a fire in which the rabbi's chemical jars begin to explode. Dragging Miriam by the hair, the golem leaves her on a rock where she is found by her father. "The whole ghetto smokes like Gemorrah." Enveloped by flames, the rabbi's tower collapses. However, the Jews are saved as the golem disappears and the people give thanks to their rabbi. Famulus promises to keep Miriam's secret about her dead lover and asks for, and receives, her forgiveness.

Galeen was left with the problem of destroying the dangerous golem. Traditionally, the one to remove the name of God from the golem's mouth or forehead was his creator, but the scenario so far has made it unlikely that Rabbi Löw could perform this act because of the golem's hostility. Galeen solves this problem with a strikingly effective scene for which the audience has been prepared by the golem's earlier interest in children. Reappearing at the city gates, the golem watches the children at play in the bright sunlight with flowers in their hair. In a symbolic act intended to bring this sunlight and joyous activity into the dark, stale ghetto, he uses his brute strength to tear down the city gates. The children flee in terror, but one girl remains. She stands there crying as the golem smiles at her gently. When she offers him an apple, he picks her up and holds her in his arms. Fascinated by the amulet on his chest, this blond Aryan beauty removes it, thus reducing the giant man to a lifeless statue. The returning children play with the amulet until they lose it. Informed by the watchman that the golem is near the city gates, Rabbi Löw finds the children sitting on the inert body, now covered with flowers. As their rabbi praises God, ten Jews pick up the remains and carry them to the room below what used to be the watch tower. The film ends with a puzzling inconsistency. The gates of the city, torn down by the golem only hours ago, are miraculously intact as they now swing shut. The white Star of David appearing on the black walls turns into "a white star in the darkness of the heavens."

In his introduction to *Masterworks of the German Cinema*, Roger Manvell sees German "art" cinema of the period following World War I as adopting the Expressionism already present in art and literature. *Der Golem*, like *The Cabinet of Doctor Caligari* (1919), is a case in point. The German Expressionist is not so much interested in the external representations of evil, such as sweatshops, ghettos, hunger, and prostitution as he is in the inner vision which produces them. The Expressionist wants to study not the temporary forms and outward manifestations of evil, but its essence and permanent meaning. Seen from this perspective, *Der Golem* is about man's victimization by those

> forces originating in his darker imaginings, creatures conjured by "Gothic" fancies—vampires, magicians, hypnotists, demented scientists, archetypal criminals and the like seeking absolute power over their individual victims or over mankind as a whole. To these forces of darkness were opposed the idealism of the soul—loyalty, love, self-sacrifice, usually demonstrated by innocent youth and beauty in the face of evil old age and foul decay.

Thus Manvell sees both the "medieval legend" of the golem and the film as "a clear case of wishful thinking which oversteps itself because of its dependence upon 'unlawful' black magic." Though the Jews are justified in seeking help to save themselves from persecution, they go too far in creating a destructive monster. In this interpretation, Rabbi Löw is the villain who brings his people further pain and suffering rather than redemption. "Only pure innocence [symbolized by the Aryan child] possesses the counter-magic to destroy the monstrous forces of evil."

Jewish audiences may not appreciate Manvell's thematic analysis of *Der Golem* and may find the film anti-Semitic. The glorification of the blond Aryan child as representing the power of innocence smacks too much of German racism. The rabbi's black, pointed wizard's hat, similar to one worn by many other Jewish males in the ghetto scenes, suggests that all of the members of this exotic race are perverted by the black magic of their ancient rituals and prayers. It is the demon Astaroth who is forced to yield the magic word which animates the golem. And it is the sensuality of the Jewess Miriam that leads her to deceive her father and entertain a lover behind his back.

However, this line of criticism is only partially valid. The film does portray the Jews as innocent victims of persecution. The emperor's expulsion order is an evil act of grave consequences. Rabbi Löw does show compassion in ordering the golem to save the fleeing Christians when the roof beams collapse, and the silly, giggling girl friend and despotic emperor are totally despicable. All of these features could be construed as eliciting sympathy for the Jews. Another mitigating factor is the golem's craving for affection and kindness and his love of children and flowers. He is less monster than the frivolous, mocking guests. In short, it is difficult to accept the Wegener-Galeen film as consciously anti-Semitic. It is more likely that the Gothic supernaturalism of the legend had great appeal to the creative artist. Manvell is certainly right when he praises the film's "stylized movements which border on slow motion," its "bizarre medievalism" suggested by its pictorialized settings and light, and its "theatrical-cinematic atmosphere" with a minimum of captions. It is also hard to fault Manvell's conclusion that *"The Golem* appears now beautiful rather than macabre, a kind of softened nightmare alleviated by the uniform beauty of its images and the unreality of its situations and characters."

From 1920 to 1972, several other golem stories were filmed. Glut describes them all briefly, including the first talkie, *Le Golem,* produced by the French in 1936, with an "almost completely bald" monster; and a Czech comedy, *Cisaruv Pekar a Pekaruv Cisar* (titled *The Emperor and the*

Golem in the United States and then called *Return of the Golem* and *The Golem and the Emperor's Baker)*, in which the golem "resembled a stone King Kong, bound at the waist by bolted metal bands, with steam shooting from the mouth." At the end of the Czech version, the golem is tamed by the emperor's baker, who then puts him to work in the bakery. Glut also lists golem films which were planned, even announced, but never made, such as *The Mask of Melog* (the golem's name spelled in reverse). Three golem films were released in the 1960s, one French, one British, and one Czech. The British film was released in the United States as *It* (Warner Brothers-Seven Arts), with Roddy McDowall as "the psychotic museum curator" who brought the golem back to life after discovering the "stone-like giant with wrinkled face and pointed head . . . in the ruins of a burned warehouse." The mad curator used the golem to kill his enemies and destroy a bridge. "Predictably the army was called upon to drop the favorite weapon of 1950s science fiction films, the atomic bomb. Although the master was destroyed, the Golem survived. With no one to command it, the Golem lumbered into the sea." The last golem film Glut lists is the German *Homo Vampire* (titled *The Golem's Daughter* in English, 1972).

Four years after the publication of Glut's book, the winter bulletin of the Berkeley (California) Film Institute featured an illustrated article on a fifteen-minute film made by Jan Taylor Blythe and Frederick Sweet called *Black Golem*. Sweet explains that he and Blythe were familiar with Wegener's 1920 film when they began their script. In addition to Galeen's version, they had books on "Jewish myths, Haitian voodoo, witchcraft and classical astrology." But basically, the filmmakers

> were attracted to the archetypal character of the Golem folktale. We wanted to maintain the social consciousness of the original story; so it was natural for us to write a script for a cast of predominantly Black actors. In our story a community of poor Blacks would be threatened with eviction. The Golem would step in to scare off the police and protect the people.

The film was shot (with a budget of just under two thousand dollars) in a film production workshop taught at Berkeley by Sweet and Robert Good. Professional actors donated their services in five days of shooting. Expensive wall hangings for the astrologer's chamber were lent by an antique dealer. Since the producers could not afford the type of masks used in *Planet of the Apes*, they used latex and cotton balls instead in creating the golem's makeup. "The lumpy consistency effectively suggest[ed] the texture of rough sculpted clay." The film was completed at the last possible instant before nightfall, with the last shot "of the Golem freezing in a menacing pose, to the Astrologer's command, 'shem ha m'forash.' " On November 14, 1977, the film was shown at the On Broadway Theater during the First Annual San Francisco Screen Actors Guild Conservatory Student Film Festival.

The Golem Meets Superman

It was inevitable for the golem to find his way into comic books as well as films. Once again Donald Glut is helpful as he supplies titles, magazines, dates (from 1960 to 1972), and even a few brief plot details. Two examples will suffice for now. In 1966, a French comic strip called *Lone Sloane,* by Philippe Druillet and Eric Losfeld, told a story about the golem, based on Wegener's portrayal, in which "the Golem was destroyed by the traditional removal of its magic sign." In 1970, "Among Us Walks . . . the Golem" appeared in Marvel Comics' *Incredible Hulk* (No. 134). Roy Thomas told the story (illustrated by Herbert Trimpe) of the Hulk, "a creature patterned after Frankenstein's Monster, . . . mistaken for the Golem by a child whose father often told the legend. Thus the Hulk became the temporary Golem of a people oppressed by a dictator."

A totally different version of the golem, conceived of simply as the tool of an evil scientist, can be found two years later as the new opponent of that all-American institution, Superman. Glut was familiar with the February, 1972 issue (No. 248), which contains the story "The Man Who Murdered the Earth," written by Len Wein and drawn by Curt Swan and Murphy Anderson, but apparently because of publication deadlines for *The Frankenstein Legend,* he was unable to mention a sequel that appeared in November of the same year (No. 258). Detailed summaries of both of these adventures will serve as examples of the appeal of the golem legend in popular culture and show how far it has come since the days of Yudl Rosenberg and Chayim Bloch. They will also show the lingering influence of Mary Shelley's novel and Wegener's film.

In the first adventure, Wein introduces the mad scientist Lex Luthor, who, frustrated by his lifelong conflict with Superman, has decided to record the story of how the latter once destroyed the earth. Insisting that he could outdo "that bumbling Victor Frankenstein," Luthor boasted that he had succeeded in creating more than "mere HUMANOID LIFE!" From the birthplace of the universe he had gathered "particles and pieces of GALACTIC MATTER," proclaiming, "Like the legendary GOLEM of old who was forged from bits of CLAY, I have molded a man-thing that'll be more than a match for my old 'friend'—SUPERMAN." In previous versions of the creation of the golem, the procedure involved a knowledge of ancient Jewish mysticism (for example, the *Sefer Yetzirah* and the *Zohar*), alchemy, astrology, and—in the Wegener film—chemical mixtures in laboratory beakers, but Wein adds a new element which he adapted from all the Frankenstein movies of the previous four decades—a terrific surge of "galactic energy." Whereas Mary Shelley was surprisingly vague in her explanation of the way in which Victor Frankenstein brought his monster to life (probably, as Glut suggests, through galvanic power and injections, productions of the scientist's own discoveries and advanced apparatus), filmed versions usually offer a spectacular display of electrical power. (Frequently there is a raging storm, which adds to the theatricality but is also needed for its electricity.) In the *Superman* version, instead of mere galvanic power, Luthor waits for the proper conjunction of the stars and then succeeds in producing, by means of his modern electronic equipment, a surge of "galactic energy" which shocks the golem to life. A design of swirling planets and stars covers the creature's huge, blue, muscular body and the center of his forehead. Appropriately named "THE GALACTIC GOLEM," it has "a single DRIVING FORCE—an ALL-CONSUMING HUNGER for the hyper-stellar energy that lent it life."

Speaking through a voice box implanted in his monster, Luthor sends the Galactic Golem after Superman, who has to flee when he feels the powerful monster sucking out his strength. Desperately trying to figure out the monster's weak spot, Superman decides to hit the Galactic Golem on the astrological design on his forehead. The blow unleashes tremendous forces, seemingly killing everyone in the world. Even Superman is gone. A remorseful Luthor, apparently the lone survivor, decides to leave earth, but the golem attacks him. To protect himself, the mad scientist sets up a force field of energy but is trapped in his laboratory with the ravenous monster. Fortunately for Luthor, Superman reappears and, with an incredible effort, is able to smash through the shield. Desperately holding off the golem, Superman gives Luthor time to shoot into space a cannon loaded with the energy the golem craves. This plan succeeds because the golem loses interest in the two men, and he heads into space in pursuit of the galactic energy.

If the comic book reader is worried at this point about the dubious victory over a golem when all human life on earth has already been destroyed, Wein has a surprising revelation. Superman explains to a stunned Luthor how he realized just in time that he could not strike the golem on the forehead because "a discharge of that much hyper-stellar energy could decimate the EARTH." Thus he used "the GOLEM'S own energy-radiation to increase [his] vibrations" and shifted earth's population "to a different dimensional plane." With all earthlings safe, Superman completed the punch, but "the GOLEM'S shimmering energy blurred [his] eyesight," with the result that he missed the mark and ended up in the other dimension also.

In the November sequel, the Galactic Golem surprises Superman with his return to earth. He explains that an alien exploratory vessel had picked him up with other space debris. Even though the astronauts had saved his life, he destroyed their laboratory. They, in turn, tricked him back into space "in pursuit of energy changed METEOROIDS," which led him back to his own planet. Superman's new strategy is to go to Luthor's laboratory to fill the galactic cannon with energy to attract the hungry golem. Taking his eye off of the dials for a second, Superman is himself caught in an energy feedback and is given a charge of galactic energy, adding to his already awesome strength but also making the monster want to feed on him. In the fight that follows, Superman hits the Galactic Golem so hard that the monster flies three miles. As Superman races in pursuit, the golem hurls icebergs at him, knocking him from the sky. Not to be outdone, Superman takes molten metal from the earth's core and uses it to trap the golem as they stand over the magnetic North Pole. Covered with a mixture of iron and nickel, "two elements highly attracted by MAGNETISM," the Galactic Golem is last seen bent over on hands and knees, chilled by Arctic winds—"unfeeling—uncaring—unmoving." Although the reader does not feel for him the pity felt for Mary Shelley's Frankenstein, her monster is also seen for the last time alone on a raft of ice floating off into the dark Arctic wilderness.

Avram Davidson and Isaac Lieb Peretz: "Less Is More"

Far less spectacular and imaginative than Superman's adventures with the Galactic Golem is a story by Avram Davidson, published by Fantasy House in 1955 and reprinted in both *The Jewish Caravan* (1965), edited by Leo Schwarz, and *Wandering Stars: An Anthology of Jewish Fantasy and Science Fiction* (1974), edited by Jack Dann and introduced by Isaac Asimov. "The Golem" is an attempt to give a venerable Jewish legend a light, humorous touch. The result is a banal, tedious story with a contrived ending.

The setting of Davidson's "Golem" is an autumn afternoon in suburban California. An elderly couple, Mr. and Mrs. Gumbeiner, are seated on their porch when they are suddenly joined by a mysterious stranger. Mr. Gumbeiner, the stereotypical Jewish senior citizen, jokes that this man "walks like a golem." Ignoring the stranger's ominous comments (" 'When you learn who—or rather what—I am, the flesh will melt from your bones in terror' "), the couple talk about the stranger, the need to mow the lawn, and a sick friend with a generous son. When the stranger tries to tell the couple about a Professor Allardyce's experiments which, in creating him, have finally made mankind "superfluous," the Gumbeiners ignore him with their ridiculous and irrelevant comments. Had they been listening, they would have been the first to hear the ominous news of Allardyce's mysterious death and that his library had "a complete collection of stories about androids, from Shelley's *Frankenstein* through Capek's *R. U. R.* to Asimov's ———." Provincial Mr. Gumbeiner, who cannot see beyond his front lawn, is reminded of a " 'Frankenstein who had the soda-wasser place on Halstead Street: a Litvack, nebbich.' " Reacting to the stranger's threatening announcement that he has come on an errand of destruction, Gumbeiner gives him a slap which knocks him out as the golem's head hits a pillar on the porch.

To Gumbeiner's amazement, the stranger's head is covered with a " 'gray, skinlike material' " but is " 'all springs and wires inside!' " To his disbelieving wife he says, " 'I told you he was a *golem,* but no, you wouldn't listen.' " At this point the old couple remember the legend of Rabbi Loew and his golem, how the rabbi " 'erased the Shem Ha-Mephorash from the *golem's* forehead and the *golem* fell down like a dead one. And they put him up in the attic of the *shule* and he's still there today if the Communistern haven't sent him to Moscow.' " Since there is nothing on this golem's forehead, Gumbeiner takes some clay, adjusts his yarmulka, and writes four Hebrew letters on the gray skin. When nothing happens, he studies the golem's exposed springs and wires, tinkers with them a little, and then asserts his authority. This time the golem responds, repeating what was said to him. The story ends with Gumbeiner's ordering the golem to mow the grass, while the couple continue to discuss their many relatives.

A remarkable contrast to Avram Davidson's contrived effort is a one-page gem by Isaac Lieb Peretz. Though Peretz's story was written in the last quarter of the nineteenth century, it merits inclusion in this study because it was translated into English by Irving Howe in 1953. Peretz's simple retelling of the legend of Rabbi Loew—whom Peretz calls Loeb—and his creation of the golem is a perfect example of the meaning of the dictum "less is more." In Peretz's hands, the tale becomes, says Irving Howe, "a cryptic little parable on the decline of faith, the loss of ancient wisdom, the dust of skepticism."

The parable begins with a one-sentence paragraph: "Great men were once capable of great miracles." It goes on to tell how, in time of a pogrom in Prague, Rabbi Loeb "blew into the nose" of an image molded from clay and "whispered the Name into its ear," thus bringing the golem to life. He sent it on its mission to destroy the enemies of the Jews, until fear was expressed that, as Friday began, " 'there [would] not be a gentile left to light the Sabbath fires or take down the Sabbath lamps.' " Rabbi Loeb tamed the golem by singing the psalm "A Song of Sabbath" and then, whispering again into its ear, restored it to clay. Peretz explains that the golem still remains in the attic of the Prague synagogue, covered with cobwebs.

> No living creature may look at it, particularly women in pregnancy. No one may touch the cobwebs, for whoever touches them dies. Even the oldest people no longer remember the *golem,* though the wise man Zvi, the grandson of the great Rabbi Loeb, ponders the problem: may such a *golem* be included in a congregation of worshipers or not?

Peretz concludes his parable on the growth of secularism by observing that with such tales we can see that the golem has not been forgotten.

> It is still here! But the Name by which it could be called to life in a day of need, the Name has disappeared. And the cobwebs grow and grow, and no one may touch them.
> What are we to do?

Three Versions of the Golem Legend for Children

Further evidence that the golem legend has not been forgotten, even in a secular age, is the appearance of three children's books published in the United States in the 1970s. The first, *The Master of Miracle: A New Novel of the Golem* (1971), by Sulamith Ish-Kishor, seems to have been written for junior high school students. The second, *The Golem* (1976), by artist-writer Beverly Brodsky McDermott, is for preschoolers and is by far the best of the three. The third, and most recent, *The Return of the*

Golem: A Chanukah Story (1979), by Peter Ruggill, is probably for preschoolers and children in the first few grades.

Ish-Kishor's novel is told by Gideon ben Israyel, a figure similar to Coleridge's Ancient Mariner. He is an ageless man, condemned to live until the Jewish people are freed from exile and allowed to return to Jerusalem. He must dwell in the attic of the small Pincus Synagogue in Prague and keep watch over the pile of reddish black clay and ashes which is all that remains of the golem. This is his punishment for not having obeyed the orders of Rabbi Loewe in the late sixteenth century.

Ish-Kishor, in her attempt to write a suspenseful melodrama for Jewish teenagers, takes many liberties with the familiar plot of the legend. Gideon, for example, the author's major invention, is an orphan whose stepmother died when he was fourteen. A slow learner, but tall and very strong, the boy is taken in by Avraham ben Hayim, one of Rabbi Loewe's disciples. The ghetto Jews at this time are being made scapegoats for the poor economic conditions in Bohemia, but they are declared innocent of the Blood Libel after Rabbi Loewe's ten-day public debate with the Catholic church. Nevertheless, an increase in anti-Semitism makes Rabbi Loewe decide that it is time for him to create a golem. It is difficult for the reader to suspend disbelief when Gideon is invited to help dig up the riverbank clay with his stepfather, the rabbi, and the rabbi's son-in-law, Yitzak Kohen. But when the time comes to shape and animate the clay in the rabbi's house, Gideon is replaced by the rabbi's pupil Jacob. No matter! Gideon is present anyway, as he spies on the four men performing the ritual and sees a deep blue flame in Rabbi Loewe's hand touch the golem's forehead. The resulting crash hurls Gideon to the ground, but the rabbi, having known all along that he was there, orders him to help dress the golem and become his guide. Even though the golem towers over the youth, the man of clay smiles at him in friendship.

By now it is evident that Ish-Kishor has turned the golem legend into an Encyclopedia Brown mystery adventure, with Gideon as the boy detective. Gideon's job is to accompany the invisible golem in searching the ghetto at midnight for a missing girl, whom a villainous count has accused the Jews of killing. In an incredible dilution of Rabbi Loewe's role, Gideon is even entrusted with the secret words which will restore the golem to clay after the successful completion of their mission.

The golem is as delighted as a child to play detective with Gideon, placing him on his invisible shoulders and making it appear as though the youth is sailing through the air. This amazing duo find not only the missing girl alive but also the carcass of a slaughtered pig, some labeled stone bottles, and the count's instructions for carrying out another Blood Libel. More intelligent than Gideon, the golem realizes that they must take all of the evidence back to the ghetto, where the girl identifies herself on the steps of the synagogue, disappointing the Christian mob, which then disperses. While the joyous Jews are celebrating the first seder, Gideon realizes at dawn that he has forgotten the rabbi's orders to restore the golem to clay. Finding the golem at the gates of the Altneu Synagogue, he orders him to the cellar, noticing that the creature has grown to twelve feet. His face has grown more human and his movements less awkward, as he looks trustingly and proudly at Gideon, expecting praise for a job well done. Gideon begins the procedure as he was told, but the clay man seems to be pleading for his life, apparently experiencing the human emotions of love, hope, and fear. When the compassionate Gideon relents, disobeying Rabbi Loewe's orders, the golem goes wild and breaks out of the cellar. He uproots trees, flings horses and cats into the air, splits houses, and crushes people. Only Rabbi Loewe is able to stop him, but the collapsing giant falls on Gideon, knocking him unconscious. When he awakens, a contrite Gideon takes the blame for the golem's frightened, destructive actions. Gideon's mistake was one of pride, thinking that he was wiser than the rabbi.

Ish-Kishor resolves her complicated plot by defeating the villainous count with revelations of hidden identities, pirates, and sunken ships. Gideon, however, must pay the penalty for his vanity; his head heals, but not his mentality. He will always have the brain of a child and remain alive until the Jews return to their homeland. His one reward is marriage to the rabbi's granddaughter, who will not let the Jews of Prague make fun of him.

The second children's version is *The Golem: A Jewish Legend,* a beautifully illustrated, unpaged storybook by Beverly Brodsky McDermott, who, like Peretz, realizes that less can be more. With only the barest retelling of the story, she lets her fascinating paintings speak for her. In a prefatory note to the book, Mrs. McDermott explains that she had seen the German film based on the legend and researched her subject for two years, studying the symbolism of the Hebrew alphabet and the magical qualities attributed to letters and numbers by Jewish mystics.

> As I explored the mysteries of the Golem, an evolution took place. At first, he resembled something human. Then he was

transformed. His textured body became a powerful presence lurking in dark corners, spilling out of my paintings. In the end he shatters into pieces of clay-color and returns to the earth. All that remains is the symbol of silence.

In Mrs. McDermott's version, a Rabbi Yehuda Lev ben Bezalel tells his wife, Rivka, of his dream in which the Jews are accused of the Blood Libel. With the help of two of his pupils, Isaac and Jacob, he creates a golem from the clay remains found in the attic of the synagogue. Whereas the movie and comic book versions stressed the use of astrology and science, Mrs. McDermott goes back to the religious ritual involving the chanting of secret words. The golem eventually takes shape with flames and steam. He is mute because " 'only God can give the gift of speech.' " When the rabbi breathes life into the clay, the golem remembers "another time and another Rabbi long ago" (Rabbi Loew, of course). After animating the golem, Rabbi Bezalel places the name of God in his mouth.

This nameless golem, divinely created but as imperfect as his legendary predecessors, might have been content to visit the synagogue, listen to the songs of his people, and light the hearth fires in Jewish homes, but his wrath is kindled when, on the eve of Passover, he hears a man arouse a crowd to attack the Jews, whom he blames for the poor economic conditions. The Blood Libel is invoked and a Jewish home burned to the ground in the ghetto. At this point the golem grows into a giant and crushes the mob with one blow, but he is not satisfied, destroying houses, uprooting trees, and hurling boulders. Rabbi Bezalel orders him to return to dust, and as the golem looks at his master, the name of God falls from his gaping mouth. Picking up the clay remains, Rabbi Bezalel hides them once again under the holy prayer books.

Wallace Markfield reviewed Mrs. McDermott's *Golem* in the May 2, 1976 *New York Times Book Review* in glowing terms, claiming that few authors of children's books could succeed

in retelling this elusive, enigmatic legend; and those few, I fear, even if they possessed Beverly Brodsky McDermott's prodigious gifts, would set about converting it into a sweet-tempered, squeaky clean plea for interfaith harmony or a pious parable directed against the abuse of power in general and the C.I.A. in particular.

Mrs. McDermott avoids these risks and uses her remarkable talents with paint and prose to retell the story. Markfield's perceptive appreciation of the "rich and resonant" pages of this unusual book merits full quotation.

> Her ghetto, at first a dreamy, langorous alternation of Chagall-like colors and contours, presently takes on oppressive, killing mass and density, drawing the eye deeper and deeper inside by its profusion of brilliantly muted details—the implacably malign moon that appears to consume more light than it emits; the thick burnished gateposts that suggest crossbows, pikes and knouts; the two desiccated, genderless human figures backlighted by a spectral candle who underscore the gross force of the distant battlements; the houses shaped like grave-stones and inscribed with imploring, despairing hands, with Hebrew characters representing life, eternity, rapture, the absolute and nothingness; the cast-iron soup pot transfixed in the air and holding only a tiny sickly-green chick.

Markfield's own sensitivity and sharp eye catch some of the endless dualities of dream and reality, beauty and malignity, despair and hope, death and life which have intrigued readers of this legend since its inception.

Peter Ruggill's adaptation of the golem legend, *The Return of the Golem: A Chanukah Story*, combines science fiction and a Jewish festival with heavy moralizing. While the family of Rachel and Benni are celebrating a quiet Hanukah at home, a rocket ship with unfriendly creatures lands nearby. The children go to Rabbi Yosef for help. He removes a "shiny lump of clay" from a wooden box and begins to recite the Hebrew alphabet, reading from a special book. As each letter is read, it dances in the air over his head and forms words, culminating in a big explosion and the appearance of the golem. Although the primitivistic pen-and-ink drawings are generally too busy, distorted, and disappointing, the one of the golem, whose mummylike form consists of many Hebrew letters, is surprisingly effective. Climbing on a table, Rabbi Yosef draws an aleph on the golem's forehead, explaining to the children that it stands for "truth." When he explains, " 'Only when we are dedicated to the truth are we strong and truly alive,' " the golem comes to life.

Ruggill's golem saves the synagogue from the alien invaders but then goes berserk as he lifts a horse and cow and must be stopped.

Rabbi Yosef has Benni climb on his shoulders while Rachel climbs on Benni's and erases the aleph from the golem's forehead. "There was a giant explosion in reverse," and the golem is restored to clay. Rabbi Yosef supplies the moral. " 'Sometimes we need force to fight evil, . . . but then force by itself runs wild and becomes evil.' " The children's parents, refusing to believe them when they describe their nighttime adventures, send them to bed. The story ends with the family lighting the menorah on the second night of Hanukah, one candle for each night "plus one extra standing guard." Thus Ruggill imaginatively connects the golem legend with the miracle of the oil in the victory of the Maccabees over the Syrians commemorated during this holiday.

"Apropos of the Golem": Poems by Borges and Hollander

In 1961, when Jorge Luis Borges, one of South America's finest writers, carefully selected those works of his which he wanted to include in *A Personal Anthology,* one of the poems he chose was "The Golem" (1958). In "An Autobiographical Essay," published later, Borges explains that he first encountered the legend of the golem in Gustav Meyrink's novel, which he read after he had taught himself German while living in Europe. Many years later, when he was visiting Israel in 1969, he "talked over the Bohemian legend of the Golem with Gershom Scholem, . . . whose name I had twice used as the only possible rhyming word in a poem of my own on the Golem." Borges's interest in imaginary creatures, in different systems of belief, and in what Anthony Kerrigan calls "the epiphanies of racial and folk evolution," drew him inevitably to the subject of Rabbi Loew and his homunculus. The entire poem, as translated by Anthony Kerrigan, appears below.

The Golem

If (as the Greek asserts in the *Cratylus*)
The name is archetype to the thing,
The rose is in the letters of "rose"
And the length of the Nile in "Nile."

Thus, compounded of consonants and vowels,
There must be a terrible Name, which essence
Ciphers as God and Omnipotence
Preserves in consummate letters and syllables.

Adam, and the stars, knew it
In the Garden. The iron rust of sin
(Say the cabalists) has effaced it
And the generations have lost the word.

The artifices and candor of man
Are endless. We know that there came a day
On which the People of God sought the Name
In the vigils of the ghetto:

The memory is still green and vivid—
Not in the manner of other memories like
Vague shadows insinuated in a vague history—
Of Judah Lion, rabbi of Prague.

Burning to know what God knew,
Judah Lion gave himself up to permutations
Of letters and complex variations:
And at length pronounced the Name which is the Key,

The Portal, the Echo, the Host, the Palace,
Over a doll which, with torpid hands,
He wrought to teach the arcana
Of Letters, Time, and Space.

The simulacrum raised its heavy
Lids and saw forms and colors
It did not understand, lost in a din,
And attempted fearsome movements.

Gradually it saw itself (even as we)
Imprisoned in that sonorous net
Of Before, After, Yesterday, While, Now,
Left, Right, I, Thou, Those, Others.

(The cabalist who officiated as divinity
Called his farfetched creature "Golem":
These truths are related by Scholem
In a learned passage of his volume.)

The rabbi explained the universe to him
(*This is my foot; this is yours; this, the rope*)
And, after many years, taught the aberration
To sweep the synagogue, as best he might.

There must have been some error in graphics
Or in articulating the Sacred Name:
For despite the most bizarre wizardry
The apprentice man never learned to talk.

Its eyes—less a man's than a dog's,
And even less a dog's than a thing's—
Would follow the rabbi through the equivocal
Twilight of the dim unworldly retreat.

There was something too untoward in the Golem
For at his approach the rabbi's cat
Would hide. (This cat does not appear in Scholem
But I intuit it across all these years.)

Raising its filial hands to God
It copied the devotions of its god
Or, stupified and smirking, it would bend
Into the concave salaams of the Orient.

The rabbi gazed fondly on his creature
And with some terror. *How* (he asked himself)
Could I have engendered this grievous son,
And left off inaction, which is wisdom?

Why did I decide to add to the infinite
Series one more symbol? Why, to the vain
Skein which unwinds in eternity
Did I add another cause, effect, and woe?

At the hour of anguish and vague light
He would rest his eyes on his Golem.
Who can tell us what God felt,
As He gazed on His rabbi in Prague?

Borges's "Golem" consists of eighteen quatrains. (It is quite likely that he chose this number of stanzas because of his interest in the symbolism of Hebrew letters and numbers. The number 18 (*Hai*) means "life," and both Borges and John Hollander, in his poem "Letter to Jorge Luis Borges: Apropos of the Golem," may have chosen this number to suggest that this old legend still lives.) The tone is light, even playful, as the poet deals with serious philosophical and theological questions which remain unanswered. The poem's ultimate ambiguity is the product of Borges's healthy skepticism. "The Golem" begins with the word "If," and the last three quatrains end with question marks.

First Borges probes the Platonic belief in archetypes ("The name is archetype to the thing"). To the Greeks, every rose, whether white or red, tea or floribunda, is included in the letters *r-o-s-e*. To the Platonic mind, the essential quality is more important than the mutant form. From this premise, Borges proceeds to the Jewish mystics' belief in the secret combination of vowels and letters which spell out the name of the archetypal God, a name the very articulation of which expresses all of His omnipotence. Adam also learned the power of expressing the essence of things by giving them names, but after centuries of sin, man can no longer remember the Word.

These reflections bring Borges to the subject of his poem: Rabbi Judah Loew's decision to create a golem. Like Leivick, Borges thinks that Rabbi Loew may have suffered a great intellectual pride, "Burning to know what God knew." This master of the Kabbalah knew the right combination "Of letters and complex variations; / And at length pronounced the Name which is the Key." Thus he succeeded in animating the "doll," "the simulacrum," which "He wrought to teach the arcana / Of Letters, Time, and Space." The bewildered golem found himself, like other men, ensnared in a heavy net of temporal, physical, and social restraints ("Before, After, Yesterday, While, Now, / Left, Right, I, Thou, Those, Others").

It is at this point, a little beyond the halfway mark of the poem, that Borges playfully uses his first exact rhyme in a parenthetical aside.

> (The cabalist who officiated as divinity
> Called his farfetched creation "Golem":
> These truths are related by Scholem
> In a learned passage of his volume.)

It is interesting to note that Borges followed Gershom Scholem's early error (which Scholem later corrected) in claiming that the golem was incapable of speech. Although the golem had no real place in the chain of being ("Its eyes—less a man's than a dog's, / And even less a dog's than a thing's—"), he was eventually taught to use a broom to keep the synagogue clean.

Borges cannot resist adding his own small contribution to the golem legend, using an old literary trick to imply the frightening appearance of this monstrous "abberation" without supplying any explicit description of it.

> There is something too untoward in the Golem
> For at his approach the rabbi's cat
> Would hide. (This cat does not appear in Scholem
> But I intuit it across all these years.)

The parenthetical aside, with its second "Golem"-"Scholem" rhyme, undercuts the horror and shows once again the fun Borges is having.

Borges sees the golem as imitating Rabbi Loew in his daily prayers, but the poet adds a delightful ambiguity as he suggests the possibility of rebellion: the "stupefied and smirking creature" would sometimes "bend / Into the concave salaams of the Orient." Rabbi Loew looked fondly at his creation, but at the same time felt fear. He wondered how he could have created a golem without having given him wisdom. Why to the infinite mystery and pain of life did *I add another cause, effect, and woe?*" These troubled thoughts prepare the reader for the final stanza of the poem, in which Borges lays bare the core of his skepticism, as he imagines God's possible disappointment in the imperfection of His creation, the scholarly mystic Judah Loew, and, by a logical extension, in man.

> At the hour of anguish and vague light
> He would rest his eyes on his Golem.
> Who can tell us what God felt,
> As He gazed on His rabbi in Prague?

Among those who enjoyed the Borges poem was the American writer John Hollander, who credits the Argentinian poet with jogging his memory and reminding him of tales and myths he had thought long forgotten. Hollander published his response as a poem in *Harper's Magazine* (June, 1969). The full text is given below.

> Letter to Jorge Luis Borges:
> Apropos of the Golem
>
> I've never been to Prague, and the last time
> That I was there its stones sang in the rain;
> The river dreamed them and that dream lay plain
> Upon its surface, shallow and sublime.
>
> The residues of years of dream remained
> Solidified in structures on each bank;
> Other dreams than of Prague and Raining sank
> Under dark water as their memory waned.

And far beneath the surface of reflection
Lay a deep dream that was not Prague, but of it,
Of silent light from the gray sky above it,
The river running in some dreamed direction.

O Borges, I remember this too clearly—
Staring at paper now, having translated
Your poem of Prague, my flood of ink abated—
To have recalled it from my last trip, merely.

Three mythical cronies my great-grandfather
Was known to speak of nurture dark designs
Against my childhood: from between the lines
Of what was told me of them, I infer

How Haschele Bizensis, Chaim Pip,
The Bab Menucha and his friends, conspire
Over old pipes; sparks in a beard catch fire,
The smoke grows heavier with each slow sip . . .

I scream and wake from sleep into a room
I only remember now in dreams; my mother
Calms me with tales of Prague back in another
Time. All I remember is a tomb

Near what was called the Old-New Synagogue;
Under a baroque stone whose urn and column
Emerge in the first dawn lies, dead and solemn,
My ancestor, the Rabbi Loew of Prague.

He made The Golem (which means "embryo,"
"Potential person," much more than "machine")
And quickened him with a Name that has been
Hidden behind all names that one could know.

We have our family secrets: how the creature
Tried for the Rabbi's daughter, upped her dress
Till nacreous and bushy nakedness
Shone in the moonlight; groped; but failed to reach her—

How once, when heat throbbed in the August skies
And children were playing hide-and-seek, the Golem
Trailed the one who was It, and nearly stole him
Before the shadows rang with all their cries.

But was he circumcised? What glimmering rose
In his thick face at evening? Were they sham?
Did he and nine men make a quorum? I am
Not, alas, at liberty to disclose.

(But how he saved the Jews of Prague is told
In a late story—from a Polish source?—
Not to be taken seriously, of course,
No more than one about the Emperor's gold.)

These tales jostle each other in their corner
At the eye's edge, skirting the light of day
(The Bab Menucha lurks not far away,
As if around a grave, like a paid mourner).

Too dumb to live, he could not touch, but muddy:
Lest the virgin Sabbath be desecrated,
The rabbi spoke. It was deanimated;
Half-baked ceramic moldered in his study . . .

Save for the Fire of process, elements
Mix sadly: Mud is born of Water and Earth;
Air knows Water—a bubble comes to birth;
Earth and Air—nothing that makes any sense.

But bubble, mud and that incoherent third,
When animated by the Meta-Name
That is no mere breath of air itself, became
The myth whose footsteps we just overheard

Together, shuffling down a hallway, Borges,
Toward its own decreation, dull and lonely,
Lost in the meager world of one and only
One Golem, but so many Johns and Jorges.

Hollander's eighteen stanzas, unlike Borges's, rhyme *a b b a, c d d c,* and so on, and are written in fairly regular meter, basically iambic pentameter. Like Borges, Hollander playfully uses feminine rhymes (for example, "Golem"-"stole him") in the final stanza, even rhyming the poet's last name with the plural of his first ("Borges"-"Jorges"). Missing from the Hollander poem is Borges's religious skepticism, but Hollander's love of the legend is evident throughout. Where Borges devoted many stanzas to Rabbi Loew's creation of the golem and its education, using this old legend as a vehicle to question God's displeasure with man, Hollander is more personal, more reminiscing, more intent on exhuming buried memories just for the sheer pleasure of recollection and exploring old roots. He is proud to be a descendant of Rabbi Loew.

Hollander's poem begins with an arresting paradox. "I've never been to Prague, and the last time / That I was there its stones sang in the rain." The poet has been to Prague only in dreams and memories of his family, nurtured by his mother's stories, and, after he translated Borges's poem, such dreams and memories became more real to him than an actual visit to the old city. He remembers childhood nightmares brought on by his great-grandfather's "mythical cronies," whose beards caught fire from the sparks of their pipes. He remembers being calmed at night by his mother, who told him tales of Prague "in another Time," about the Altneuschul and their "ancestor," Rabbi Loew, who "made The Golem." Like Borges, Hollander explains that Rabbi Loew animated the golem by invoking God's secret "Name that has been / Hidden behind all names that one could know."

Borges invented his own details about the horrified cat; Hollander adds some titilating details about "family secrets" which reveal the golem's terrifying behavior. In a delightful parody of golemania, the extensive commentary of learned men over the centuries arguing the attributes of the golem, Hollander asks, "But was he circumcised?" and "Did he and nine men make a quorum?" The answers to these questions "I am / Not, alas, at liberty to disclose."

Hollander alludes only obliquely to the Blood Libel and the threatened pogrom from which the golem saved the Jews of Prague, a story which is "Not to be taken seriously, of course." More interesting to him is the fate of the golem, his mission accomplished. "Too dumb to live, he could not touch, but muddy: / Lest the virgin Sabbath be desecrated, / The rabbi spoke." With the golem reduced to "half-baked ceramic" moldering in Rabbi Loew's study, Hollander philosophizes about the nothingness of the natural elements as they are mixed in nature, until "the Meta-Name" is added; then, and then only, is shape given to shapeless matter, is myth created. Thus the world needs the poet, the mythmaker extraordinary, as men move down the hallway of life. It comforts Hollander to be part of the brotherhood of artists. He is grateful to his colleague Borges because in a world in which there is "only one Golem," there are "so many Johns and Jorges."

Even while the final paragraph of this book is being read, some creative person is sitting at an easel or typewriter thinking of a new way to reanimate the golem in comic strip, short story, novel, play, scenario, painting, or poem. The spirit of the golem refuses to remain quiescent in the garret of the Altneu Synagogue, covered with tattered prayer shawls or ripped pages of discarded siddurim. The idea of man's being able to create life in a test tube or through cloning, or his being able to freeze bodies for future reanimation when medical technology can cure old diseases, will continue to intrigue audiences dreaming of human perfection and immortality. The robot as servant has also been part of this fantasy, whether he be one of Rossum's Universal Robots in Capek's *R. U. R.* (1922) or a Hollywood automaton in *Westworld* (1973) or *Star Wars* (1977). Sometimes he is seen in a museum, a technology exhibit, or on the evening's televised news as a pair of mechanical arms performing dangerous tasks in factories, nuclear plants, or laboratories. But the danger of the mechanism's breaking down or going berserk will always haunt the minds of the viewers and creators. Perhaps Walt Disney (with an assist from Goethe) caught the image best in *Fantasia,* with the endless multiplication of broomsticks frantically out of control, to the dismay of the sorcerer's apprentice. Whatever the scene, man will always be searching for the magic word, the hidden talisman that will turn the robot off at his command. The difference that one letter makes between *emet* and *met* can be the difference between a world of hope and a world of despair, between true knowledge and destruction. The legend of the golem will always serve as a reminder to man of the need to know the difference.

Bibliographic Commentary

Full publication information for the works cited is given in the Selected Bibliography.

Introduction

Three books by Gershom Scholem (as well as his entries in the *Encyclopaedia Judaica*) are especially useful to the reader interested in the development of the golem legends. See, for example, "The Idea of the Golem," in *On the Kabbalah and Its Symbolism*, pp. 158-204, where Scholem carefully distinguishes between black and white magic in the early history of the golem. To the Hasidim,

> the magic effected by application of the instruction found in, or read into, the *Book Yetsirah* [was considered] as a natural faculty with which man within certain limits is endowed. Creation itself, in this view, is magical through and through: all things in it live by virtue of the secret names that dwell in them. Thus magical knowledge is not a perversion, but a pure and sacred knowledge which belongs to man as God's image [p. 174].

Scholem believes that this view "must be rigorously distinguished from the specifically Kabbalistic view of magic underlying, for example, the *Zohar*. For here is magic represented as a faculty first manifested in the fall of Adam and originating in the corruption of man, in his bond with the earth from which he came" (pp. 174-75). See also "Golem," in *Kabbalah*, and *The Messianic Idea in Judaism and Other Essays on Jewish Spirituality*. Quotations from *On the Kabbalah and Its Symbolism* can be found on pp. 200-201, 201, 190-91, 180-81, 167, 169, 174; the quotation from *Kabbalah* is from p. 353. Scholem's speech, "Prague and Rehovot. Tale of Two Golems," was first published in the *Jerusalem Post* (June 18, 1965) and reprinted in *Commentary* 41, no. 1 (1966):62-65, and in *The Messianic Idea in Judaism*, pp. 335-40.

Other examples of scholars and writers who have shown an interest in the development of the golem legends are Joshua Trachtenberg, *Jewish Magic and Superstition*, pp. 84-86, and Nathan Ausabel, ed., *A Treasury of Jewish Folklore*, p. 604. The most recent is Gershon Winkler, whose adaptation of the Rosenberg tales, *The Golem of Prague*, was published while my book was going to press. In his introduction,

Winkler discusses such things as "A Torah Perspective" on the occult, "Kabbalah vs. Black Magic," "Witchcraft and Voodooism," and "The Golem of Prague: Fact or Fiction." In Winkler's opinion, the stories allegedly first written by Rabbi Loew's son-in-law are true. I take the opposite stand in chapter 2 of this book.

For more information on Rabbi Judah Loew, see Rabbi Ben Zion Bokser, *From the World of the Cabbalah.* The passages quoted can be found on pp. 7, 57, 58.

An interesting and unusual article, "The Golem and Ecstatic Mysticism," was written by Bettina Knapp and published in the *Journal of Altered States of Consciousness* 3 (1977-78):355-69. According to Knapp,

> The initiate intent upon creating a Golem is said to have experienced altered states of consciousness when reciting permutations of letters, vocalizing sounds or other phonemes (gutterals, labials, velars, dentals, sibilants), each of which he sensed as endowed with divine energy. If he were successful in his exercise, he would undergo an ecstatic experience [p. 357].

Using a Jungian approach to "the psychological, alchemical, and metaphysical aspects of the Golem-making process," Knapp argues that Rabbi Loew's golem "was a phantasm which emerged into the phenomenological world when this holy man was in a state of *ecstatic mysticism*—a soul in the process of ascending divinity" (p. 355). Psychologically, Rabbi Loew was tapping "an enormous transcendental power within him" in the golem-making ritual. This psychic energy forced up "contents from his collective unconscious" (p. 360).

Chapter One

From the World of the Cabbalah, by Rabbi Ben Zion Bokser, supplies much helpful information on the historical background of the period and Rabbi Loew's ideas. Quotations from this book are from pp. 153, 151, 18, 19, 23, 194.

Frederic Thieberger's *Great Rabbi Loew of Prague* supplements historical and biographical information with excerpts from Rabbi Loew's books and includes some of the early legends about the golem and his creator which appeared in *Sippurim* and elsewhere in the nineteenth century. Quotations from Thieberger are taken from pp. 1, 2, 3, 40-41, 39, 39-40, 40, 46, 52, 53, 75, 44, 77, 78-79, 79, 79-80, 80, 87, 83, 175. Thieberger himself supplies a beautiful example of an oral source making its way into print. In his parents' house in Prague, he heard the following legend about Rabbi Loew, perhaps the only one of the tales not involving magic. Because of his strict observance of dietary laws, Rabbi Loew always brought his own food when he was invited to eat with Emperor Rudolf. One day the emperor decided to test him secretly and ordered the imperial chef to prepare the same dish that the rabbi brought. Soon after the meal began, Rudolf rose and asked his guest to join him in the next room to see a new instrument. In Rabbi Loew's absence, the chef's dish was substituted for his.

> When they again sat at the table, the Rabbi did not touch any more of the food. In reply to the Emperor's question he asked to be forgiven, but there was a regulation that one must not continue to eat a dish, once one had risen from the table. The Emperor, ashamed, confessed what he had done, and expressed his admiration of the wisdom of the rabbi's laws [p. 88].

There is some uncertainty as to the date of Rabbi Loew's birth. His first biographer, Nathan Gruen, lists 1522 in *Der hohe Rabbi Löw*, but Meir Perles and Rabbi Bokser think it was 1512, as does Thieberger. Yudl Rosenberg and Chayim Bloch give the date as 1513, while the *New Jewish Encyclopedia* records 1520. Another discrepancy involves the famous Altneuschul, where so many of the tales take place. Actually, Judah Loew spent comparatively little time there in the course of his entire career. There has also been some confusion over the date of Rabbi Loew's meeting with Emperor Rudolf. In "Rabbi Loew and the Golem," *Jewish Spectator* (Summer 1977), p. 47, Byron L. Sherwin gives 1552 as the year of this important event, but, replying to my inquiry, he explains in a letter dated October 3, 1977, that 1552 is a printer's error; the correct date is 1592. For another translation of Yitzchak Kohen's recording of his father-in-law's visit with Emperor Rudolf, see Thieberger, pp. 38-40.

The reader interested in seeing how the oral sources first found their way into print should consult the following works mentioned by Thieberger: the Warsaw (1869) and London (1902) editions of the Perles family chronicles; *Bilder aus meiner Knabenzeit*, by L. Kalisch (1872); *Old Bohemian Tales*, by the Czech writer Alois Jirásek (1914); and *Böhmische Sagen* (1919), by a Prague Jew, Oscar Wiener.

In an interesting article on "The Golem and the Robot" in *Literature and Psychology* 15 (Winter 1965), Robert Plank claims, "Outside of any Jewish literature that may have existed secretly, the oldest reference [to a golem] . . . is in a book by Johann Jakob Schudt, *Judische Merkwür-digkeiten,* published in 1714. Grimm seems to have used Schudt as his source and to have thought primarily of the golem of Rabbi Elia ben Judah, the 'Baal-Shem of Chelm (1514-1583)' " (p. 14).

Chapter Two

Students of Jewish folklore and legend will find Joachim Neugro-schel's two-volume *Yenne Velt* very useful. Neugroschel's translation of Rosenberg's Yiddish inscription to *Nifla'ot Maharal im ha-Golem* is basically correct, but he leaves out three things: 1) the reference to "the wisdom of the Cabbala" which aided Rabbi Liva in his fight; 2) Rosenberg's claim that the Blood Libel was common during Rabbi Liva's lifetime; and 3) the Jewish people's need to cleanse themselves from this shame. Surprisingly, Neugroschel does not indicate to his readers major editorial changes that he has made in his translation of Rosenberg's book. Neugroschel's translation contains twenty-two (counting the foreword) unnumbered sections; in Rosenberg's book, where the chapters are numbered, there are twenty-five (also including the foreword). First of all, Neugroschel drops Rosenberg's second chapter, the alleged bill of sale. Neugroschel then moves up Rosenberg's chapter 23 to the third position to flesh out the introductory section, and he eliminates chapters 24 and 25 entirely. The translation of *Nifla'ot Maharal im ha-Golem* can be found on pp. 162-225 of vol. 2. All quotations are from these pages.

For additional information on the use of the Rabbi Landau story to help establish the date for the beginning of the legend of Rabbi Liva and the golem between 1730 and 1740, see Thieberger, *Great Rabbi Loewe of Prague,* p. 96. The other quotations from Thieberger are from pp. 80-81, 81, and 81-82.

In *The Golem of Prague,* Gershon Winkler defends Rosenberg against criticism of topographical and other errors in his translation of Rabbi Kohen's eyewitness report, arguing that "the Slavic intonations were commonly integrated within the 'Yiddish' of even Bohemian Jewry" (p. 66) and that "there is a good possibility that R. Rosenberg implemented some minor editorial altercations [sic] on the Katz manuscript before publishing it. By the time he obtained the manuscript, it had been lying in storage for nearly three hundred years and certainly required some work in preparation for its printing." Other quotations from Winkler's book are from pp. 68 and 69.

Chapter Three

Sándor Várhely is quoted at some length by Harry Schneiderman in "Chayim Bloch, An Interpreter of the East to the West, The Story of Chayim Bloch, Who Has Created a Sensation in Literary Europa," Introduction to Chayim Bloch, *The Golem: Legends of the Ghetto of Prague*, trans. Harry Schneiderman. Bloch's "War Diary of a Jew" is also printed in this introduction. In a prefatory note to *The Golem*, Hans Ludwig Held explains that he found "much that is new and explanatory" in Bloch's collection, feeling that the reader is "much nearer to the cabbalistic mystery of the Golem" (p. 28), the emphasis in the developing legend now being on the spiritual rather than the magical. To Held, "the problem of the Golem does not only represent a Jewish question but, above all, a universal popular one which, like so many other universal human questions, has found it's [sic] best solution in Judaism" (p. 29). The "universal popular" question Held speaks of is "a deep and tragic desire of mankind, the possibility of the creation of artificial beings" (p. 28). One year after the publication of the original German edition (1919) of *The Golem*, Bloch published in Berlin *Israel der Gotteskämfer: Der Baalschem von Chelm und sein Golem*, which has not been translated into English.

A puzzling error appears in the English texts of Bloch's "Romance of Rahle and Ladislaus." After a slight break on p. 118, Bloch resumes the tale, writing, "It was not long before Ladislaus also learned of the tragic death of his fiancee." But Rahel is not dead, nor does she pretend to be. Apparently a section of the story in which the golem rescues the girl and Thaddeus's servant concocts a plot to pretend that she has died in a fire was left out by the printer (see Rosenberg's "The Wondrous Tale That Was Widely Known as the Sorrows of a Daughter," pp. 186-88).

Chapter Four

The Golem: A Dramatic Poem in Eight Scenes is the only one of H. Leivick's plays to be translated into English. It has been published as one of five dramas edited and translated by Joseph C. Landis in *The Great Jewish Plays*, which also contains *The Dybbuk*, by S. Anski; *God of Vengeance*, by Sholem Asch; *Green Fields*, by Peretz Hirshbein; and *King David and His Wives*, by David Pinski. Landis provides an excellent short introduction to Yiddish literature and theater, along with perceptive headnotes to each play. Quotations from Leivick's *Golem* are all taken from this edition.

For additional information on the Yiddish theater, see Charles A. Madison, *Yiddish Literature*; Sol Liptzin, *The Flowering of Yiddish Literature*; and Mendel Kohansky, *The Hebrew Theatre: Its First Fifty Years*. Quotations from Madison are from pp. 350, 357, 353, 354, 354-55, 364, 368, 379, 353, 355; quotations from Liptzin are from pp. 220, 222, 229, 307, 231, 302, 226; quotations from Kohansky are from pp. 50-51, 50, 115.

Three of Leivick's Yiddish works other than *The Golem* merit special mention here because of their autobiographical or thematic relevance. One of Leivick's early prison poems is "A Soul in Hell or Job the Second." According to Madison, it describes

> a spirit in revolt—a youth who rebels against God and strives to become his own master—grieving to see the suffering of his people and impatient for their salvation. Largely autobiographical, the poem is composed of the elements of folklore, poverty, social satire, inner struggle, and the messiah complex— components which were to dominate much of his mature work [pp. 351-52].

In *The Salvation Comedy—The Golem Dreams* (1932), Leivick returns to the subject of the golem, using the word "comedy" in his title the way Dante did in his *Divine Comedy*. In Leivick's drama, the golem awakens after four hundred years, is given the name Yosel, unchains the messiah whom he remarkably resembles, and eventually is acclaimed the messiah after Hanina ben David reluctantly uses violence to kill his rival, ben Joseph. In Madison's opinion, *"The Salvation Comedy* does not measure up to the poetic fervor of *The Golem"* but is still "a major achievement and completes Leivick's artistic near-monopoly of the messiah theme in Yiddish literature" (pp. 359-60). Liptzin sees this drama as a political parable, with Stalin and Lenin as the false messiahs from the house of ben Joseph (p. 227). The third of these other works by Leivick is "He," described by Madison as a long "monologue by Jesus on visiting the poet in time of a pogrom." According to Madison,

> Leivick regarded Jesus sympathetically: "The Nazarene himself, as a man of suffering, attracted me. I saw in him simply a prisoner. . . . I am excessively pained by the figure of Jesus Christ. He is to me the expression of all who find salvation through pain [p. 360].

Chapter Five

The Golem, by Gustav Meyrink, was first published serially (1913-14) in Germany in *Die Wiessen Blätter* and appeared in book form in 1915. The first English translation, by Madge Pemberton in 1928, was reprinted in 1964; in 1976 it was again reprinted in *Two German Supernatural Novels,* with an introduction by E. F. Bleiler. All quotations from *The Golem* in this chapter are taken from the 1928 edition; quotations from Bleiler's introduction are taken from pp. iv, v, vii, viii, x, xi of the Dover edition.

Very little critical analysis of Meyrink's writing is available in English. Of some value is William R. van Buskirk's dissertation, "The Bases of Satire in Gustav Meyrink's Work" (University of Michigan, 1957), available on microfilm. Quotations from van Buskirk in this chapter are taken from pp. 1, 2, 26.

A very attractive edition of *L'Herne,* edited by Yvonne Caroutch, is devoted entirely to Meyrink, whose picture is on the cover; it was published in France in 1976. Especially helpful are the chronology of Meyrink's life and the chronologically arranged bibliography, compiled by Francois d'Argent, which lists all of Meyrink's writings, translations of his works, and even films based on *The Golem.* The only film which is based on the adventures of Athanasius Pernath is a French production made for television in 1971. In chapter 5 I have quoted specifically from Manfred Lube, "La Genèse du 'Golem,' " p. 67, and Lambert Binder, "Essai sur l'Histoire du roman 'le Golem,' " p. 75. Lube believes that one of Meyrink's golem sources was Michael Klapper, whose "Rabbi Paltiel or le chumizig Borchu" was published in the 1853 edition of Pascheles's *Sippurim.*

Gershom Scholem does not think highly of Meyrink's knowledge of the Kabbalah, stating, "Behind the facade of an exotic and futuristic Prague ghetto Indian rather than Jewish ideas of redemption are expounded. The alleged Kabbalah that pervades the book [*The Golem*] suffers from an overdose of Madame Blavatsky's turbid theosophy" (*On the Kabbalah and Its Symbolism,* p. 158).

For an illuminating study of literary use of the alter ego, see Robert Rogers, *The Double in Literature.* My one quotation from this book comes from p. 58.

Chapter Six

Abraham Rothberg is the author and editor of many works, including magazine articles, short stories, essays, poems, reviews, children's books, history, literary analysis, and novels. Among the latter are *The Thousand Doors* (1965), *The Heirs of Cain* (1966), *The Song of David Freed* (1968), and *The Other Man's Shoes* (1969). His *Aleksandr Solzhenitsyn: The Major Novels,* was published by Cornell University Press in 1971.

Except for some very favorable reviews (see, for example, *The New York Times Book Review,* 14 Feb. 1971, and the *Saturday Review,* 30 Jan. 1971), there has been no published criticism of *The Sword of the Golem* in English. All quotations from this novel are taken from he first edition, published in December, 1970. Rothberg's autobiographical statements are quoted from the final page of the Bantam edition (1973) and his personal essay on the genesis of his novel, "What Time Is It Now?" (*Southwest Review* [Summer 1973]). In a letter to me dated May 13, 1980, Rothberg explains that he read Chayim Bloch, Gustav Meyrink, and H. Leivick in his youth, but that he read parts of Yudl Rosenberg's collection of tales only after he had finished writing his novel.

The quotation from Donald F. Glut, *The Frankenstein Legend,* is from p. 17.

Chapter Seven

For more information on the opera *Der Golem,* by Mr. and Mrs. Abraham Elstein, see Alan Rich, "Golem's Mr. and Mrs." (*New York Times,* March 18, 1962). Rich's article is accompanied by three large photographs of scenes from the opera. The quotation from Scholem, *Kabbalah,* is from p. 355. The quotations from Glut, *Frankenstein Legend,* are from pp. 70, 74, 71, 73-74, 76, 79.

Henrik Galeen's complete scenario for *Der Golem: Wie er in die Welt Kam* can be found in Roger Mandell, ed., *Masterworks of the German Cinema.* All quotations from the scenario are from this edition. Quotations from Manvell's introduction are from pp. 10, 12. Irving Howe's translation of Isaac Lieb Peretz, "The Golem," appears in Irving Howe and Eliezer Greenberg, eds., *A Treasury of Yiddish Stories.* Howe's translation was also reprinted in Saul Bellow, ed., *Great Jewish Short Stories.* "An Autobiographical Essay," by Jorge Luis Borges, was published in *The Aleph and Other Stories, 1933-69.* The quotation from Borges is found on p. 216. The quotation from Anthony Kerrigan appears on p. vii of his foreword to Borges's *Personal Anthology.* "Letter to Jorge Luis Borges: Apropos of the Golem," by John Hollander, can also be found in *The Night Mirror: Poems by John Hollander.* Hollander's own translation of Borges's "Golem" can be found in *Jorge Luis Borges: Selected Poems: 1923-1967* (1972), with an Introduction and Notes by Norman T. Di Giovani. In this bilingual edition, Hollander's translation appears opposite the original Spanish on pp. 111, 113, 115.

Selected Bibliography

Ausabel, Nathan, ed. *A Treasury of Jewish Folklore: The Stories, Traditions, Legends, Humor, Wisdom, and Folk Songs of the Jewish People.* New York: Crown Publishers, 1964.

Binder, Lambert. "Essai sur l'histoire du roman.'le Golem'." In *Gustav Meyrink,* edited by Yvonne Caroutch, pp. 73-75. Paris: Éditions de l'Herne, 1976.

Bloch, Chayim. *The Golem: Legends of the Ghetto of Prague.* Translated by Harry Schneiderman. Prefatory Note by Hans Ludwig Held. Vienna: John N. Vernay, 1925. Reprinted Blauvelt, N.Y.: Rudolf Steiner Publications, 1972. First published in German in 1919.

Bokser, Rabbi Ben Zion. *From the World of the Cabbalah: The Philosophy of Rabbi Judah Loew of Prague.* New York: Philosophical Library, 1954.

Book of Formation (Sepher Yetzirah), The. Including the Thirty-two Paths of Wisdom, Their Correspondence with the Hebrew Alphabet, and the Tarot Symbols. Translated by Kurt Stenring. London: W. Rider, 1923.

Borges, Jorge Luis. *The Aleph and Other Stories, 1933-1969.* Translated by Norman T. Di Giovanni. New York: E. P. Dutton, 1970.

———. "The Golem." In *A Personal Anthology,* edited by Anthony Kerrigan, pp. 77-79. New York: Grove Press, 1967.

Caroutch, Yvonne, ed. *Gustav Meyrink.* Paris: Éditions de l'Herne, 1976.

Davidson, Avram. "The Golem." In *Wandering Stars: An Anthology of Jewish Fantasy and Science Fiction,* edited by Jack Dann, pp. 41-47. New York: Harper and Row, 1974.

Douglas, Alfred. *The Tarot: The Origins, Meaning, and Uses of the Cards.* New York: Penguin Books, 1973.

Ginzberg, Louis, ed. *Legends of the Bible.* Introduction by Shalom Spiegel. Philadelphia: Jewish Publication Society of America, 1972.

Glut, Donald F. *The Frankenstein Legend: A Tribute to Mary Shelley and Boris Karloff.* Metuchen, N.J.: Scarecrow Press, 1973.

"Golem." In *Encyclopaedia Judaica,* 7:501-7.

Gorion, Emanuel bin, ed. *Mimekor Yisrael: Classical Jewish Folktales.* Bloomington, Ind.: Indiana University Press, 1976.

Gruen, Nathan. *Der hohe Rabbi Löw und sein Sagenkreis.* Prague: Verlag von Jacob B. Brandeis, 1855.

Hoeller, Stephan A. *The Royal Road: A Manual of Kabbalistic Meditations on the Tarot.* Wheaton, Ill.: Theosophical Publishing House, 1975.

Hollander, John. "A Letter to Jorge Luis Borges: Apropos of the Golem." In *Night Mirror: Poems by John Hollander,* pp. 37-39. New

York: Atheneum, 1971. First published in *Harper's Magazine* 238 (June 1969):79.

Ish-Kishor, Sulamith. *The Master of Miracle: A New Novel of the Golem.* New York: Harper and Row, 1971.

Jirásek, Alois. *Old Bohemian Tales.* Omaha, Nebr.: Nová Doba, 1914.

Kalisch, Ludwig. *Bilder aus meiner Knabenzeit.* Leipzig: E. Keil, 1872.

Knapp, Bettina. "The Golem and Ecstatic Mysticism." *Journal of Altered States of Consciousness* 3, no. 4 (1977-78):355-69. Reprinted in *The Prometheus Syndrome.* Foreword by Salo W. Baron. Troy, N.Y.: Whitson Publishing, 1979.

Kohansky, Mendel. *The Hebrew Theatre: Its First Fifty Years.* New York: Ktav Publishing House, 1969.

Leivick, H. [Leivick Halper]. *The Golem: A Dramatic Poem in Eight Scenes.* In *The Great Jewish Plays,* edited and translated by Joseph C. Landis, pp. 217-356. New York: Avon, 1972.

Liptzin, Sol. *The Flowering of Yiddish Literature.* New York: Thomas Yoseloff, 1963.

————. *A History of Yiddish Literature.* Middle Village, N.Y.: Jonathan David, 1972.

Lube, Manfred. "La Genèse du 'Golem'." In *Gustav Meyrink,* edited by Yvonne Caroutch, pp. 66-72. Paris: Éditions de l'Herne, 1976.

McDermott, Beverly Brodsky. *The Golem: A Jewish Legend.* New York: J. B. Lippincott, 1976.

Madison, Charles A. *Yiddish Literature: Its Scope and Major Writers.* New York: Frederick Ungar, 1968.

Manvell, Roger, ed. *Masterworks of the German Cinema: "The Golem," "Nosferatu," "M," "The Threepenny Opera."* "The Golem," pp. 18-51. New York: Harper and Row, 1973.

Markfield, Wallace. Review of *The Golem: A Jewish Legend,* by Beverly Brodsky McDermott. *New York Times Book Review,* 2 May 1976, p. 25.

Mayer, Sigrid. *Golem: Die literarische Rezeption eines Stuffes.* Utah Studies in Literature and Language. Bern and Frankfurt: Herbert Lang, 1975.

Meyrink, Gustav. *The Golem.* Translated by Madge Pemberton. Boston: Houghton Mifflin, 1928. Reprinted in *Two German Supernatural Novels,* Introduction by E. F. Bleiler, pp. 3-190. New York: Dover Publications, 1976.

Neugroschel, Joachim. *Yenne Velt: The Great Works of Jewish Fantasy and Occult.* 2 vols. New York: Stonehill Publishing, 1976.

Pascheles, Wolf, ed. *Sippurim.* Prague: W. Pascheles, 1847. Four additional collections of these Jewish tales were subsequently published with the same title.

Peretz, Isaac Lieb. "The Golem." Translated by Irving Howe. In *A Treasury of Yiddish Stories*, edited by Irving Howe and Eliezer Greenberg, with drawings by Ben Shahn, pp. 245-46. New York: Viking Press, 1954. Reprinted in *Great Jewish Short Stories*, edited by Saul Bellow, pp. 140-41. New York: Dell Publishing, 1963.

Perles, Meir. *Megillath Yuchasin*. 1745.

Plank, Robert. "The Golem and the Robot." *Literature and Psychology* 15 (Winter 1965):12-28.

Rich, Alan. " 'Golem's' Mr. and Mrs." *New York Times*, 18 March 1962.

Rogers, Robert. *The Double in Literature*. Detroit: Wayne State University Press, 1970.

Rosenberg, Rabbi Yudl. *Nifla'ot Maharal im ha-Golem*. Warsaw, 1909. English text: *The Golem or the Miraculous Deeds of Rabbi Liva*. Translated by Joachim Neugroschel. In *Yenne Velt: The Great Works of Jewish Fantasy and the Occult*, edited by Joachim Neugroschel, 2:162-225.

Rosenfeld, Beate. *Die Golemsage und ihre Verwertung in der deutsche Literatur*. Breslau: H. Priebatsch, 1934.

Rothberg, Abraham. *The Sword of the Golem*. New York: McCall Publishing, 1970. Reprinted New York: Bantam Books, 1973.

———. "What Time Is It Now?" *Southwest Review* (Summer 1973):193-208.

Ruggill, Peter. *The Return of the Golem: A Chanukah Story*. New York: Holt, Rinehart and Winston, 1979.

Scholem, Gershom. "Golem." In *Kabbalah*, pp. 351-55. New York: Quadrangle, New York Times Book Co., 1974.

———. "The Idea of the Golem." In *On the Kabbalah and Its Symbolism*, translated by Ralph Manheim, pp. 158-204. New York: Schocken Books, 1965.

———. "Prague and Rehovot. Tale of Two Golems." In *The Messianic Idea in Judaism and Other Essays on Jewish Spirituality*, pp. 355-40. New York: Schocken Books, 1971. Reprinted in *Commentary* 41, no. 1 (1966):62-65.

Sherwin, Byron L. "Rabbi Loew and the Golem." *Jewish Spectator* (Summer 1977):47-49.

Thieberger, Frederic. *The Great Rabbi Loew of Prague: His Life and Work and the Legend of the Golem, with Extracts from His Writings and a Collection of the Old Legends*. London: Horovitz Publishing, 1955.

Tractenberg, Joshua. *Jewish Magic and Superstition: A Study in Folk Religion*. New York: Atheneum, 1970.

Van Buskirk, William R. "The Bases of Satire in Gustav Meyrink's Work." Ph.D. dissertation, University of Michigan, 1957.

Wein, Len. "The Man Who Murdered the Earth." Illustrated by Curt Swan and Murphy Anderson. *Superman.* (National Periodical Publications, Feb. and Nov. 1972).

Wiener, Oscar. *Bömische Sagen.* Warnsdorf i B.: E. Strache, 1919.

Winkler, Gershon. *The Golem of Prague.* New York: Judaica Press, 1980.

Arnold L. Goldsmith was educated at Boston University (B.A., 1948) and the University of Wisconsin (M.A., 1949; Ph.D., 1953). In 1953, he joined the faculty of Wayne State University as an instructor; he is currently professor of English. Professor Goldsmith's previous publications include several articles in the fields of nineteenth- and twentieth-century American literature, as well as *Publication Guide for Literary and Linguistic Scholars*, which he coedited with Milton Byrd (Wayne State University Press, 1958), and *American Literary Criticism: 1905-1965* (G. K. Hall, 1979).

The manuscript was edited by Sherwyn T. Carr. The book was designed by Gary Gore. The type face for the text and the display type is Mergenthaler's VIP Palatino, based on an original design by Hermann Zapf in 1950.

The text was printed on Glatfelter B-31 paper. The book was bound in Holliston Mills' Kingston natural finish cover cloth over binder's boards. Manufactured in the United States of America.

DEMCO